WINSTON CHURCHILL

AND THE SECOND FRONT

1940–1943

WINSTON CHURCHILL
and the SECOND FRONT
1940-1943

by Trumbull Higgins

GREENWOOD PRESS, PUBLISHERS
WESTPORT, CONNECTICUT

Library of Congress Cataloging in Publication Data

Higgins, Trumbull.
    Winston Churchill and the second front, 1940-1943.

    Reprint of the ed. published by Oxford University
Press, New York.
    Bibliography: p.
    Includes index.
    1. World War, 1939-1945--Campaigns. 2. Strategy.
3. Churchill, Sir Winston Leonard Spencer, 1874-1965.
I. Title.
[D744.H5 1975]   940.54'012   74-14025
ISBN 0-8371-7782-0

Originally published in 1957 by Oxford University Press,
New York

Reprinted with the permission of Oxford University Press

Reprinted in 1974 by Greenwood Press,
a division of Williamhouse-Regency Inc.

Library of Congress Catalog Card Number 74-14025

ISBN 0-8371-7782-0

Printed in the United States of America

940.54
H636

To my father

Preface

'War, which used to be cruel and magnificent, has now become cruel and squalid. In fact it has been completely spoilt. . . . From the moment Democracy was admitted to, or rather forced itself upon the battlefield, war ceased to be a Gentlemen's game. To Hell with it!' [1]
— Winston Churchill

'We have to make war as we must and not as we would like to.' [2]
— Lord Kitchener
(on Winston Churchill)

'But the age of chivalry is gone. That of the sophisters, economists, and calculators, has succeeded: and the glory of Europe is extinguished for ever. . . . The unbought grace of life, the cheap defence of nations, the nurse of manly sentiment and heroic enterprize, is gone.' [3]
— Edmund Burke

'Soldiering, my dear madame, is the coward's art of attacking mercilessly when you are strong, and leaping out of harm's way when you are weak.' [4] — George Bernard Shaw

SIR WINSTON CHURCHILL figures here neither as hero nor as villain. Nevertheless, the author may hope that something of the stature of the magnificent British War Minister will be reflected in these pages. The gravest charge leveled against Sir Winston will be that after achieving a well-deserved reputation before the First and Second World Wars through his efforts to ready Great Britain for the military trials ahead, thereafter, like so many decent patriots, he resisted carrying out the logical implications of what he had helped set in motion. The parallel for today is obvious.

Certainly this will not be official history with its inherent fear of fundamental or even explicit conclusions. In Acton's phrase,

vii

the historian must not only be a judge, but a 'hanging judge' as well.[5] Neither will this be a history of the Left, as represented, apart from the official Soviet line, in such polemicists as Ralph Ingersoll, Elliott Roosevelt, and Emrys Hughes; nor will it be of the Right, which is often, as Russell Grenfell, Chester Wilmot, and Sir James Grigg have demonstrated, more royalist than Churchill himself. Indeed, this will be something of an anomaly, a military approach to the career of Sir Winston Churchill.

Possibly such an approach will not please those disillusioned with the means of war and prone to exaggerate the significance of Sir Winston's political ends. It should not be forgotten that, however political his conception of war, Churchill remained, in Admiral Fisher's phrase, pre-eminently a 'war man.'[6]

At the start it will be shown why, following the drastic clearing of the strategic decks brought about by the fall of France in the late spring of 1940, the Axis powers refused to carry through a campaign in the Mediterranean, directed against the British Empire, to its logical conclusion. The failure of the Axis in the Mediterranean gave Churchill an opportunity to initiate somewhat prematurely the development of his long-held desire for a British offensive on the periphery. Notwithstanding the entrance into the war of the United States and the Soviet Union in 1941 as active allies of Great Britain, Sir Winston would continue to maintain his strategic conceptions until after the Casablanca Conference in January 1943, and in the process to push through his own idea of a second front — in Africa rather than in France.

Essentially, this narrative ceases upon the triumph of Churchill's philosophy of war in 1943, although the consequences of the disillusionment of the U. S. Army with the policies of the British Prime Minister will be made clear in both the political and military realms. In the long run, one may conclude that the strategic conflict between Great Britain and the United States over a second front to aid Russia was a most important cause of the emergence of the Soviet Union as the real victor of the Second World War.

An examination will also be made of the background of Churchill in his role as advocate of a traditional, limited, or British Conservative warfare, in opposition to that more democratic, absolute, or Jacobin philosophy of war stemming from Cromwell, Napoleon, and Clausewitz. Characteristic exemplars of this last-named doctrine among the soldiers discussed here may be found in Kitchener, Marshall, and Eisenhower. This particular friction will, in turn, be related to the perennial conflict between an opportunist exercise of free will and long-range, determinist planning, or between war waged chiefly for the sake of domestic public opinion or prestige and war motivated principally by a desire for external results.

Since what might be called the recent desecularization of history, most prominently carried through by Niebuhr and Toynbee, it should now be possible to talk in terms not just of philosophies, but indeed of theologies of war. If George Kennan has implied the existence of a characteristically Calvinist foreign policy in the United States,[7] today such a war policy may well be discerned in more secular soldiers than Oliver Cromwell. In such a light what Captain Liddell Hart advocated as the 'British' way in war [8] can, perhaps, be better defined as an Anglican way — a conception of war upheld by certain Englishmen, including Sir Winston Churchill, but not by the whole of British society. In this sense the strategic disagreement between Churchill and the Americans in the Second World War can be considered as a continuation of the basic split in English Protestantism, manifested in the British and American Civil Wars, between its Anglican Right and Puritan Left.

Samuel Eliot Morison has declared that there is a compelling need for a more complete and profound synthesis of the several elements of war in an era when the ideology prevailing, at least until 1940, tried as much to rationalize the causes of war as its conduct. This book is an attempt to go further than simply to create a synthesis which includes only realized plans or actual coalition strategy; it is particularly an effort to consider what did not happen. Consequently, the reader cannot be granted the vulgar securities of historical determinism, let alone the peculiar moral satisfactions of a plot or conspiracy interpretation of events. So aberrant a Marxist as Leon Trotsky has put it, 'war itself is no science — it is a practical art, a skill . . . a savage and bloody art.' [9]

It is remarkable how quickly official documentation of the Second World War has become available, not to mention memoirs and interpretations in embarrassing abundance. The millions of words that so articulate a statesman, historian, and journalist as Sir Winston Churchill has written also afford us a surfeit of riches. It is already possible, therefore, to obtain a great variety of accurate and reasonably unbiased information on the resources and capabilities of the different belligerents at the time of their more important strategic decisions, which permits judgments upon the wisdom and rectitude of these decisions, upon their calculation of risks, and, especially, upon alternative decisions.

The tendency to accept as correct whatever was done in a victorious war must be particularly resisted in military history. The brutal examination of poor judgment and error conducted by the Germans in the period of the 1920's laid one basis for the tremendous renaissance of German military success thereafter. The military rigidity prevalent in France after the First World War may, in part, be explained by the satisfying influence of victory. Although they employed in grand strategy far more economy of force than the Axis in World War II, the inadequacies in the execution of this basically sound strategy on the part of Great Britain and the United States must not be overlooked nor understated. The odds may be much less favorable in the future.

T.H.

New York
June 1957

Contents

10.   ARCHITECT OF STALEMATE, 183

WINSTON CHURCHILL

AND THE SECOND FRONT

1940–1943

1

FELIX AND IL DUCE UNDONE

THE AXIS AND THE MEDITERRANEAN

1939-1941

*'To gain England's favor, no sacrifice should have been too great. . . .
We terminate the endless German drive to the south and west of
Europe, and direct our gaze towards the lands in the east.'* [1] — Adolf
Hitler in 1924

*'Empires are made by the sword, by superior force — not by alli-
ances.'* [2] — Adolf Hitler in 1934

*'Herein was Bonaparte's error. His attempt upon India was strategically
a fine conception, it was an attack upon the flank of an enemy whose
center was then too strong for him; but as a broad effort of military
policy — of statesmanship directing arms — it was simply delivering
blows upon an extremity, leaving the heart untouched. The same error
pervaded his whole career';* [3] — Admiral Mahan

*'There is a school of British strategists who hold that in a world
struggle with Nazidom it would be a positive advantage to have Italy
as an enemy.'* [4] — Winston Churchill in April 1939

IN 1924 Adolf Hitler, the embodiment of Jacob Burckhardt's
terrible simplifiers,[5] had written in criticism of the foreign
policy of his predecessors: 'The correct road would even then
have been the . . . *strengthening of continental power by the
winning of new soil and territory in Europe*, precisely by which
means an expansion through subsequent colonial regions would
have appeared raised to the realm of what is . . . possible. This
policy, of course, would have been possible of realization only
in alliance with England, or under . . . an abnormal development of instruments of military power. . . .' [6]

By 1938, the year of the British capitulation at Munich, Hitler

3

had become so hopeful of the realization of his plans for a new Österreich, or revivified Eastern German Empire, that in return for her continued acquiescence he was willing to lend Great Britain some twelve German divisions for her own defense. If in 1939 Hitler had reluctantly decided that the West must be made to 'quiver with horror' before any further German expansion would be possible, with the fall of France in 1940 he was again prepared to maintain the British Empire as one of the 'essential cornerstones in the framework of Western Civilization.' [7] He would declare in all sincerity in 1941: 'I have offered Britain my hand again and again. It was the very essence of my programme to come to an understanding with her.' [8]

The swift and unexpected collapse of a world power such as France naturally disrupted the careful calculations of a dozen general staffs and evoked an immediate change in the foreign policies and in the military planning of the remaining great powers. As a remarkable survivor from the days of old Bolshevism, Mme Kollontay, the Soviet Minister in Stockholm, put it privately, henceforth it was in the common interest of the European powers to oppose German imperialism. It had become obvious that the German threat was far greater than had been anticipated.[9]

Stalin's great gamble that the Anglo-French coalition equaled Germany in strength had failed in a most spectacular manner, and a shattered balance of power could not be relied upon to reinsure Russia. It would take more than that well-worn instrument of security; it would take a New World to redress the lost balance of the Old, and that, in turn, would require time, perhaps too much time. Victory seemed close for Adolf Hitler in June 1940.

Officially, of course, Russo-German relations remained friendly enough. On June 18, just four days after Mme Kollontay's distress, Soviet Foreign Minister Molotov congratulated Count Schulenburg, the German Ambassador in Moscow, on 'the splendid victories' of the German Armed Forces.[10] As in 1917, it appeared that Germany had conquered one front — on this occasion, her Western Front. In the words of the triumphant Nazi Fuehrer: 'We did not "bleed to death" as Russia anticipated . . . Russia's calculations went wrong.' [11] It may be, Winston Churchill once remarked, that in life 'the only wise course is to follow the course of duty and not of interest. Every man knows what his duty is. But it is not given to many to know their true interest.' [12] For the moment the Politburo was forced to rely upon the dubious advantage of seizing the Baltic States and parts of Roumania, in somewhat approximate accord with its 1939 agreement with the Reich.[13]

The military results of the too clever Soviet Realpolitik of August 1939 had been rather well anticipated on the German side. In November 1939, following his pact with Russia and conquest of Poland, Hitler informed his generals: 'For the first time in 67 years, we do not have a two-front war to wage. That which has been desired since 1870, and which we had previously considered impossible of achievement, has come to pass.' Hitler concluded that Germany could oppose Russia only when she became free in the West.[14] Here he was acting upon the warning in 1938 of his General Staff against a prolonged or two-front war, a warning which even the reckless Nazi Fuehrer could not dismiss out of hand as he had dismissed its sponsor, General Ludwig Beck.[15]

Italy was the first to be affected by the German successes in France. In spite of the almost universal opposition of both the population and the military leaders, Mussolini hurriedly advanced his schedule some two or three years in order to attack France before her surrender.[16] Always afraid that Italy might be defrauded of her territorial ambitions in favor of prompter participants, the Duce may now have believed what he said to Ribbentrop in March 1940 — that the British would disappear from the Mediterranean as soon as a conflict broke out there.[17] He may also have assured the Chief of Staff of the Italian Army, Marshal Pietro Badoglio, that he needed a few thousand dead in order to attend the peace conference because, in any event, the war would be over by September.[18]

In a fruitless final appeal to Mussolini, Winston Churchill had written: 'Is it too late to prevent the shedding of blood between the British and Italian peoples? Of course, we could annihilate each other and redden the Mediterranean with our blood . . .

but I wish to say that I have never been an enemy of the Italian people, nor have I in my heart ever been opposed to the man who rules Italy.' [19] On the other hand, Hitler, who at the start of the war had raged that the Italians were behaving just as they did in 1914, was pleased to gain an ally with a navy admirably placed to threaten the communications of the British Empire in the Mediterranean. But his intimates among the German Army Chiefs did not agree with the Fuehrer on the desirability of having Italy as an active and, therefore, more demanding partner.[20]

Perhaps the primary cause for Mussolini's previous reluctance was that, notwithstanding some seventeen years of Fascism, Italy was to no serious extent prepared for a large-scale war. After some hesitation at the outbreak of the war in August 1939, the mortified Duce had informed Hitler that since Germany had been unable to furnish Italy the new materials she required, active participation on his part was ruled out. In fact, although the Italian Navy had one year's supply of oil, the Italian Army had only enough for one month of combat at that time.[21] Even more pertinently, Mussolini's son-in-law and Foreign Minister, Count Galeazzo Ciano, had added that the Italian Navy was still greatly inferior to those of Britain and France and that Italy was especially vulnerable in her colonies.[22]

As a somewhat belated Germanophobe, Count Ciano had much to do with drawing up the list of requirements which Italy made the conditions of her entry into the war. Indeed, he had boasted that he had made his list long enough to kill a bull — 'if a bull could read it.' He may also have agreed with Marshal Badoglio — not to mention the similar views of the British military leaders — that entry into a large-scale war would be suicide for Italy. For that matter, Mussolini himself had told Hitler in January 1940 that Italy did not wish to become involved in a long war. In any event, with some justice Ciano felt that the Germans had betrayed the terms of their alliance with Italy by going to war both without Italian approval and earlier than they had previously led Rome to expect.[23]

It is clear why Hitler had concluded: 'If something happens to him [Mussolini], Italy's loyalty will no longer be certain. The basic attitude of the Italian Court is against the Duce. . . .

The Duce is the man with the strongest nerves in Italy.' [24] Mussolini, however, had to be shamed into a mood for war by such remarks as Hitler's in March 1940 that Italy need not enter the war if she was content to remain a second-class power. With the collapse of France it is not surprising that the Duce's fear of defeat was overcome, as much by his chagrin at continuing to seem a 'welsher' in German eyes as by his greed for spoils.[25]

The decision for war was to profit Mussolini little enough even in the short run. To his distress the German-dictated armistice with France gave Italy neither elements of the French fleet nor more than crumbs from France's territories. Avowedly, Hitler had refused any major cession of French territory, such as Tunisia, to his importunate ally for fear of driving the Vichy French into the eager arms of Winston Churchill. General Halder has recorded that soon enough, thereafter, the growing German conviction that Italy was 'an unreliable partner' became the determining factor in Hitler's decision to favor France over Italy in Africa.[26]

France had rudely snatched the fruits of victory from Il Duce by two principal techniques — surrender and bluff. The regime at Vichy hoped to mesmerize the Reich with the supposed potentialities of French North Africa and with what the German Foreign Minister called that 'elusive factor,' [27] the French fleet, but this ambiguous tactic almost backfired at once in the face of the insistent British demand at Oran in early July for a more clear-cut French naval status. Fortunately for Great Britain, Marshal Pétain's government managed as usual thereafter, to gloss over this inauspicious overture to Mr. Churchill's Mediterranean policy.

As to the third major Latin nation, Sir Samuel Hoare, the new British Ambassador in Madrid, reported that the arrival of the Germans on the Pyrenees was a tremendous event in the eyes of every Spaniard. Like everyone else, Sir Samuel wondered whether this would mean the passage of German troops through Spain to Portugal or Africa.

Generalissimo Francisco Franco had made his decision under the impact of the British evacuation of Dunkirk. On June 12, two days following the Italian declaration of war, the Spanish Cau-

dillo offered to participate himself in return for certain territorial and economic concessions at the expense of France and,
more important, of the Reich herself.

As a preparatory move Franco adopted the status of nonbelligerency, a foreboding posture legitimized by Mussolini in
1939. Soon after he claimed British-held Gibraltar and asserted
that two million soldiers were ready to revive the glorious past
of the Peninsula. But, unlike his incorrigibly romantic mentor in
Rome, at the height of the staggering German victory the Spanish
chief was to surrender his freedom of action only for something
concrete and immediate. Fortunately for the West, although
Hitler wanted to pull Spain into the war in order to build up a
European front against Britain, he was too hopeful at this time
for a truce with the British to feel any particular need for another
weak and hungry ally in the Mediterranean.[28]

As for his remaining enemy, Great Britain, it soon developed
that Hitler was facing a problem. In 1939 he had divulged an
essential postulate when he had declared: 'It is nonsense to say
that England wants to wage a long war.' Consequently the German Armed Forces were unprepared for an invasion of the
British Isles.[29] Again, in his speech to the Reichstag on July 19,
1940, Hitler declared that he could see no reason why the war
should go on, particularly with an Empire which he had never
intended to destroy or 'even to harm.'[30] He also initiated peace
overtures to the British through Stockholm, Washington, and
the Vatican.

Hitler was greatly puzzled by the persistent refusal of Great
Britain to make peace. General Franz Halder has noted that the
Nazi leader saw an explanation for this strange intransigence in
British hopes for Soviet aid. Hitler also did not wish to continue
the war with Britain because he felt that the dissolution of her
Empire would not bring any advantage to the Reich. On the con-
trary, in his opinion German blood would have been shed to
accomplish something that would only benefit other powers.[31]

It is difficult to treat Sea-Lion, the formal German plan for
an amphibious invasion of Britain, with quite the deference which
many authorities manifest to this day, in view of Hitler's much
more profound interest in the continental alternatives open to

him. For example, in June, with victory in France still incomplete, Hitler may have told General Jodl of his fundamental decision to attack the U.S.S.R. the moment the military situation made it possible.[32] With the French capitulation, General Halder received orders to do some operational thinking about Russia. On July 21, as soon as the British had rejected his final peace offer, Hitler and his military aides discussed plans concerning a campaign against Russia scheduled for the autumn of 1940. To his intimates, at least, the reason given by the Fuehrer for his new attitude was that now the conquest of Britain could only be achieved in the East.[33] Napoleon had employed the same rationale.

The General Staff of the German Army greeted this new decision with open consternation, since an assault upon the U.S.S.R. in 1940 was out of the question so soon after the great campaign in the West. Field Marshal Keitel finally prevailed upon Hitler to postpone the proposed attack until the spring of 1941.[34] As the younger Moltke had been forced to explain to William II in 1914, the deployment of a host of millions of men could not be improvised; it would mean a whole year of laborious work.[35]

By July 31, Hitler had given in, declaring, *'Russia's destruction must . . . be made a part of this struggle. . . .* The sooner Russia is crushed, the better. Attack achieves its purpose only if the Russian state can be shattered on its roots with one blow. . . . If we can start in May '41, we would have five months to finish the job in. Tackling it this year still could have been the best, but unified action would be impossible at this time.' [36]

On August 9, Aufbau Ost, the first directive for a campaign against Russia in 1941, had been promulgated, and during the next two months the German forces in East Prussia and Poland were increased, although great efforts were made to conceal this from the Soviets. In August, Germany also guaranteed Roumania's frontiers against further Russian aggression and began to arm the Finns.[37] Obviously Hitler was still faithful to the policies he had delineated sixteen years earlier in *Mein Kampf*.[38]

In this summer of increasing uncertainty for the Reich, the thoughts of many men in several nations began turning toward the Mediterranean. By no coincidence, among Hitler's advisers the advocates of German action in the Mediterranean included the heads of the German Navy and Air Force. Preferring, as service arms so generally do, a form of war which emphasized their respective abilities, Raeder and Goering soon had still another bias — the inability of their commands to undertake Sea-Lion. Thus by the autumn both were driven to exalt the virtues of campaigns to the south, although at first each was evidently unaware of the similarity of the other's views and they were, therefore, unable to present a united front to Hitler.[39]

In the German Army as well, such a generally pro-Nazi tank general as Heinz Guderian felt that after the surrender of France Malta should have been seized and the Italian colony of Libya reinforced with German troops. As early as June 30, 1940, Hitler's personal adjutant, General Alfred Jodl, had considered extending the war to the Mediterranean periphery as an alternative to Sea-Lion.[40] At the end of July General Halder expressed the strong desire of the Army High Command to preserve friendly relations with the Soviets so that Germany could deliver a 'decisive blow' to the British in the Mediterranean.[41]

With the frustration of his desire to attack Russia in 1940, and with his increasingly obvious inability to invade Britain, at least for several months Hitler was compelled to regard the Mediterranean with an ostensibly acquisitive eye. Nonetheless, his European predispositions were to lead first to an otherwise inexplicable lethargy and ultimately to comparative failure in operations in the south. Certainly Hermann Goering attributed Hitler's hesitancy in the Mediterranean to his thinking exclusively in continental terms.[42] His colleague, Mussolini, complained later that in the presence of the French the Germans acted 'like provincials before the aristocracy . . . [whose] outlook is completely warped.'[43]

Similarly, the British critic and military historian, General Frederick Fuller, has condemned Hitler because he did not see where the center of gravity of the war lay and was unable to recognize that he was well situated to cross the Mediterranean and, by conquering Egypt, to strike a 'devastating blow' against British sea power.[44] Whether the center of gravity of the war — a useful, if often misleading phrase from Clausewitz — really lay in the Mediterranean, as so many British authorities affirm, is a moot point; the center of gravity of the only power which could seriously threaten the Reich in the autumn of 1940 lay unmistakably to the east.

With the beginning of August 1940, Generalissimo Franco renewed his offer to participate in the war in return for economic aid and the Spanish annexation of Gibraltar, Morocco, and Western Algeria. It should be noted that Franco's new offer was now dependent upon a successful invasion of Britain. Although for Germany in the halcyon summer of 1940 the Spanish terms were still too high, Hitler had come to favor the assistance of Spain in the Mediterranean.[45] He may have seen that it was only through an assault on Gibraltar that the danger of leaving northwest Africa under the French could be averted.

In mid-summer, Italy would also call herself to the Fuehrer's attention in a manner that was to subdue Berlin's temporary elation. Mussolini was now overcome with anxiety that peace might come before he had gained any territory. Since his claims on France had been thwarted, the Duce had returned to his Balkan alternatives. He believed himself faced with the curse of governments at war, the political necessity for action.

In July, however, Mussolini had found that Hitler was opposed to a joint Axis assault upon Yugoslavia until after the defeat of Britain, so he began to consider a private campaign against Greece. Unfortunately, by the time everything had been prepared for such an attack, Metaxas, the aspirant Fascist dictator of Greece, was so inconsiderate as to appeal to Hitler. On August 17, Ribbentrop, with a tactlessness unique even for the German Foreign Minister, halted Mussolini's Balkan projects all along the line.[46]

If the Axis powers as a whole found it difficult to think along the same lines and to work in mutual agreement, the same cannot be said of the identical service arms within the different states, whether Allied or Axis. For example, in the autumn of 1940, German naval thinking was quite capable of perceiving the intentions of the British and Americans. On September 6, Grand Admiral Raeder warned Hitler that the United States might seize the Spanish and Portuguese islands in the Atlantic in an attempt to influence and perhaps to seize the French West African colonies. On September 26, Raeder stated: 'The British have always considered the Mediterranean the pivot of their world empire . . . Italy, surrounded by British power, is fast becoming the main target of attack. Britain always attempts to strangle the weaker.'

The German Grand Admiral stressed that in the forthcoming winter months action should be taken against Gibraltar, the Suez Canal, and Dakar before the United States was in a position to reinforce the British in this region. To substantiate his conclusion further, Raeder told his Fuehrer that it seemed doubtful to him that a land invasion of Russia would be necessary.[47] The remark of a great British naval historian can be appreciated anew: 'Once to grasp the Mediterranean point of view is to be dominated by its fascination.'[48]

In Berlin in September, a representative of Generalissimo Franco, Serrano Suñer, notified Ribbentrop that Spain wished to invade and conquer Gibraltar by herself. Apart from economic aid, Spain would require no more than special German troops and equipment.[49] In conversation with Suñer Hitler reached the more or less parallel conclusion that the conquest of the rock was possible, but only if the Spaniards were given a considerably larger German military force than they desired or dared to accept.[50]

Ribbentrop then brought up those details too blunt for the personal attention of the Fuehrer. Since, in the opinion of Hitler, the islands off West Africa had to be made secure, Ribbentrop asked for German military bases at Agadir and Mogador in French Morocco, a territory zealously desired by Spain. What was more infuriating to a hypersensitive and suspicious Castilian chauvinist such as Suñer, Ribbentrop went on to solicit a military base on the so-called home territory of Spain, the Canary Islands. While this was a normal enough request from one wartime ally to another, for Spain it was a demand which Suñer refused point-blank to transmit to his chief. He would only advise the German Foreign Minister that Germany could perfectly well establish her bases in West African ports such as Dakar or Saint

Louis, without touching upon Morocco, and still less upon the Canary Islands.

In short, the Reich was offered the privilege of defending French West African territory in which she had little interest rather than the much more essential Moroccan region, so appealing to France, Spain, Germany, and the Anglo-Americans. Ribbentrop cannot be blamed for maintaining that once the Americans had landed in French Morocco it would be too late for the Spanish to claim it. On the other hand, Suñer was rational enough to distrust the German ambitions in Morocco as well as her too widely advertised promises to Pétain.[51] Concerning this latter complication, the German Undersecretary for Foreign Affairs would subsequently point out that not even Hitler could bring off the conjuring trick of satisfying both sides by giving each of them the possessions of the other.[52]

Not surprisingly, Hitler decided that co-operation with a defeated France was easier than with so sovereign a potential ally as Spain, since the latter power not only demanded a great deal more than France, but offered Germany very little in return. Unlike the Spaniards, however, the French could not be relied upon to resist the Americans; here Hitler's proclivities toward the East and his irresolution before such a plethora of conflicting ambitions in Africa had led him into a grave miscalculation, notwithstanding his desire to organize a European coalition against Great Britain.[53]

On the Spanish side, Suñer returned home by way of Dunkirk, where he observed that the Germans were not taking Sea-Lion seriously. The opportunity for Germany in Spain thus passed with the disappearance of the proposed German attack on Britain, and for Suñer, as for other Spaniards, henceforth 'our rule had to be to do nothing and to gain time. This was an axiom whose evidence was imposed upon all future Spanish negotiations.'[54]

Apparently the results of the disappointing Suñer mission induced Ribbentrop to warm up Italy to obtain an alternative bridge across the Mediterranean. In a phrase evocative of 1914, he now advised his weaker ally that Yugoslavia and Greece were zones of Italian interest in which Italy could follow whatever policy she chose 'with Germany's full support.' The Duce gratefully replied to Berlin that he was preparing to liquidate Greece, forthwith.

Aware of the Tripartite Peace among the Axis powers in the offing, Mussolini had also favored an alliance with Japan to paralyze American action, although he found it desirable to add that the United States Navy must be considered an 'amateur organization like the English Army.' Still, the Duce's confidence in victory could not affect the future of the Axis so dangerously as did that of Ribbentrop and his master. By 1940 Mussolini had only the pretensions; Germany, the power.[55]

Thus, with Italy as with Spain, the Reich was again denying any of her friends' attempts to protect the still vulnerable French North African colonies as well as supporting the Italians in unnecessary diversions. Undertaken, perhaps, so far as the Balkans were concerned, without Hitler's full assent, this extraordinary German policy in the autumn of 1940 frustrated both Spain and Italy and filled them with perfectly justifiable suspicion regarding the real Nazi motives. As Suñer remarked, and it went for Italy almost as well as for his Spanish homeland, 'to the absence of any desire for war . . . was joined an absence of any reason for war.' [56]

On the 4th of October, Hitler met Mussolini at the Brenner Pass to explain to him that to give in to Spain's demands would result in a British occupation of the Canary Islands and the loss of French North Africa to de Gaulle. Such an outcome would involve the Axis in the extension of its own operational fronts.[57] This, indeed, was the rub. In 1940, Hitler was still thinking of that Russian state to the east whose immense manpower had offered such a threat to the old Austrian Empire. Eventually, to be sure, he may have been planning to rectify Bülow's failure and obtain a place in the Moroccan sun for the Reich, but, like Bülow in 1905, at the present juncture he had no intention of waging a war for it.[58] At least, in the Brenner meeting, Hitler offered Mussolini special units for the latter's proposed Egyptian campaign,[59] a gesture which was to pay for itself many times over in the future.

Yet, in spite of Hitler's lack of interest, the views of the German Air Force and Navy staffs gathered headway, and the outlines of a vast three-headed southern offensive, energetically sponsored by Goering, gradually took shape in the German war plans. The Spanish end — Operation Felix — under the command of Marshal von Rundstedt, was assigned Gibraltar and Morocco as immediate objectives. The center attack under Bock was intended to reinforce Libya, and after receiving the code name of Aida, was actually to be initiated, although under the leadership of Erwin Rommel. The third assault, headed by Marshal List, was scheduled to invade northern Greece, Turkey, and the Middle East, under the code name of Marita.[60] This operation was to be carried out to some extent in the forthcoming year.

Sent in October to report on the middle or Libyan route, German General Thoma testified of the Italian Army there: 'Every last man is scared of the British. The two opponents barely hurt each other.' Thoma concluded that nothing less than four armored divisions would suffice and these could be provided only by replacing Italian troops with German since large numbers could not be supplied.[61] To help Italy, or indeed any of her weaker allies, Germany was often willing to send her troops, but rarely her equipment.

The need which General Thoma stressed for elite forces in Africa helps explain why the Axis, to whom it seemed so efficient to compel Britain to supply an army around Africa while supplying its own forces from nearby Italy, actually found the shoe on the other foot. Despite naval theory, the Italian Navy was neither in equipment nor in training, morale, or sea-air power up to the job of protecting Italy's communications with Libya. Mussolini himself was to confess: 'I don't know anything about naval matters so I let the Navy take care of itself.' [62] Consequently, Britain, with an exceedingly limited strength in Egypt in 1940, was able to fight an inexpensive war so far as her most desperate shortages, tanks and artillery, were concerned, although the price she paid in terms of shipping would, in time, become exorbitant.

Thus, in 1942–43 the Germans were to derive a progressively greater advantage from these essentially colonial campaigns. In North Africa they helped keep the cream of the British Army occupied in the limited and indecisive Mediterranean theater until 1944, and did so at a cost to the Reich of only four active divisions during most of this period. As General Jodl put it in 1943: 'Employing our forces in this way — incidentally no great force was involved — appeared all the more justified since by this means strong British land, sea and air forces and a very considerable tonnage . . . would be kept . . . from Germany's "living space." ' [63]

Hitler initiated the preliminaries to Marita with more determination than he had displayed regarding Africa, for this Balkan operation involved the occupation in early October of Roumania, a country as well situated for an eastward as for a southern assault. It should not be overlooked that in the Roumanian oilfields lay the principal German source of natural petroleum. Perhaps as an excuse, Hitler claimed to be much disturbed by the threat of the bombing of these fields by the British from their new Greek air bases.[64]

Hitler's colleague in Rome, however, was furious, since he had long cherished dreams of his own exploitation of the resources of eastern Europe.[65] Savagely the Italian dictator told Ciano: 'Hitler always faces me with a fait accompli. This time I am going to pay him back in his own coin. He will find out from the papers that I have occupied Greece. In this way the equilibrium will be re-established.' [66] In this way, also, wars are lost.

The competitive aspirations of the two Axis dictators toward eastern Europe had stemmed from the days of the old role of Mussolini as the protector of Austria. Hitler had been overcome with relief at winning the Duce's consent to the Anschluss of Germany and Austria in the spring of 1938, but immediately thereafter the negotiations for the so-called Pact of Steel between Germany and Italy had broken down, in part from German fears of Italian adventures in eastern Europe. That such fears were justified could be seen when, to compensate for the Nazi annexation of most of what remained of Czechoslovakia after Munich, Mussolini invaded and seized Albania during Easter 1939.[67] Eventually Hitler was to pay a high enough price for treating his great power Allies in the same irresponsible fashion in which he handled lesser powers or domestic affairs.

Presumably the Soviets were even more distressed than Mussolini over the German occupation of Roumania in 1940. Unwisely they put pressure upon the Russophile Bulgars to resist a further German advance in the Balkans — an advance away from the frontiers of Russia, although toward the only slightly less precious Dardanelles. Hitler may not have been too irritated at this move, since he would be furnished with another excuse for an eastern campaign through accusing Moscow of collusion with the British in the Balkans. But his fury was intense when at last Mussolini launched his attack on Greece at the end of October. Notwithstanding his own admission on October 25 to the effect that he did not wish to oppose the Duce on the issue of Greece, hereafter Hitler was to pretend that the invasion of Greece had caught him entirely by surprise. It is possible, of course, that he had not taken the frequent warnings from Rome very seriously, and Mussolini's last-minute letter announcing the invasion caught up with him only at Montoire in France, too late for action.[68]

Arriving in Florence some hours after the actual campaign in Greece had commenced, Hitler controlled himself very well and exchanged only friendly words with the smug Duce.[69] But a month later, after the collapse of the Italian campaign, in a letter — and the Duce was to admit he had been rapped over the knuckles like a schoolchild — the Nazi leader wrote concerning his visit to Florence: 'I wanted, above all, to ask you to postpone the operation until a more favorable season, in any case until after the presidential election in America. In any event I wanted to ask you not to undertake this action without previously carrying out a blitzkrieg operation on Crete.'[70] At almost the same time Hitler complained to Suñer that the Italians had committed 'a grave and inexcusable error' in initiating a war against Greece.[71]

Hitler may have anticipated to some extent the trouncing Mussolini's armies were to receive in their Balkan offensive. In this period General Halder observed in the privacy of his diary that the Fuehrer had little confidence in Italian generals and that he felt that Italy wanted the Germans only for the sake of saving the lives of her own soldiers. Concerning aid for Italy in Africa, Halder himself had already concluded: 'From the operational standpoint it is dangerous to use German troops in operations across seas which we do not control, and with an ally who does not put in his last ounce of effort.' [72]

On October 23, in the same week in which he saw Mussolini and Pétain, the busy Fuehrer had already met Francisco Franco at Hendaye. The latter had sought to prepare for this uneasy encounter by appointing his brother-in-law, the chief of the Falange, Serrano Suñer, as Foreign Minister. Purportedly more acceptable to Berlin than his Anglophile predecessor, Suñer appears in Halder's disillusioned record as the best-hated man in Spain. Halder noted that the new Foreign Minister was opposed not only by the Spanish Army, but also by the police and government bureaucracy.[73] Even before Hendaye, Suñer had been described by Hitler himself as 'the worst kind of business politician' who bargained so closely that he reduced the sensitive Nazi leader to feeling 'like a little Jew.' [74] Few love an avaricious neutral at best, and Suñer scarcely represented the best in neutrals.

Of course, there was another side to this story. In June 1939, visiting in Rome, Suñer had told Ciano that Spain feared a new war in the near future because she was at the end of her resources. Indeed, actual famine conditions prevailed in parts of the war-ravaged country. Suñer had been delighted to learn that the Axis powers were also in favor of postponing any general conflict for some years, an illusion fostered in Italy in this period by Ribbentrop in order to push through the Pact of Steel with Rome. Under these circumstances of common Latin deception by the Germans it becomes more apparent why Ciano had decided that Suñer was the factor on which Italian policy in Spain must be based.[75]

With the aid of this conveniently unpopular Foreign Minister, Franco received Hitler's proposal for a military alliance between their respective countries and for a Spanish entry into the war on a date fixed for January 10, 1941. So far as Franco's generous territorial aspirations upon French African and, in fact, upon French metropolitan territory were concerned, the Fuehrer continued to profess that any news regarding German support for such claims might precipitate a de Gaullist movement in Algeria and French Morocco. But without positive and unrestricted Nazi fulfillment of both their territorial and economic demands, the cautious Spaniards refused to enter what was to them too obviously a war designed chiefly for the benefit of the Reich.

Hitler's disinclination to deliver Spain much economic assistance before her entry into the war stemmed in some measure from a feeling that during the Spanish Civil War he had already been gulled into providing Franco with an excess of unrequited aid. On the other hand, Halder noted that Spain was completely dependent for food and fuel upon the favor of the British fleet, and that the domestic position of Franco was so precarious that the Generalissimo could not afford to take great risks.[76]

Hitler was furious at his inability to pin Franco down to any binding commitment, and he subsequently told Mussolini that his chief impression of Spain was one of great disorder. Franco appeared to him as 'a brave spirit, but a man who has become a leader by chance'; rather than go through with meeting the Spanish Caudillo again, Hitler said that he would prefer to have three or four of his teeth out.[77] All the way back from Hendaye, Ribbentrop could only curse the 'Jesuit' Suñer and the 'ungrateful coward' Franco who 'owes us everything and now won't join in with us.' It is easy to see why the Spanish leader found the Germans boorish and overbearing[78] to a point where the prospect of playing the role of a new Godoy had few attractions — it was safer instead to watch Il Duce's rendition of that thankless part.

Notwithstanding Hendaye, Hitler continued to nurse certain illusions regarding Operation Felix, illusions no doubt fostered by a pact signed with the Spanish Foreign Minister in mid-November concerning the eventual entry of Spain into the war. In War Directive No. 18, issued on November 12, 1940, Hitler ordered the Army to hold an armored division in reserve for Libya (Operation Sunflower). For Operation Felix he now asserted that the political steps necessary to bring about an early Spanish entry had been taken, that Gibraltar would be seized and the British prevented from occupying the Canary Islands.[79]

In Madrid the object of this attempted deception had been stalling so effectively that it was now almost too late for Germany to resolve the African problem before undertaking the eastern campaign. By mid-November Suñer found himself in complete agreement with the Spanish military chiefs that it was necessary to avoid entering the war regardless of circumstances. Italy's difficulties were already all too apparent.

Notwithstanding this phenomenal Iberian unanimity, Hitler persisted in his bluff that the political conditions for the Spanish entry had been arranged, and he acquainted Suñer again on November 18 with this supposedly fixed resolve: 'I have decided to attack Gibraltar and my operation is prepared in the utmost detail. It remains only to undertake it and it is necessary to do that . . .' [80] To Mussolini, however, the Fuehrer was decidedly less self-assured, declaring to him on the 20th that Spain must be persuaded to enter the war immediately.[81] To Halder came the real admission, one not vouchsafed to his ally. Before November 24 Hitler told his general: 'We can do the Straits only after Russia has been beaten.' [82]

In 1945 Goering felt that the attack on Gibraltar had been so fully prepared that it could not have failed. Goering added: 'We would have then pushed through to Casablanca and Dakar, which would have foiled the deployment of American forces in North Africa. . . . With the Mediterranean closed we could have struck across Tripoli to Suez and the long Italian coastline would have been no longer endangered.' Field Marshal Keitel, likewise, found it expedient to agree with Goering after the war. 'Instead of attacking Russia,' stated the Marshal, 'we should have strangled the British Empire by closing the Mediterranean. The first step in the operation would have been the conquest of Gibraltar. That was another great opportunity we missed.' [83] Hitler's refusal to forgo Russia and to consider the Mediterranean his foremost strategic objective, as his Naval Command repeatedly urged,[84] unquestionably constituted a grave blunder, if no longer an inexplicable one.

On November 12, 1940, the Fuehrer had again acted upon his penchant for the East by ordering the continuation of planning for a campaign in the Soviet Union regardless of the conse-quences of the forthcoming conference between the German and Russian Foreign Ministers.[85] Previously Ribbentrop had invited Molotov to Berlin, possibly to lull Soviet suspicions regarding a German attack, or perhaps honestly to attempt to divert Russia from Europe toward India and Persia. One may well suspect that the sincerity of Hitler's intention to reach a modus vivendi with his only possible rival on the Continent was doubtful, to say the least. In any event the German effort failed, ostensibly over Balkan and Finnish issues.[86]

With Molotov the German Foreign Minister indulged in a series of characteristically arrogant statements. Said Ribbentrop: 'The entry of the United States into the war was of no consequence at all to Germany. Germany and Italy would never again allow an Anglo-Saxon to land on the European Continent. . . . Any attempt at a landing . . . on the European Continent by England . . . backed by America was doomed to complete failure at the start. This was no military problem at all. This the English had not yet understood . . . [in part] because the country was led by a political and military dilettante by the name of Churchill, who throughout his previous career had completely failed at all decisive moments and who would fail again this time.' [87]

According to Goering, Hitler was disturbed by Molotov's persistent interest in the Dardanelles and by the possibility of undue Soviet influence upon Roumania. The Fuehrer claimed that Britain must have come to a secret agreement with Russia to justify her continued resistance.[88] The British were not playing that role in which Hitler (and Stalin) had cast them — the protagonists in a phony war or revivified Munich. No doubt these rationalizations made it simpler for Hitler to justify his War Directive No. 21. Code-named Barbarossa, and issued on December 18, 1940, this famous directive embodied his fundamental mistake in the Second World War, his decision to crush Soviet Russia in a quick campaign before the end of the war against England.[89]

Hitler may well have felt the need for justification, since all of his military commanders opposed this campaign from the moment of its inception.[90] Unfortunately the confidence of these circles concerning the chances of victory was greater than their distaste for such a gamble. Moreover, their confidence in victory in the East was the only consideration Hitler regarded as in any way relevant. After all, on matters of general policy, he had guessed right and they wrong on too many previous occasions. Finally, almost all foreign military opinion considered this German confidence regarding Russia more than justified.[91]

The same consideration cannot be extended to the errors of Hitler concerning Japan and America. With these errors Barbarossa was always intimately connected. In January 1941, defending his Russian decision, Hitler reasoned that in order to avoid a simultaneous war with Soviet Russia and the United States, the Russians should be eliminated as soon as possible. Hitler wound up on the cheerful note that in the event of a Russian defeat, Japan, in her turn, would be 'greatly relieved.' This would then divert America with an Asiatic threat.[92] On the other hand, as the Nazi leader did not foresee, should the Soviets not collapse, an unrelieved Japan would not be able to threaten the United States nearly so much. Yet Japan did so anyway. Nazi strategic policy was to founder upon the rock of Russia's unexpected survival, a survival not fully apparent even after the fatal Japanese action at Pearl Harbor.

It is amazing to watch the logic of Hitler in action — that of a paranoid creating precisely those conditions he purports to avoid. Far too frequently the Nazi leader would believe his own propaganda. It is no surprise that Stalin was to characterize Hitler 'as a very able man but not basically intelligent . . .'[93]

The German declaration of war upon the United States a year after the Ribbentrop-Molotov conversations, carried out presumably to relieve Japan, caps the irony. Here also Ribbentrop had already indicated the existence of Nazi illusions, perhaps more natural than those implicit in Barbarossa. In the autumn of 1940, speaking as if he were inspired 'by an oracle,' Ribbentrop informed Serrano Suñer that the Americans could not remove their fleet from the Pacific and that the United States program for a two-ocean navy involved, if it were to be realized at all, a delay of not less than eight or ten years.[94] Such opinions were, of course, common judgments stemming from the experiences of previous twentieth-century wars, in which the time required for the creation of a large navy generally had exceeded the length of the war itself.

The abandonment of Felix also may have been a precipitant of the formal, or Barbarossa, decision on Russia. On December 5, Hitler had written Mussolini expressing anxiety over the equivocal position of General Weygand, the Vichy commandant in North Africa. The Fuehrer declared that under the present conditions safety for the Axis lay only in recognizing that the possession of the Straits of Gibraltar was of 'capital importance.' Hitler added: 'It is only in these circumstances that we could face a French insurrection and crush the British should they attempt to disembark.' [95]

On December 7, the strange and disconcerting Admiral Canaris, chief of the German Abwehr, or Army Counter Intelligence, officially transmitted to Generalissimo Franco the desire of the Fuehrer to enter Spain at the head of his troops on January 10. It is possible that because of his opposition to Hitler's aggressive plans, Canaris may have advised Franco against entering the war at all.[96] Franco replied that a Spanish entry at such a date was impractical, since no preparation had been made to defend Spain's insular possessions against the British or to replace her food imports from overseas. Franco also brought up a new prerequisite; Suez must be in Axis hands before he could move. As Suñer remarked: 'Could anything be more clear?' [97]

On December 9, Hitler admitted that Spain had finally declared her stand. Two days later Keitel gave the order: 'Operation Felix will not be undertaken, the desired political conditions not having been fulfilled as yet. Studies will be pursued for it, but its . . . preparation will be deferred.' Continued studies were to save face for abortive war plans among the Allies as well.

On New Year's Eve Hitler's bitterness overflowed in another letter to Mussolini: 'I am very upset by the decision of Franco which does not correspond to the aid which we — you, Duce, and I — rendered him when he found himself in difficulties.' [98] Shortly thereafter, following an assertion that the possibilities of action by Germany were exhausted, Ribbentrop asked Mussolini to put pressure once again upon the Spaniards in view of his much warmer relations with Franco and Suñer.

The end of Operation Felix was hastened by the Italian loss of the initiative to the British and the Greeks in the Mediterranean. Possibly because of this new concern, Hitler insisted upon carrying through the Balkan wing, Operation Marita, of his far-flung southern schemes. On December 13, War Directive No. 20, the final order for Marita, was promulgated. Three days previously in War Directive No. 19, Operation Attila, Hitler had tried to prepare for the possible consequences of his still unlatched door at Gibraltar. Attila involved the seizure of the French unoccupied zone should the British land in French North Africa or should the French colonials there revolt against Vichy. This tantalizing directive terminated with the typical Nazi injunction that it must remain a secret, even from Italy.[99]

The Italians were at last paying in full for what Mussolini had admired so audibly and for so long — a real war. In the previous century the prophetic Swiss, Jacob Burckhardt, had written: 'The enormous falsity which lies in Italy's desire to be a great power and a military and centralized state must revenge itself.' [100]

On December 21, General Halder recorded that the Italian Tenth Army in Libya had been virtually wiped out by the unexpected British offensive launched under General Wavell. Hereafter the Germans were plagued by what Halder enjoyed calling insane Italian demands for arms.[101] In Rome, Count Ciano heard that the jealousies among the generals were worse than those among women. 'Geloso has softening of the brain, Perugi is a disaster, Trionfi is bankrupt . . . Poor Vercellino. He is such a dear. He came to see me and he wept.' Yet Ciano himself had been responsible for the appointment of the incompetent and unpopular Ugo Cavallero as Chief of Staff of the Italian Army, when he replaced Badoglio after the latter's resignation as scapegoat for the fiasco in Greece.

The King of Italy declared that, like the Italian Army divisions, for too long a time a chair had been called a palace in Italy. Mussolini consoled himself with the notion that Greece was a political masterpiece, undone only by the complete failure of the Italian Army. The Duce told Ciano that he recognized that 'the Italians of 1914 were better than these. It is not flattering for the regime, but that's the way it is.' [102]

Hitler was now of the opinion that while the war in Africa need not disturb Germany very much, nevertheless it was neces-

sary to send some modern matériel to stave off an internal collapse in Italy.[103] Consequently, he ordered larger German units
to be sent to North Africa as quickly as possible. Nevertheless
the bias of Hitler on behalf of action only in Europe is perfectly
obvious at this time. He continued to assert that the situation
could not develop unfavorably for Germany, even if she lost all
of North Africa, because he remained convinced that the only
British hope of victory, namely beating Germany on the Continent, was impossible.[104]

These grim sentiments had been uttered at a general military
conference on January 8–9, 1941, three long months after the
Battle of Britain, and six months after Dunkirk. At the end of
January, Hitler spoke in a similar mood of unconscious self-
revelation, this time publicly asking: 'Does England think I have
an inferiority complex with regard to her?'[105]

On January 11, War Directive No. 22 detailed the embryonic
Afrika Korps to Libya and several Luftwaffe squadrons to Sicily;
both of these small forces were to become acute if often over-
estimated factors in future Anglo-American planning. But very
little of the tremendous potential of the German southern war
plans was ever realized. Indeed, Hitler hoped to have the Luftwaffe units which he had sent to Sicily returned to the Reich by
February, and it was only in the winter and spring of 1941 in the
whole course of the war that the German Air Force in the Mediterranean amounted to a major threat.[106]

During the latter half of January 1941, Goering's men inaugurated the first of a series of air attacks.[107] At the same time Hitler
was forced to admit that the blocking of the Straits of Sicily by
the Luftwaffe was only a 'poor substitute' for the possession of
Gibraltar. Once there, Germany could have placed strong forces
in North Africa and thus put an end to what Hitler termed Weygand's blackmail.[108]

At the end of January, after regretting the fact that to him
the purpose of Barbarossa was not clear, General Halder went on
to express the fear that an Italian collapse would soon create a
southern front for Germany. The German Army Chief of Staff
concluded sadly: 'If we are then tied up in Russia, a bad situation
will be made worse.'[109]

Halder was already involved in the perplexities of co-ordinating the German plans for Africa and the Balkans with the plan for Russia. He noted that a complicated shuttle plan to reconcile these differing projects had to be worked out, and Attila, the emergency plan for occupying Vichy France, henceforth could be executed only with difficulty. Finally, Felix was no longer possible because the artillery and troops set aside for it were needed in Russia.[110] Even in early 1941 it was obvious that German resources were not unlimited.

In February, Hitler was to reiterate that a British capture of North Africa could be withstood militarily, but that it would have a bad psychological effect on Italy. He concluded that Britain could then hold a pistol at Italy's head and force her either to make peace . . . or after the loss of North Africa to be bombarded.'[111] Nonetheless, in the same month the Luftwaffe, although now supported by Grand Admiral Raeder, failed in an attempt to induce the Fuehrer to seize that most efficient British submarine base, Malta, before staging Barbarossa. Hitler vacillated a great deal on the subject of islands at best, and assaults on British islands won his fancy even less. As he later professed: 'On land I am a hero, but at sea I am a coward.'[112] Unlike William II, Hitler had no desire to posture as Admiral of the Atlantic or of any lesser sea.

While the German Navy would continue a long succession of expostulations urging the occupation of the island, general German interest in Malta markedly diminished. Indeed, the Luftwaffe would soon divert Hitler's attentions from Malta to Crete. In a final appeal to Franco on February 6, Hitler threatened the Generalissimo with a horrendous picture of his status in the event of an Allied victory, saying that Spain would be completely isolated and would be forced to throw out Franco's regime. In an equally futile personal meeting with the Spanish leader, Mussolini declared that the French in North Africa were only waiting for the opportune moment to join the Allies. In vain the Duce stressed to Franco: 'Today America can help France only through Morocco. . . . The possibility will disappear when French Morocco is no longer in the power of France.'[113]

More than a century before, in contemplating the failure of his rather more maritime ambitions, Napoleon had complained that no one had seen in his Peninsula War the mastery of the Mediterranean.[114] Yet it can be understood why, following Hitler's feint at Britain in 1940, and given his intention to undertake an immense campaign in the east, the prospect of a Spanish ulcer as well would hardly appeal to the Nazi Fuehrer. In fact, using the Napoleonic analogy himself, in 1943 Hitler maintained that the Spaniards were 'the only tough Latin people' with a population which in the event of a forcible Nazi invasion would carry on guerilla warfare in the German rear. In addition, Admiral Canaris claimed that a German occupation of the whole of the peninsula would not necessarily have closed the Straits of Gibraltar to Allied shipping.[115] It also should not be forgotten that the feeding and defense of such an extensive and hungry countryside would have immediately constituted a greater burden on the Reich than that ultimately imposed by Italy.

One day before undertaking that root and cause of his Mediterranean frustrations, the attack on the Soviet Union, Hitler wrote Mussolini as follows: '(1) France is, as ever, not to be trusted. Absolute surety that North Africa will not suddenly desert does not exist. (2) [Italian Libya] . . . is probably out of danger until fall . . . (3) Spain is irresolute and — I am afraid — will take sides only when the outcome of the war is decided . . . (6) Whether or not America enters the war is a matter of indifference, inasmuch as she supports our opponent with all the power she is able to mobilize . . . (7) . . . The elimination of Russia means . . . a tremendous relief for Japan in East Asia, and thereby the possibility of a much stronger threat to American activities through Japanese intervention.'

Hitler concluded: 'Since I struggled through to this decision, I again feel spiritually free. The partnership with the Soviet Union . . . was . . . often very irksome to me, for in some way or other it seemed to me to be a break with my whole origin, my concepts, and my former obligations. I am happy now to be relieved of these mental agonies.'[116]

2

'MARLBROUCK S'EN VA T'EN GUERRE'

WINSTON CHURCHILL AND THE MEDITERRANEAN

1939–1940

'It was the Kingdom's misfortune, that the Sea was not the Duke of Marlborough's Element, otherwise the whole Force of War would infallibly have been bestowed there to the Advantage of his Country, which would thus have gone hand in hand with his own.' [1] — Jonathan Swift

'If he [Churchill] ever goes to the Admiralty it will be sixteen battleships we'll need, not eight.' [2] — John Morley

'So much do I consider offensive operations against the colonial possessions of our enemies as the first object to be attended to in almost every war in which Great Britain can be engaged, that I have no hesitation in laying it down as a fundamental maxim in the policy of this country, that at the breaking out of hostilities, exertions of that nature ought to admit of no limitation, except what may arise from the necessary reserve of force to be kept at home for the security of the United Kingdom of Great Britain and Ireland.' [3] — Henry Dundas

'What on earth is the use of our risking our existence for France if we get no return . . . Move Malta to Alexandria at once — now that the Italian War is still on. Alexandria is the key of Islam, and Islam is the key of the British Empire.' [4] — Admiral Fisher in 1912

ON May 10, 1940, the day on which the German storm broke over Western Europe, Winston Churchill finally achieved the post of the first of His Majesty's Ministers. Never had the top of Disraeli's greasy pole seemed less promising or less secure.

Lord Randolph's son was now Prime Minister, because — among other reasons — of his supposed influence upon the Americans. If this influence had not existed when he re-entered the

Cabinet in September 1939 at his old stamping grounds, the Admiralty,[5] Winston Churchill quickly put the matter aright. Having critized his predecessor, Neville Chamberlain, for his aloof laxity toward the American connection,[6] Churchill had responded with unabashed enthusiasm to a deliberate overture which President Roosevelt had made upon the outbreak of the war.

A letter which Roosevelt then sent Churchill set the keynote for the extraordinarily successful relationship which was to govern the future: 'It is because you and I occupied similar positions in the World War that I want you to know how glad I am that you are back again in the Admiralty. Your problems are, I realize, complicated by new factors, but the essential is not very different.' Graciously Roosevelt concluded by expressing pleasure that 'you did the Marlborough volumes before this thing started — and I much enjoyed reading them.'[7]

For Winston Churchill was a man of parts — few of them small — and such an essentially sympathetic person as Franklin Roosevelt was the first to appreciate them. But it was probably fortunate that Franklin Roosevelt's personality was not so similar to Mr. Churchill's as that of his more strenuously romantic cousin, Theodore. Churchill's break-up with his former intimate at the Admiralty, Jacky Fisher, had demonstrated as much.

In the opening volume of his tremendous military panorama of the Second World War, Mr. Churchill has disclosed one of his basic strategic postulates, a postulate which goes to the heart of the controversies that have raged about Churchill's role in both World Wars. Throughout 1939 Churchill advocated that, in the event of hostilities with Italy, Britain's first battlefield must be the Mediterranean. In accordance with the basic Allied war plan of the spring of 1939 the new First Lord of the Admiralty felt that 'a series of swift and striking victories in this theatre . . . would have a most healthy and helpful bearing upon the main struggle with Germany. Nothing should stand between us and these results, both naval and military.'[8]

Nothing indeed except, of course, that persistent main struggle with Germany. Churchill's analysis and foresight were brilliant; yet, as usual, the main question of how to defeat Germany was begged. But in 1939 the French backed up the thesis of a Mediterranean offensive; moreover, in agreement with the British, they favored the creation of a Balkan bloc to divert German interest from the West.[9] Since Verdun, France, too, had been afraid of a bloody victory, if a real one.

As we have seen, Churchill lost no time after his accession to the Cabinet in September 1939 in involving himself with the United States. But not for the first time, circumstances soon outstripped him. On May 15, 1940, only five days in the seat of Britain's highest power and with the Germans five days advanced on their drive to the Channel, Churchill asked President Roosevelt to proclaim a state of American nonbelligerency. He asked this heretofore neutral power to furnish forty or fifty destroyers, planes, guns, and steel. He also suggested that Singapore become a United States naval base, a bold modification of earlier Anglo-American discussions.[10]

With his new approach toward the United States, Churchill simultaneously reversed another Chamberlain policy: following the raid on Rotterdam by the Luftwaffe on May 14, he initiated the strategic bombing of German industry. To be sure, the Allied governments had agreed in April 1940 to bomb such objectives in the event of a German invasion of the Low Countries, but the devastation of Rotterdam afforded a more satisfactory justification for the new program.[11] The day of dropping leaflets, of twilight war, was over, and a type of limited war begun, notwithstanding what may be considered its absolute implications for the future.

On May 13, 1940, the Prime Minister proclaimed in the House of Commons that his was a policy of 'victory at all costs, victory in spite of all terror.' [12] To one British critic, General Frederick Fuller, this inauguration of a strategy of exhaustion in the air — at the same time that Hitler forced through the traditional German strategy of annihilation on land — was morally comparable with the terrorism of the Seljuk Turks. If in the piping days of pacifism Mr. Churchill had held views similar to Fuller's, by 1945 he had come to approve of atomic bombing.[13]

Certainly, by the end of 1940, the ineffectiveness of this initial expression of the doctrines of strategic air power led to the outright British acceptance of indiscriminate area bombing, purportedly to make up for the failure of the R.A.F. to hit industrial targets.[14] But prewar estimates of the casualties resulting from area bombing turned out to be dangerously misleading. For example, in 1938 Captain Liddell Hart, then at the height of his influence, had estimated that the Luftwaffe could drop two thousand tons of bombs daily on London with the resulting casualties approximating 250,000 for the first week alone. In 1939 a British psychologist had written for the British Armed Services journal that 'wars are won and lost on the psychic front' and that London would be untenable in a modern air raid.[15] Predictions of this order were better at bringing about political victories for the enemy than military victories for Great Britain, as Churchill himself had evidently come to appreciate after Munich.[16]

On May 23, two days after the German Panzer divisions reached the Channel, thus splitting the British and Belgians from the bulk of the French forces in Western Europe with consequences for the Allied coalition which were soon enough clear, President Roosevelt and his chief military advisers were already considering the effect of this situation in the United States. General Marshall and Admiral Stark agreed with the President that the loss of Wake, Guam, and the Philippines must be tolerated in order to hold South America. On the next day, May 24, a convenient warning from Winston Churchill concerning a possible Nazi coup in Brazil accentuated Washington's anxiety concerning the east coast of South America. On the 25th President Roosevelt acted. To the great distress of his Chiefs of Staff and Naval Operations he ordered the rapid preparation of a large naval force (code-named Pot-of-Gold) to be ready to sail for Natal and Pernambuco within thirty days.

Although the United States probably lacked the resources to mount even such a limited expedition, the position of the bulk of the U. S. Pacific fleet at Pearl Harbor was now thrown into doubt. General Marshall and his aides initiated the basic American strategic readjustment almost immediately. On June 17, the Army Chief of Staff asked his War Plans Division an already rhetorical question: 'If the French Navy goes to Germany and Italy

we will have a very serious situation in the South Atlantic . . .
Are we not forced into a question of reframing our naval policy
. . . into purely defensive action in the Pacific with a main effort
on the Atlantic side?' On June 22, after consultation with the
President, Marshall and Stark agreed that if Germany should
obtain effective control over the French fleet, the bulk of the
United States Navy should be transferred to the Atlantic.[17]

Meanwhile in the climactic week of Dunkirk, Winston Churchill showed his countrymen how to live with adversity. No doubt
Churchill's endeavors to save Europe through his example were
reinforced by the fact that the British national forte is a morally
exalted defensive. 'If France is still our ally after an Italian
declaration of war,' wrote the new Prime Minister on the first
day of the evacuation of the British Army from the French Channel ports, 'it would appear extremely desirable that the combined fleets, acting from opposite ends of the Mediterranean,
should pursue an active offensive against Italy. It is important
that . . . we can see what their quality really is, and whether
it has changed at all since the last war. The purely defensive
strategy contemplated by Commander-in-Chief Mediterranean
ought not to be accepted.' Perhaps Mr. Churchill was aware that
in 1918 Assistant Secretary of the Navy, Franklin Delano Roosevelt, had failed to persuade the Italian Navy to fight under the
still more favorable circumstances of that time.[18]

Churchill was still all for exposing Mussolini, whom he char-
acterized in the words of the poet as one of:

> Those Pagod things of sabre way
> With fronts of brass and feet of clay.[19]

But to his military commanders, soon enough burdened under
the staggering implications of the collapse of France, the passionate and inveterate advocate of Mediterranean action, at last
ensconced in the highest post of power above them, must have
seemed another Nelson, liable to confuse new problems with
new opportunities in his favorite sea. And, like the Admiral of
the Fleet, Sir George Rooke, in his disputes with the Duke of
Marlborough in the eighteenth century, the British naval chief

in the Mediterranean, Admiral Cunningham, felt that the 'ungracious and hasty' pressure for premature action in the Mediterranean on the part of another Churchill was doing positive harm in mid-1940.[20]

If Mr. Churchill's spirit was eager, British muscle in June 1940 was weak, a result of twenty years of the embittered illusion (popularly considered disillusionment) in the West that since war was an evil it was, therefore, unnecessary. Nor did British morale always measure up to Churchill's standard.

The new Prime Minister wrote at this time: 'Our weakness, slowness, lack of grip and drive, are very apparent on the background of what was done twenty-five years ago.' [21] But it is perfectly clear why a United States Assistant Secretary of War could recognize that 'Britain stood resolute, if shaky . . . Her stand signified the preservation of the great bastion in the Atlantic by which re-entry to the Continent was possible.' [22] Britain's defiance of Nazi Germany seemed possible, as Churchill was to point out later, only because the British understood the difficulties of crossing the Channel without control of the sea or the air, and without landing craft.[23] In due course Churchill was to employ this understanding as a two-edged sword.

Desperate and essential as was the position of the United Kingdom itself, the Prime Minister's eyes remained fixed on the south. Having failed in his valiant effort to keep France in the fight, an effort which if successful, he felt, might have resulted in the complete conquest of Libya by the Allies in 1941, in early July 1940 Mr. Churchill inaugurated a new phase in his Mediterranean policy. Like the younger Pitt, the Prime Minister contemplated an aggressive colonial policy to compensate for the collapse of his continental Allies. Following what his naval chief in the Mediterranean has considered the 'almost inept' attempt by the Royal Navy to Copenhagen [24] or immobilize the now neutral French Fleet at Oran, Mr. Churchill declared that it was vital to set up a friendly French regime in Morocco, with control of as much of the French Navy as possible.[25]

Unfortunately, as General de Gaulle anticipated, after witnessing Winston Churchill's version of the Nelson touch at Oran, the proud and bitter French forces at Casablanca proved more angered than dazzled by this particular demonstration of British seapower. As in Norway, the Prime Minister might well have evoked the naval threat that he professed to fear.[26] At the same time British fears of a Spanish reaction to an intervention on their part in Morocco were growing and Churchill was forced to divert his dreams of action further south of the entrance to the Mediterranean.

Nevertheless, in retrospect, Mr. Churchill has continued to maintain that had Hitler invaded Spain and Africa, the British could have moved superior forces by sea more rapidly than the Germans into Morocco and Algeria. In 1949 the Prime Minister concluded that, assuming the aid of the French, he should certainly have welcomed a campaign in northwest Africa in the autumn and winter of 1940.[27]

Considering the strain imposed upon both Britain and her great American ally of the future in mounting a similar project after two years of additional preparation, this assertion of Churchill regarding the possibilities of 1940 is all the more astonishing. To be sure, some French opposition was encountered in November 1942, but Mr. Churchill himself might concede that the tying down of the bulk of German offensive power in Russia far more than compensated for such a brief and feeble resistance.

Yet throughout July 1940, instead of leaving well enough alone in northwest Africa, the Prime Minister continued his efforts to win over bases in French Morocco and Algeria. On July 25, Churchill informed his Foreign Secretary: 'I want to promote a kind of collusive conspiracy in the Vichy Government whereby certain members . . . will levant to North Africa in order to make a better bargain for France. . . .' Unless, of course, the Prime Minister hoped in this fashion to divert the Germans from the poorly defended British Isles themselves, such a policy in the Mediterranean in the lean and hungry summer of 1940 bordered upon the irresponsible.

Simultaneous with his rash but ineffective activities in the western Mediterranean, Churchill successfully opposed an attempt by the Admiralty to abandon the eastern Mediterranean. He recorded: 'I resisted this policy, which, though justified on paper by the strength of the Italian Fleet, did not correspond to my impressions of the fighting values, and also seemed to spell the doom of Malta. It was resolved to fight it out at both ends.'

Hereafter a running argument in London between Churchill and his more cautious naval commanders paralleled the engagements between the Royal Navy and Mussolini's quickly tarnished fleet in the Mediterranean. The Prime Minister simply could not bring himself to accept the absolute closure of his favorite sea, a refusal facilitated by the immense strain which the voyage around the Cape imposed upon British convoys to Asia and the Middle East. To the Middle East, the Cape of Good Hope route was almost four times as long as the dangerous passage through the Mediterranean; to India, however, the Cape passage was only 40 per cent longer. In addition, the heavy German naval losses in the Norwegian campaign had released more British cruisers for the Mediterranean.

On July 15 Churchill informed the First Sea Lord: 'It is now three weeks since I vetoed the proposal to evacuate the Eastern Mediterranean . . . Warships are meant to go under fire. . . .' [28] In justifying his dispute with the Admirals over the Dardanelles in the First World War Churchill had then complained: 'The public does not understand naval warfare. They criticise naval losses more severely than military losses. The loss of a ship is regarded as a crime.' [29]

Yet it was not officially for this reason, but in protest against Churchill's gradual draining of British naval resources from the main theater of the war for the benefit of the Dardanelles that Admiral Fisher had resigned in 1915.[30] There is little doubt that, in striking contrast to the British generals at that time, the excessive caution of certain British admirals in the First World War [31] would tend to lead Mr. Churchill into pushing the Royal Navy perilously far in the Second. Contrary to the situation in 1915–16, after 1939 the Royal Navy would hardly have to seek action; its enemies were both more numerous and widespread.

Throughout August, Churchill complained because the few tanks which heroically he had decided were more needed in Egypt than in England were unable to play a part in the defense of either of these gravely menaced regions — they were, in fact, being tediously convoyed around the Cape. The Former Naval

Person — as Winston Churchill was wont to sign his letters to President Roosevelt — had not been able to induce either the Admiralty or his commanders in the Mediterranean to undertake the risks of convoying these precious British tanks through the Mediterranean. But as he had told Wilfred Blunt in 1909: 'We shall continue to hold it [Egypt] whatever happens; nobody will ever give it up — I won't — except we are driven out of it at the end of a war. It will all depend upon whether we can hold command of the sea.' [32]

Winston Churchill's strategic conclusions for the second half of 1940 and for 1941 are well summarized in a memorandum of September 3. 'The Navy,' stated the Former Naval Person, 'can lose us the war, but only the Air Force can win it. Therefore our supreme effort must be to gain overwhelming mastery in the air. The Fighters are our salvation, but the Bombers alone provide the means of victory. . . . In no other way at present visible can we hope to overcome the immense military power of Germany.' [33] As under Neville Chamberlain, the Royal Air Force would continue to maintain its primacy over the Army and Navy.

For the British Army the Prime Minister now naturally foresaw a mainly defensive role, although there remained possibilities of limited amphibious warfare of the kind once advocated by Admiral Fisher against the coasts of Europe or North Africa.[34] Nevertheless, even though Dunkirk had revivified limited liability as a viable policy for the Cinderella Service, Mr. Churchill still favored a force for the Empire of fifty-five divisions. But although the British Army in the United Kingdom was nominally building up toward some thirty-six divisions, the Chief of the Imperial General Staff no longer favored a large-scale force for active use in France.[35]

Indeed, in the great speech to the House of Commons of August 20, the Prime Minister had already emphasized a happier theme for all the world to hear and to hope for — provided they were not so foolish as to live on the continent of Europe. As another conservative nationalist, Charles de Gaulle, had advocated for the war-weary French several years earlier,[36] Mr. Churchill now postulated 'a conflict of strategy, of organization,

of technical apparatus, of science, mechanics and morale . . .
a war of this kind will be more favorable to us than the somber
mass slaughters of the Somme and Passchendaele.' Great Britain, declared Mr. Churchill, had suffered about one-fifth of the
casualties, excluding civilians, in the first year of the Second
World War that she had sustained in the first year of the First
World War.[37] Unfortunately, as so prominent a scapegoat for
the Dardanelles as Winston Churchill was the first to proclaim,
wars are not won by successful evacuations.[38]

Given such a variety of military interests and of strongly held
opinions, it is apparent why the Prime Minister had also felt the
absolute necessity for becoming Minister of Defence as well.
In this post he could exclude the three Service Ministers from
the War Cabinet and attach the Chiefs of Staff to his own person
for all purposes of strategy. Moreover, by annexing the Chiefs'
planning section he could secure for himself the initiative in the
formulation of all war plans. Thus, as his admirer, Leopold
Amery, put it, Churchill had only to inform the British War
Cabinet of his and his military chiefs' plans and they usually were
'well content' to accept them.[39] Indeed, in 1942 David Lloyd
George would refuse to join the War Cabinet on the grounds that
it was, in reality, no more than a Churchill Cabinet.[40] Obviously
the new Prime Minister was in a position to dominate the conduct
of the war so far as Great Britain was concerned.

In the late summer of 1940, when the Prime Minister's restless
glances again began to move south down the African coast, he
began to develop an interest as keen as President Roosevelt's
in the Vichy French port of Dakar. Having translated his defensive concern for Brazil in May into an offensive-defensive interest in the west coast of Africa opposite the Brazilian bulge at
Natal, Roosevelt was already well on his way toward his eventual
strong disposition on behalf of action in Morocco.

Possibly from considerations of practical domestic politics and
on State Department advice, in the summer of 1940 the President
had decided that Africa was the best place to resist another
Axis breakthrough to the Atlantic. Dakar could be plausibly
represented as a great threat to Latin America, a continent
made much of by both American isolationists and interventionists

in 1940–41, although for very different reasons. At the moment, the hasty departure of a United States consul for Dakar was the limit of the administration's activities, but the State Department had been sufficiently aroused to initiate consideration of its own type of collusive conspiracy with the Vichy French in these regions.[41]

In a revealing passage Winston Churchill has written: 'Once it was clear that Casablanca was beyond our strength, my mind naturally turned to Dakar.' On August 3 the Prime Minister gave his approval to an expedition, code-named Menace, involving General de Gaulle's Free French in a seaborne assault against the West African capital. The British leader felt in his fingertips that the Vichy French would not declare war, a tactile perception no doubt convenient since he has admitted that he had undertaken in an exceptional degree the advocacy of this expedition.[42] Had Churchill's gamble failed and Vichy entered the war on the Axis side, as Pierre Laval actually advocated after Dakar, Britain would have been threatened much more terribly by the German U-boat campaign already moving seriously against her. On the other hand, had de Gaulle gained possession of Dakar, according to General Weygand, the Germans would have countered by immediately occupying French North Africa.[43] Weygand's opinion, of course, cannot be substantiated. However, the hopes and policy of Admiral Raeder in this period and Hitler's impulsive occupation of Tunisia in 1942 following the Allied invasion of northwest Africa lend it support.[44]

Through a chain of mischances, Menace failed to achieve its ill-defined purpose, yet the struggle for Africa had begun. On the same day that the luckless Allied expedition was diverted from Dakar southeast to the French Cameroons, the War Plans Division of the United States Army submitted a memorandum which said, in part, that the United States might need to occupy Dakar and the Azores even if the British fleet were not lost.[45] The unfavorable criticism which broke out in the United States following the abandonment of the assault on Dakar may have made President Roosevelt all the more receptive to the idea of action along the lines suggested by the War Plans Division.

The embarrassingly visible fiasco at Dakar did not induce Mr.

Churchill to forget his hopes for an approach to the Mediterranean; he simply fell back again upon less military methods of
obtaining his ends. In October he wrote to Sir Samuel Hoare,
the British Ambassador in Madrid, in a vein of frustration: 'It
passes my comprehension why no French leaders secede to
Africa . . . If this had been done at the beginning we might well
have knocked out Italy by now. But surely the opportunity is the
most splendid ever offered to daring men.'

At the same time the Prime Minister asked President Roosevelt to put pressure upon the less daring men of Vichy not to
surrender to the Axis either military bases in North Africa or
French naval ships.[46] In this matter the President had already
acted. Secretaries Stimson and Hull had become as alarmed as
Winston Churchill in the month of the Nazi Fuehrer's mysterious
visits with Franco, Pétain, and Mussolini.

The Prime Minister also undertook a policy with reference to
Marshal Pétain which is still rather cloudy. He received a Pro-
fessor Louis Rougier, representing the Marshal, and evidently
pressed upon him the desirability of active resistance on the
part of General Weygand in North Africa. Although subsequently he has not liked to admit it, and notwithstanding his
formal commitment to de Gaulle, Churchill was always as eager
to further his 'collusive conspiracy' with Vichy as was Cordell
Hull.

Whatever the outcome of these surreptitious negotiations, General Weygand, the new Vichy commander in Algiers, treated
them with discretion. He was supposed to have said: 'If they
[the British] come to North Africa with four divisions, I'll fire
on them; if they come with twenty divisions, I will welcome
them.' [47] In this era Mr. Churchill was hopefully planning for at
best a force of six divisions with which to enter French Morocco
by July of 1941 should the French attitude there become favorable.

In late November Churchill wrote the President concerning
Britain's now recognized inability to take on the defense of the
western Mediterranean in addition to that of the recently active
eastern Mediterranean theater. Should Hitler enter Spain and
by-pass Gibraltar, he said, there would be no force to prevent

the Germans' crossing the narrow Straits and entering Africa at Tangier and Ceuta. 'Once in Morocco,' warned the Prime Minister, 'the Germans will work southward, and U-boats and aircraft will soon be operating freely from Casablanca and Dakar.' Churchill has revealed that, so early as 1940, he had sensed the President's interest in Morocco and French West Africa.[48]

While the Americans appointed Admiral Leahy, a close advisor of Roosevelt, ambassador to France in order to tighten their connections with Vichy and Algiers, Lord Halifax proposed to Marshal Pétain that a state of 'artificial tension' between Vichy and Britain be maintained to deceive the Germans (not to mention General de Gaulle). Nonetheless the ultimate object of the British remained that of bringing Pétain or elements of his regime over to the Allied side. Since there was no serious chance of such a possibility, one American authority has argued that it is very surprising that the British government persisted in ignoring that fact.[49] In the future Winston Churchill was to manifest the ability to ignore much more obvious facts than the petty obduracy of the regime at Vichy when the future of his strategy in the Mediterranean basin was at stake.

3

RAINBOWS ACROSS THE ATLANTIC

GRAND STRATEGY AT HOME AND POLICY OVERSEAS

1940–1941

'Desirous of doing many things at once, the British government easily accepted the assurance of a few royalists as to the political dispositions of a most excitable and changeable race. . . . It was an exact repetition of the blunder which led to the invasion of the Southern colonies during the American Revolution; and the gist of the mistake is in the dependence upon unorganized forces to supplement the weakness of the organized force, which is not by itself alone sufficient to its undertaking.' [1] — Admiral Mahan

'The defect of brilliant brains is not necessarily a want of courage — daring there usually has been in plenty — but they are apt to lack fortitude. They are apt to abandon the assault upon positions which are not really invulnerable, and go off, chasing after attractive butterflies, until they fall into quagmires. Dispersion of effort has always been the besetting sin of British statesmen and the curse of British policy.' [2] — F. S. Oliver

'He [Churchill] carries great guns, but his navigation is uncertain.' [3] — Harold Begbie

'There's Winston, he has half a dozen solutions to it and one of them is right, but the trouble is he does not know which it is. [4] — David Lloyd George

I N the summer and fall of 1940, coincident with the increasing interest of President Roosevelt in the northwest coast of Africa, a more general and more objective approach to the issue of grand strategy against the Axis was initiated. At the suggestion of Lord Lothian, the British Ambassador in Washington, Admiral Stark sent Rear Admiral Ghormley to London in

July for exploratory conversations with the British Chiefs of
Staff. With the full approval of the President this useful staff
relationship with Great Britain was broadened by August to include representatives of the U. S. Army and Air Forces.[5]

In London the American emissaries quickly discovered that
the British Chiefs regarded the conquest of Italy as a strategic
aim of the first importance, although at the same time they maintained that all actions should be related to their 'main object,'
the defeat of Germany. In reply to Admiral Ghormley's question as to whether land warfare against Germany was necessary
to achieve a decision, the British declared that they hoped for
a serious weakening in the morale and combat efficiency of
the Germans, if not a total collapse, before the British Army delivered a *coup de grâce*.[6]

In 1941, General Marshall would send General Chaney to
London as his permanent personal representative, but almost
until Pearl Harbor, the United States Navy was the bolder and
more energetic American service. Toward late October, 1940,
Captain Kelly Turner came from the Naval War College to head
the Navy War Plans Division, bringing with him certain fruits of
his previous labors. These were the conclusions, reached from
studies undertaken in the spring of 1940 at the War College,
that in a two-ocean war priority should be given to the defeat
of Germany, that American aid to Great Britain would hasten that
defeat, and that action against Japan in the event of war in the
Pacific should be initially defensive.

Captain Turner may have provided the impulse for Admiral
Stark's Plan D (or Dog) memorandum, a plan which deliberately
was not allowed to see the light of day until November 12,
that is to say, until the results of the presidential election were
known. In accord with his new Chief of War Plans, Admiral
Stark propounded his belief that in the event of war an offensive
strategy in the Atlantic with a defensive in the Pacific would be
the correct course. Already in prospective opposition to Winston
Churchill's emphasis of September 3 upon bombers alone as
Britain's means of victory, this unusual American admiral stressed
that purely naval assistance would not assure victory for Great
Britain. The United States would have to send large air and land

forces to Europe or Africa, or both, and participate strongly in a land offensive in these regions.

Yet it is important to notice that these American naval plans were continuing to include Africa as a perfectly acceptable alternative or approach to Europe. Even the most able minds in the British and American navies did not apply the principle of ruthless concentration of force to land armies nearly so consistently as they did to sea power.[7]

As a preliminary to possible entry of the United States into the war, Stark recommended that secret and detailed staff talks be immediately undertaken with Great Britain, an opinion which paralleled that of the First Sea Lord, Admiral Sir Dudley Pound. Thus it was the naval chiefs of Britain and the United States who propounded the bases for and urged the speedy formulation of the eventual grand strategy of the Western Allies, a strategy soon to be embodied in the principles of the ABC-1 Staff Agreement.

General Marshall was, of course, in essential agreement with these proposals of his colleagues, although on November 27 he wrote the Chief of Naval Operations suggesting what was to become a perennial source of conflict with the United States Navy, namely the readjusting of war plans on the basis that 'we avoid dispersions that might lessen our power to operate effectively, decisively if possible, in the principal theater — the Atlantic.'[8] Of significance for his future maneuvers was the fact that Marshall had already warned that 'a serious commitment in the Pacific is just what Germany would like to see us undertake.'[9]

As so often before Pearl Harbor, Prime Minister Churchill lost no time in accommodating himself without argument to a strategic outlook relatively well-suited to his own concepts of the future. He wrote the First Sea Lord on November 22: 'In my view Admiral Stark is right and Plan D is strategically sound, and also most highly adapted to our interests. We should, therefore, so far as opportunity serves, in every way contribute to strengthen the policy of Admiral Stark, and should not use arguments inconsistent with it.'[10] There were no qualifications to Winston Churchill's enthusiasm for a plan which led both away

from the Pacific and, quite possibly, toward the Mediterranean.
In accordance with Admiral Stark's recommendation in Plan
D that detailed and secret staff conversations be undertaken at
once with Great Britain, representatives of the various service
War Plans Divisions of the two powers gathered on January 29
in Washington for a series of conferences which were to last until
the end of March. In their final report, submitted on March 27,
1941, and entitled the ABC-1 Staff Agreement from the names
of the participating states, the conferees laid down the first
declaration of common strategic principles between the British
Commonwealth and the United States.[11] Wisely, after reading
the agreement, the President declined to sign it before America's
entry into the war.[12] Yet his approval was obviously essential
for the making of a *de facto* military agreement with another
country.

The American delegation, headed by Admiral Ghormley and
General Embick, was bound rather closely by instructions issued
by Stark and Marshall, instructions which revealed that the eastward emphasis behind what would soon be called Rainbow No.
5 was already dominant in the thought of the administration in
Washington. Ghormley's and Embick's orders read: 'The objective of the war will be most effectively attained by the United
States exerting its principal military effort in the Atlantic or
navally in the Mediterranean regions.'

In their final report, therefore, the delegates reiterated this
stress upon American action in the West rather than in the
East. They promulgated what was to be at least the official
strategy for the United States in the next four years, however
much it would be violated in practice. 'Since Germany is the
predominant member of the Axis Powers,' affirmed the conferees,
'the Atlantic and European area is considered to be the decisive
theater. The principal United States military effort will be exerted
in that theater, and operations in other theaters will be conducted in such a manner as to facilitate that effort.' This fundamental statement concluded: 'If Japan does enter the war, the
strategy in the Far East will be defensive.'

Under the heading 'General Strategic Concepts,' ABC-1 placed
four plans for an offensive in the West on a seemingly equal

plane. The first involved the increase of the air offensive against Germany, the second the concentration of Allied naval power in the Mediterranean to eliminate Italy early in the war, the third advocated concentrations of American and British troops in England to prepare to invade the Continent 'as the opportunity offers' in accord with joint Allied plans to be formulated at a later date, while the fourth proposed the 'capture of Mediterranean or other bases from which one or more invasions of Europe could be launched at the appropriate moment.' [13]

A program of this character was well-calculated to satisfy all service arms equally, as well as to please Mr. Churchill by its emphasis upon the conduct of the war in ways not inconsistent with his viewpoint. Unfortunately these diverse proposals, so often hereafter to be presented as complementary to each other, would in practice turn out to be savagely competing alternatives. The lack of a sharper Allied strategic focus in the West, embodied particularly in ABC-1's implicit acceptance of the British encircling ring strategic theory,[14] was to plague Anglo-American relations for the next three years.

Another aspect of the potential conflict between the British Isles and North Africa as bases for land offensives against the European Axis may be seen in the assertion by ABC-1 that each of these regions was essential for a defensive Allied strategy. Great Britain, of course, had to be held, but whether it was necessary 'to maintain the present British and Allied military positions in and near the Mediterranean basin, and to prevent the spread of Axis control in North Africa' as well was another matter.[15] Certainly, to the dismay of Mr. Churchill, even in 1941 the United States War Department was to have grave doubts concerning the desirability of holding the Middle East.[16] In 1942 when the great bastion of the British Isles was already held in much more than adequate strength, Churchill would successfully urge the necessity of defending North Africa, using this as an effective argument for a deployment of forces that would later validate his concept of land offensive against Italy instead of the Reich.

If the specific geographical outlook of the ABC-1 Staff Agreement on the conduct of warfare against the European Axis was lacking in sufficiently clear-cut definition, the clauses setting up a Supreme War Council for Britain and the United States in the event of the formal entry of the latter into the war can also be easily confused with the subsequent strictly military body known as the Combined Chiefs of Staff. Nevertheless the affirmation of such a supranationalist political concept by itself testified to the immense superiority of the conduct of coalition warfare on the Allied side by 1941; none of the more or less absolute major Axis rulers would ever have seriously entertained such a grave limitation upon their sovereignty.

Another aspect of this flexible Anglo-American outlook, likewise born from bitter experience in France in the First World War, was the insistence in ABC-1 upon unity of command in each theater, and integrity of the forces of each nation in such theaters. The English-speaking democracies, so accustomed to compromise and limited authority at home, were temperamentally capable of effective coalition warfare overseas.

A new temptation besetting the planners in Washington may be found in the Aladdin's lamp of strategic bombing. Submitted almost simultaneously with ABC-1 was a report on air collaboration between the potential allies. Known as ABC-2, this report recommended that the production of heavy bombers be increased in order to support a sustained air offensive against Germany of all areas within range of the United Kingdom.[17]

It is abundantly evident that there is a close conceptual relationship between Mr. Churchill's direct expressions of opinion to President Roosevelt and this ABC-2 Agreement. In December 1940, in accord with his memorandum of September 3 of that year, Churchill had written the President that heavy bombers were Britain's principal offensive weapon against Germany. In February 1941, in a public radio broadcast in connection with the pending Lend-Lease Act, the Prime Minister had denied wanting an American army of millions in Europe, even in the later stages of the war.[18]

Certainly this was not a view which Mr. Churchill expounded exclusively for the sake of mollifying the American isolationists. So early as the opening of the twentieth century the youthful Winston Churchill had informed a House of Commons concerned with acting upon the unpleasant lessons of the Boer War: 'In putting our trust in an army, are we not investing in a shaky concern — in a firm that could not meet its obligations when called on? . . . The honour and security of the British Empire does not depend and can never depend, on the British Army.' As a rather unorthodox participant in several recent British colonial wars, Winston Churchill then believed that Great Britain should abandon any 'servile imitation of continental operations.' Instead of trying 'to make a miniature German Army in England,' the young Mr. Churchill advocated the raising of 'a force as would represent the natural and military characteristics of the British people.' [19]

It can be seen why so reluctant a progenitor of Haldane's 'Hegelian' and Kitchener's mass armies as Lord Esher would conclude that if much of what Mr. Churchill had said about the British Navy was both interesting and valuable, all that he had to say in this period about the Army was worthless.[20] Even in the Second World War his own Chief of the Imperial General Staff, Sir Alan Brooke, would find Churchill sometimes 'unconsciously unjust' to the British Army because of his earlier experiences.[21]

As in the German Navy, so also in the United States Navy could thinking parallel to Churchill's be found. More representative of the Pacific-minded American Navy than Admiral Stark, in a memorandum dated January 9, 1941, Admiral Yarnell anticipated the British Prime Minister's public disclaimer of the need for a large American Army or its corollary, the possibility of large American casualties. Yarnell proposed an American Navy and Air Force equal to that of any hostile nation or coalition; for the Army, apart from some outlying garrisons, Yarnell saw no need for any force larger than 600,000 men. He asserted that the United States should never send a large army abroad in any future war and that the American military frontier must stop at the enemy coast.[22] It may be concluded that a military apparatus organized along these lines was inherently defensive in its composition; given the technological conditions prevailing in 1941 the war could not be won with it.

During the formulation of Allied grand strategy, consideration of North Africa had not been forgotten either in London or in Washington. General Wavell's easy victory over the Italians in Egypt and Cyrenaica at the end of December 1940 again raised Prime Minister Churchill's African hopes and dreams to a high pitch. Churchill hastened to appeal to the Italians to dispense with their Duce, publicly affirming that 'one man and one man alone' was responsible for the 'river of blood . . . flowing between the British and Italian peoples.'[23] Hereafter Wavell and his successors in the Middle East would be subject to constant pressure by the Prime Minister to launch attacks before they were fully prepared.[24]

On December 31, in a more private communication to Marshal Pétain, Churchill wrote: 'If at any time in the near future the French Government decide to cross to North Africa or resume the war there against Italy and Germany, we should be willing to send a strong and well-equipped Expeditionary Force of up to six divisions to aid the defence of Morocco, Algiers and Tunis . . . delay is dangerous. At any time the Germans may, by force or favour, come down through Spain . . . and . . . establish themselves on the Moroccan coast. . . .'[25] The Prime Minister received no reply for his pains from either the aged Marshal or from General Weygand in Algiers to whom a similar message had been sent.

Actually by early January Churchill appears to have sensed that the German threat to the western Mediterranean, however useful it might be as a debating point in correspondence with Vichy and Washington, was noticeably less than that brewing before the eastern Mediterranean. Consequently he urged the revival of Workshop, a plan of the Director of Combined Operations, Sir Roger Keyes, to seize the small Italian island of Pantelleria, which, like Malta, was located directly athwart the Axis convoy route in Tripoli. After the condemnation of this plan by Admiral Cunningham, who subsequently in terms worthy of Kitchener described it as a 'wild-cat scheme' of little value, the British Chiefs of Staff vainly attempted to divert the attention of the Prime Minister to the island of Rhodes, which commanded the safest maritime route to the Balkans.[26]

Rhodes, the objective of Operation Mandibles in its 1941 form,

lay on the Aegean flank of Turkey, a neutral state whose large
and poorly equipped army would continue to attract Winston
Churchill's encouraging smiles and ultimately futile favors for
three full years more. Long before the Second World War
Churchill had written in a striking exposition of his political
conception of war, 'At the summit politics and strategy are one.
The manoeuvre which brings an ally into the field is as service-
able as that which wins a great battle.' [27]

Although unenthusiastic concerning the seizure of so useful
a logistic stepping stone as Rhodes, the Prime Minister was still
itching to mobilize the armies of Turkey and Yugoslavia and
with the aid of these small allies to open up a new front in
southeastern Europe. As in the First World War numerous
Balkan allies were integral to Winston Churchill's concept of
limited British land warfare on the continent of Europe. Indeed,
so early as 1901 Mr. Churchill had emphasized that such famous
British victories as Blenheim and Waterloo had been won 'mainly
by foreigners.' [28]

The Turks were not, however, so incautious as to play the role
shortly to be assumed with so little warning by the more febrile
Serbs, namely that of the gambit in the Prime Minister's ambitious schemes. Sensibly, the Ankara Government refused the
British offers of a few Royal Air Force squadrons from the already overstrained Middle East Command on the grounds that
these units were too small to resist a German assault — but were
large enough to provoke such an attack.[29] Turkey had no illusions that the seventy-odd British and lesser power divisions
theoretically available to resist the Germans at this time could
in any real sense equal twenty or thirty divisions from the Reich,
quite apart from the fact that in the spring of 1941 Germany
could have reinforced her fine units in the Balkans indefinitely
while the Allies could not.

Unfortunately, as a result of the German occupation of Bulgaria on March 1, the Greek Government at last succumbed to
the repeated British offers of an inadequate force of ground
troops. To the keen regret of the Greek commander himself, in
order to release a British corps for this purpose, a promising offensive of the Eighth Army against Tripoli was called off on the eve

of final success.[30] In addition, although the seizure of Rhodes had always been considered an essential logistic precursor of any major British commitment in Greece, such an operation, as well as even more ambitious projects already involving Sicily (Operation Influx), were shelved in favor of the landing in Greece. As Antwerp and the Dardanelles expedition in 1914–15 had demonstrated,[31] logistics were not Winston Churchill's strong point. In this he differed from the Duke of Marlborough.[32]

In the First World War, the failure of the Dardanelles assault had cost the Australians and New Zealanders heavily in blood. When in April 1941 Hitler responded to the inflammatory but feeble British gesture on a continent which he now regarded as his own, it must have been peculiarly galling to the next generation of Anzacs to witness the dissipation of their volunteer manpower once again in an unsuccessful venture by Mr. Churchill in the Balkans.[33] In any event, when the superior German Army and Air Force drove them into the sea the British lost some 25,000 men, mostly Australians and New Zealanders, their still more valuable equipment, and many then irreplaceable planes and warships. The Greeks and Serbs lost everything.

Nor was this all. Largely because his command had been denuded to supply Greece, General Wavell was to meet a defeat in Cyrenaica, predicted by his subordinates, at the hands of Rommel's newly arrived Afrika Korps.[34] Moreover, it should be noted that Hitler's last-minute decision to include Yugoslavia in his invasion of northern Greece, an impromptu action which along with bad weather seems to have delayed his attack on the Soviet Union for several weeks, was precipitated by the revolt of the Serb officers against the Axis rather than directly by the arrival of British troops in Athens.

But to this extent Churchill's rash Balkan policy might be said ultimately to have paid off by contributing to the delay of the Nazi drive into Russia and hence by reducing its depth of penetration in 1941, although in the opinion of one disillusioned British military planner very much concerned with this whole operation, the Prime Minister may not retrospectively claim credit on this account. Certainly, unlike his characterization of the Norwegian campaign,[35] Mr. Churchill would not call Hitler's invasion of Greece a strategic blunder until Barbarossa had given him a leg to stand on in this respect.[36] David Lloyd George's prophecy to the effect that Churchill's future depended upon whether he could establish a reputation for prudence without losing audacity assumes a more concrete meaning in this context — a context in which in the Second World War, as in the First, Mr. Churchill would display an excess of audacity in the Aegean and of prudence in the West.[37]

The motive for this particular incursion by Mr. Churchill into a region in which by 1943 he would have faced humiliation four times has been described as political by both the proponents and opponents of the Greek operation. In an explanation by the Foreign Secretary, evocative of Neville Chamberlain's chivalric war-making, Britain was fighting 'not for gains, but for causes.' Unfortunately for Great Britain, to Mr. Eden Greece was apparently the only acceptable 'embodiment of those causes.' [38]

Moral issues aside, experience in the Aegean and elsewhere has shown that the political benefits accruing from honorable military defeats are quite illusionary, either at home or with neutral powers. In fact, perhaps more distrustful of Foreign Office strategy than some of his military advisers, Mr. Churchill himself feared, in advance, 'another Norwegian fiasco' in Greece.[39] But with Mr. Eden and the War Cabinet he bore full responsibility for the decision in favor of what at least one general involved has termed a 'terribly unsound' military campaign.[40]

It should be recalled, moreover, that this decision was taken in the face of steadily deteriorating tactical and strategic circumstances in both Greece and Cyrenaica, the grave doubts of the British Chiefs of Staff and of the House of Commons, the fears of the Australian and New Zealand governments, the unreliability of the Greek high command, and a problem in transporting and in supplying the British forces in Greece, comparable, indeed, to either the Norwegian campaign of 1940 or that in the Dardanelles in 1915. In extenuation it may be that poor intelligence as much as wishful thinking had misled the British Government.[41] By 1941, however, as the Duke of Wellington had said after his first campaign in Flanders, Mr. Churchill's government should have at least learned what not to do in war.

The most serious criticism that can be made of Mr. Churchill's direction of the war in the Middle East in 1941 is that he desired, as always in the Mediterranean, to do too much with too little.[42] Refusing to make essential choices in priorities in the spring of 1941, the Prime Minister had ordered the Middle East Command to conquer Italian East Africa, capture Rhodes, and defend Malta, Cyrenaica, and Turkey, while at the same time he enjoined his commanders to 'let their first thoughts be for Greece.'[43] But the answer to General Sir Alan Brooke's orthodox military query at this time — 'Why will politicians never learn the simple principle of concentration of force at the vital point and the avoidance of dispersal of effort?'[44] — may be found in Brooke's own conflict with the American military in 1942; the professional military, too, often disagree on what constitutes the vital point.

During the late winter and spring of 1940–41, two influential members of Mr. Churchill's Conservative party unburdened themselves to two equally well-placed Americans on the problem of the western Mediterranean. Sir Samuel Hoare gave to Roosevelt's peregrinating military observer, Colonel William Donovan of subsequent O.S.S. fame, a message to bring back to the President. Roosevelt was requested to take the Spanish peninsula and the northwest African coast under his special protection. Later in the year Sir Samuel was to impart to the Prime Minister a view which he held in common with Colonel Donovan, that North Africa would offer the Americans the nearest and easiest way for entering the European theater of war.[45]

In London, General H. H. Arnold of the U.S.A.A.F. observed that Anthony Eden, like everyone else in the British capital, was very interested in what was happening at Dakar. To the British Foreign Secretary also it was essential that the Americans get into Morocco and win confidence before the Germans could effectively establish themselves there.[46]

If, according to one semi-official American historian, the fear of the British over a Nazi advance through Spain had now become almost pathological,[47] one may surmise from the emphases in Mr. Churchill's own post-war account that in 1941 this fear was to some degree stressed for the benefit of the United States. To be sure, on April 24 the Prime Minister did warn the President that Spain and Portugal might surrender at any time and that Gibraltar might thereby be rendered untenable, but there is less evidence to indicate that he deemed the situation hopeless. Again, on May 4, Churchill assured the President: 'You alone can forestall the Germans in Morocco. If they are once installed, it will not be necessary for them to go overland; they will soon get airborne troops to Dakar.' [48]

In mid-April Cordell Hull had already informed Lord Halifax, the new British Ambassador in Washington, that he did not believe that Britain or the United States currently had the power to intervene at either Casablanca or Dakar, regardless of how great the need for their doing so might become. Consequently the President's anxiety must have been acute when on May 11 and 12 Admiral Darlan was received by Hitler himself. On May 15 Roosevelt publicly declared that it was inconceivable that France would voluntarily deliver her North African colonies to the Germans.[49]

In Vichy the President's friend of long standing, Admiral Leahy, now found himself in despair. On May 22 Leahy wrote the White House that if an Allied army of 250,000 men could reinforce General Weygand's poorly equipped troops before a German arrival in North Africa, this would insure the Allies' control of the Mediterranean and would halve the length of the war.[50] The American Ambassador had been warned a month earlier by Marshal Pétain regarding an imminent German plan to invade Spain, a plan which the Marshal intended to resist.[51] It was, nevertheless, a most significant augury for the future of Allied strategy that such an influential military adviser should feel that the use of land troops for essentially naval purposes could shorten the war by half.

On the same day that this communication was received at the White House, the President again acted within what he believed to be his means. As in the late spring of 1940, he gave Admiral Stark a limit of thirty days to prepare the Navy for the occupation of the Azores, an action envisaged by the American armed services in the ABC-1 Agreement.[52] London was simultaneously perfecting long-standing arrangements to seize the Cape Verde Islands and the Canaries, two amphibious operations which would exploit British resources to the utmost.[53] Northwest Africa might still be beyond the strength of the Allies, but the Spanish and Portuguese islands off the coast of that continent presumably were not. A German seizure of the Atlantic coast of northwest Africa, not to mention the islands offshore, would tend to interdict the British shipping routes both through the Mediterranean and around the Cape to the Middle East and Asia. The supposed Nazi threat to Brazil ensuing might then be used to justify American assistance in a manifestly defensive Allied effort.

The United States armed services responded to this White House extension of the Pot-of-Gold plan to the Azores with something less than enthusiasm. Although, according to Admiral Stark, the Navy and Marines would have to bear the brunt of any such impromptu assault, in the graphic phrase of a subsequent service critic of the President, the War Plans Division of the U. S. Army also 'nearly went crazy.' In the opinion of W.P.D., this operation, Plan Gray in code-name parlance, would require three months to prepare as against the one month they had been given by the President.[54]

Finally it was recognized by the higher American authorities that any such concrete American action so near to the entrance of Mr. Churchill's favorite sea was impossible to carry out in view of the shortage of equipment of all kinds. So faithful an administration stalwart as Admiral Stark had come to recognize the extreme difficulty of executing any such operation in the immediate future. Indeed, at the suggestion of Harry Hopkins, General Marshall had already undertaken the education of the President in military matters. Hopkins and Marshall both felt that Mr. Roosevelt had been unduly influenced by the State Department.[55]

On May 28, Admiral Darlan signed a long-anticipated agreement with the German representatives in Paris granting the Axis the right to place certain military forces in Syria, Tunisia, and Dakar. The day before the Darlan agreement, President Roosevelt had tried to prepare domestic public opinion for a sudden United States counteraction beyond the confines of the Monroe Doctrine, e.g. in the Azores, in response to the expected German assault upon the western Mediterranean. In proclaiming an Unlimited National Emergency, Roosevelt had warned the American electorate that the Germans had the power to occupy Spain and Portugal 'at any moment' and to threaten thereby not only Morocco but also Dakar and the Cape Verde Islands. The last-named islands, concluded the President astutely, were only 'seven hours distance from Brazil by bomber or troop-carrying planes.' Their loss would bring the war 'very close to home.' [56]

On June 6, suspecting the forthcoming German attack on Russia, and by threatening to resist forceably any German intervention in the French colonies, the Vichy regime was able to back down on the Darlan accords.[57] At the same time Mr. Churchill was also convinced that Hitler intended to invade Russia and that Spain would no longer acquiesce in a German occupation of the peninsula. The most alarming phase of the fancied German threat to Africa having blown over, to the great relief of the United States Army and Navy arrangements were now made between the British and American governments to divert the U. S. Marines from the Azores to Iceland.[58]

If another essentially artificial Allied crisis regarding northwest Africa had been brought to a close without any immediate material damage having been done, this tempest in a teapot may have had the effect of increasing pressure for the movement of additional United States naval strength from the Pacific to the Atlantic. In early April Admiral Stark, conforming to the real policy of the President, had written: 'The situation . . . in the Atlantic . . . is hopeless except as we take strong measures to save it.' [59] But strong elements of the U. S. Navy as well as the State Department did not share the opinion of the Chief of Naval Operations or, for that matter, of the Secretary of War, that the Japanese risk was moderate and the need for the active employment of the fleet in the Atlantic greater than for its passive role at Pearl Harbor. As a result the President was forced to compromise this argument. In May, Mr. Roosevelt decided to transfer three battleships and an appropriate supporting force to the Atlantic, a solution which, according to his frequently mordant Secretary of War, did not leave anyone wholly pleased.[60]

President Roosevelt may have chosen to consider this revealing issue as closed hereafter; yet for a large part of the Navy Department no solution, however much in harmony with the developing Allied coalition strategy, which left the Pacific Fleet inferior to the Japanese Navy in every type of combat ship, would ever be fundamentally acceptable.[61] Nonetheless, on the eve of the cause for Hitler's loss of interest in Spain and Morocco — his proposed attack upon Russia — the chances for an efficient long-range strategy on the part of the Western Allies looked bright. Rainbow No. 5 was definitely on top and its North African facet was momentarily quiescent.

4

THE GRAND ALLIANCE

WINSTON CHURCHILL AND LIMITED WAR

June 22, 1941–December 7, 1941

'I cannot believe that the next war, if it ever comes, will be like the last one, and I believe that our resources will be more profitably employed in the air, and on the sea, than in building up great armies.' [1] — Neville Chamberlain in 1936

'The smaller the land forces that we send abroad, the larger the air strength we can concentrate . . . If we arrange to send across the Channel a complete force like that of 1914 . . . its arrival might encourage the French to take the offensive — with the fanciful idea of winning the war in a land campaign.' [2] — Captain Liddell Hart in 1938

'This country provides the greatest fleet in the world. It has a rapidly growing Air Force. It has to provide munitions . . . for its Allies, and it cannot, in addition to that, provide a great Continental Army.' [3] — Clement Attlee in 1939

'If there was a country that had particular reasons to avoid war, it was certainly Great Britain. The only way for her to keep her Empire was to have a strong air force and a strong navy. That was all she needed.' [4] — Adolf Hitler in 1942

HAVING called in a New World to restore the balance of power, again like Canning, on June 22, 1941, Winston Churchill announced his support for Russia as a fighting comrade in arms. Declared the Prime Minister generously: 'The past with its crimes, its follies, and its tragedies flashes away.' [5] He added, however, that Hitler's attack on the U.S.S.R. was no more than a prelude to a German attempt at the invasion of Britain.[6] The implication here seems clearly to suggest an expectation of a renewed German assault upon the United Kingdom following her speedy defeat of Russia. In addition, Mr. Churchill may have felt that it was necessary to hold up the Nazi threat as a club to maintain the urgency of the British war effort. It is also possible that Albion, the German cover plan for Barbarossa, involving an ostensibly continued threat against Great Britain, was responsible for the Prime Minister's anxieties on this score.[7]

Although Mr. Churchill has called attention to the fact that his first Chief of the Imperial General Staff, Sir John Dill, had manifested undue pessimism concerning the Russian chances, he has also admitted that in June and July 1941 almost all responsible military opinion believed that the Soviet Union would soon be defeated. In this instance the Former Naval Person presumably did not exclude himself from almost all responsible military opinion. But at the same time, unlike his C.I.G.S. or the United States Chiefs of Staff, Churchill had not the slightest intention of abandoning the eastern Mediterranean to strengthen still further his British home base for defensive or other reasons.[8]

Both the War Plans Division and the G-2 Section of the U. S. Army also agreed with the British that the Soviets would be defeated within a few months, views in evident agreement with those of Admiral Leahy at that time. Moreover, in late July and the beginning of August the customarily alarmist American admiral warned the President that indications in Vichy pointed to a German move in the western Mediterranean in the direction of Dakar regardless of the outcome of the German campaign in Russia.

In anticipation of such a revival of Felix as much as of Sea-Lion, the United States Chiefs of Staff believed that Britain was making too many sacrifices in trying to maintain the Middle East. Already almost half of British military production was being sent to this theater.[9] Although the President already felt that the British had to fight the enemy wherever they found him, the United States Chiefs of Staff and the United States War Department, in particular, would not change their minds concerning the dangers of Allied operations in this region in view of the possibility of a German drive through Spain to trap any Allied land forces involved inside the Mediterranean.

In reaffirming his determination to continue fighting the Axis in Africa, Mr. Churchill maintained that approximately half of everything the enemy shipped to Libya was sunk en route.[10] Of course, throughout the early stages of the war the German General Staff recognized the advantages accruing to the British in conducting what was essentially a colonial campaign on the Dark Continent, inexpensive in lives if indecisive in results, whatever Erwin Rommel might feel to the contrary. On the other hand, after mid-1942 it was the Allies who had the initiative and, as Clausewitz has suggested, it is the assailant who must reach the decision.[11] Winston Churchill was repeatedly to refuse to face the consequences of this distinction between effective offensive and effective defensive warfare.

Within a month Mr. Churchill's unsolicited recognition of the new status of the U.S.S.R. had evoked a reply from Joseph Stalin. Now also inclined to overlook the errors of the past, the Soviet leader initiated his correspondence with the British Prime Minister on July 18 with an attempt to justify his pact with Hitler as a method of gaining a protective belt of territory between the Soviet Union and Germany. Nonetheless Stalin had to recognize immediately, though not explicitly, the appalling price he had paid for this narrow strip of buffer provinces when he urged that Britain should restore the missing second front in the West. Like Mr. Churchill, apparently pessimistic concerning Russia's chances of survival,[12] the desperate Soviet Premier wrote the Prime Minister: 'A front in Northern France could not only divert Hitler's forces from the East, but at the same time would make it impossible for Hitler to invade Great Britain.' Stalin went on to point out that a British landing in Norway would be still safer.

As we have seen, Mr. Churchill, however, was less concerned with any sort of defense of Britain, least of all an offensive-defense in northern France, than with that of the Mediterranean basin. Furthermore, his probable belief at this time that the Russians would be defeated before winter would not accentuate any desire, however minute, to traverse the Channel and land in strength on the Continent simply in the futile hope of aiding his ally. Consequently he replied to Stalin with an accurate description of the German strength in France and the Low Countries as well as with a premature account of the still unconstructed German fortifications along the nearby Channel coast of France.[13] As in the next year, the Prime Minister was on safe grounds in rejecting large-scale land warfare, although as early as June 23 he had suggested a raid on the Channel coast with about 25,000 men.[14] Britain still lacked the resources for any such sustained effort, and her minimal defensive commitments in Asia and Africa, however unimportant they may have seemed to the United States or U.S.S.R., still greatly outweighed her military means.

A week after his reply to Stalin, Churchill wrote to President Roosevelt something of his own concept of how to wage war in the forthcoming years. For 1942 and 1943 the Prime Minister emphasized chiefly an augmented program of strategic bombing of Germany and Italy in the hope that such a method might evoke a domestic reaction against the Axis governments or even a collapse. Yet Churchill considered that plans ought 'also to be made for coming to the aid of the conquered populations by landing armies of liberation when opportunity is ripe.' [15] Here the skilled British historian and parliamentarian's language must be considered with extreme care; every word meant exactly what it said but it all added up to something very different indeed from what was implied at first sight.

By drawing up an invasion plan of the Continent postulated upon the principle of the liberating armies simply aiding the revolting population rather than vice versa, as in the current United States War Department concept, Churchill was actually again waiting until that uncertain time by which the R.A.F. Bomber Command and the Red Army might have cracked the will-to-fight of Hitler's Reich. The word 'also,' as employed by the Prime Minister in the statement above, reveals the subordination of even such limited plans for invasion to prior air action. The use of the plural 'armies' reflects Churchill's lack of commitment to any given geographic region such as France; in reality he was envisaging numerous weak landings all about the Axis periphery in Europe, i.e. the British strategy involving an ever-narrowing geographic ring about the European Axis. Finally, by qualifying his whole proposal with a 'when the time is ripe,' the Prime Minister avoided being pinned down to any deadline whatsoever for restoring a true second front against Hitler in the West.

To testify to his long-standing enthusiasm for a cross-Channel invasion such as took place in Normandy in 1944, since the war Churchill has stressed his own great role in pioneering the development of the landing craft essential to landing operations on a large scale against a strongly held beachhead. His letter to the President on July 25 had discussed the need for these ships and, in fact, not merely their creation but also their employment by Commando Companies originally under Sir Roger Keyes, Director of Combined Operations, had been a particular interest of the Prime Minister for over a year.[16] Nevertheless Winston Churchill was to desire these invaluable LCT's (landing craft, tank) and LST's (landing ship, tank) for purposes other than crossing the Channel, as would become unmistakably apparent in 1942–43.

At the end of July Franklin Roosevelt initiated his direct contact with Joseph Stalin by sending his intimate friend and adviser Harry Hopkins to Moscow. The President was soon greatly heartened by the optimistic conclusions Hopkins brought back from Moscow for the benefit of the ensuing Atlantic Conference. According to Hopkins' biographer, the plans of this first meeting between Roosevelt and Churchill, which had convened in early August at Argentia Bay off the coast of Newfoundland, were therefore predicated upon the belief that the Soviet Union would survive the German assault.[17] Yet if this were entirely true the continued preoccupation of those at the Atlantic Conference with the protection of the Canaries, the Azores, and the Cape Verde Islands from a German attack, presumably following the defeat of the Soviet Union, might appear difficult to understand.[18]

Indeed, in the hostile account of one of President Roosevelt's sons, Winston Churchill had not accepted the possibility, let alone the probability, of the Russians enduring another year.[19] According to official sources, so late as November 1941 American military planners likewise doubted the ability of the Russians to continue as an active partner in the field against Germany and had determined their war plans accordingly.[20] On the other hand, before October 1 the British Government had already supplied the hard-pressed Soviets with some four hundred and fifty planes, planes which if sent to Singapore might have protected the British Empire and Navy from humiliating defeats in the next year.[21] At the end of the year the Prime Minister would argue against his new Chief of the Imperial General Staff, Sir Alan Brooke, in a strong advocacy of stripping the United Kingdom of tanks for Russia.[22] Mr. Churchill was no simple anti-Bolshevik in his war policy.

In any event, at the Atlantic Conference the Prime Minister warned the Americans that the situation in Spain was going from bad to worse and that Great Britain was preparing an expedition to seize the Grand Canary by force from Spain about September 15.[23] The British Government was undertaking this expedition, known, presumably for the benefit of the Americans, as Operation Pilgrim, in full awareness that the islands had been strongly fortified and that such an act in all probability would result in a Spanish entry into the war and the British loss of the use of the harbor of Gibraltar.[24]

Probably the motive for this bold British policy lay less in Winston Churchill's degree of faith in the Russian chances than in his inveterate hope of involving the United States more actively in the war through President Roosevelt's special interest in French North and West Africa. With the intention of relieving Great Britain's shortage of shipping, Churchill informed the President at the Conference that he would rather have an American declaration of war immediately, regardless of the effect upon Lend-Lease, than twice as many American supplies without an American entry. According to the Prime Minister, Mr. Roosevelt replied: 'I may never declare war; I may make war. If I were to ask Congress to declare war, they might argue about it for three months.'[25] The President was acutely aware that to the U. S. isolationists Hitler existed merely in an irrelevant or inherently sinful European space, but not in the still too catholic and contemporary dimension of time.

Operation Pilgrim had not been discussed by Mr. Churchill in such alarming detail entirely for the sake of further disturbing the Americans with the possibility of a German attack through

Spain. In outlining this plan to their American opposite numbers the British Chiefs of Staff had already made clear that there were no British forces left for any additional projects in this area in view of Pilgrim and home commitments.[26] Very clearly the British were leaving plenty of ground for any type of American action in response to a Spanish belligerency, including an offensive action in French North Africa. Because of the supposed Germanophile inclinations of Franco, such an action could be represented to American public opinion as a defense of Latin America, regardless of what was actually done by the Reich.

Despite President Roosevelt's nautical fascination with Morocco in general, and especially Spanish Morocco, which controlled Admiral Mahan's hallowed gateway to the Mediterranean, the Straits of Gibraltar, the United States Chiefs were currently planning only a limited assault against Dakar.[27] But although Mr. Churchill did not obtain his declaration of war at the Atlantic Conference, without doubt he had laid another plank in the circuitous road which after Pearl Harbor would lead to the Anglo-American invasion of the Mediterranean in 1942 instead of France in 1943.

With respect to the Azores, President Roosevelt agreed to an American occupation in the event of a request by the Portuguese Government, but concerning the Cape Verde Islands the President had to concede his current inability to take these Portuguese possessions so close to Dakar. The Prime Minister replied that the British Government could occupy the islands with the understanding that it would transfer its protection to the American forces when they were in a position to assume it.[28] Mr. Churchill had more than a collusive conspiracy with Vichy in mind in the vicinity of North and West Africa.

At the Atlantic Conference the British also discussed over-all strategy in some detail. Since the Americans had prepared no agenda in this connection and had no authority from the President to discuss plans involving offensive action against the enemy on the continent of Europe, the British presentation was unilateral.[29]

Mr. Churchill's Chiefs of Staff recommended blockade, bombing, subversive activity, and propaganda as the four possible methods of waging war against Germany to wear her down for a direct attack. The Prime Minister's theatrical superiority over his predecessor is obvious in every respect; as is illustrated in this declaration by his Chiefs, he was a master of arranging what appeared to be war to the hilt. Neville Chamberlain had been both too ingenuous and too limited to recognize the need for seeming to do something at a time when nothing effective could be done. Yet, in actuality, Winston Churchill would not really want to face the logical consequences of an all-out war any more than had Chamberlain and so many others of their generation of Britons.

Consequently, at the Atlantic Conference the British Chiefs did not foresee vast armies of infantry as in the First World War. Abandoning Liddell Hart's essentially defensive theories of the late 1930's as they had been forced to abandon the renascent Cardwell system on which such warfare had been based, the British Chiefs now proposed to employ armored divisions equipped with the most up-to-date matériel. Local patriots on the verge of revolt were to provide the bulk of the manpower according to this obvious reiteration of the view of the Prime Minister in July 1941. In the last phase of this extraordinary proposal for the invasion of Hitler's Europe, American armored forces might also participate.[30]

The name of this British war plan was Roundup, a name which reflected its conception as a circular mop-up operation at the end of the war against nominal resistance. At that stage, and in its British version, Roundup was clearly designated not to create, but to take advantage of a German collapse.[31] At most, Roundup envisaged landing some fourteen divisions, chiefly in the region of the estuary of the Seine, as part of the general British plan of several minor Allied offensives around the periphery of a necessarily gravely weakened Axis. Yet it was upon an enlargement of this 1941 plan rather than any fundamental change in his conception of offensive warfare on land that Mr. Churchill rested his subsequent claim that he always favored a cross-Channel invasion of France of the kind exemplified by Overlord in June 1944.[32]

Of course, Mr. Churchill's entire plan for the full-scale invasion of the Continent depended upon the previous cracking of German power or morale. The most important of these morale-cracking forces was probably the Red Army, although wisely, the Prime Minister did not frankly discuss it as such. The principal reason openly expressed, however, and evidently the only other reason existing, apart from a gross and wishful overestimate of the effects of the blockade on Germany, was the possible consequences of area bombing by the R.A.F. to be supplemented with American aid of a similar kind. The United States Chiefs at the Atlantic Conference had been informed by their air observers in Britain that the British believed it was 'probably possible' to cause a German breakdown by bombing. On the other hand it was considered highly improbable in London that any land invasion could be carried out against Germany herself in the next three years. The British were seizing with enthusiasm the view that if an air offensive were successful, a land offensive would most likely be unnecessary.[33]

In July 1941, shortly before the Atlantic Conference, Mr. Churchill himself stated: 'We have now intensified for a month past our systematic, scientific, methodical bombing on a large scale of the German cities, seaports, industries and other military objectives. We believe it to be in our power to keep this process going, on a steadily rising tide, month after month, year after year, until the Nazi regime is either extirpated by us, or better still, torn to pieces by the German people themselves.'[34] Subsequent to the war Air Marshal Harris was to admit that area bombing to break the enemy's morale had shown itself to be wholly unsound, although a 'natural' opinion in 1941.[35] Natural or not, this old theory of Lord Trenchard, the father of R.A.F. strategic bombing,[36] was to prove useful in the extreme for the Prime Minister long after 1941.

Mr. Churchill's conception of war soon brought him into conflict with his ultimately successful antagonists in the Allied coalition, Joseph Stalin and George Marshall. In the same week in which the British Prime Minister resumed his uncomfortable correspondence with the Soviet Premier regarding a second front, General Marshall and Admiral Stark submitted to President Roosevelt one of the most important documents of Allied coalition strategy. This document, dated September 11, was rather innocuously entitled the *Joint Board Estimate of United States Over-all Production Requirements.*

In direct contradiction to the aspirations of Winston Churchill, it was affirmed in this American Estimate that 'the overthrow of the Nazi regime by action of the people of Germany is unlikely in the near future, and will not occur until Germany is upon the point of military defeat.' The conclusion was reached that since Germany could not be defeated by the existing belligerent powers, it would be necessary for the United States to enter the war, and to employ 'some of its armed forces in the Atlantic islands as well as in Europe or Africa.'

If Africa was still on an equal plane with Europe, the Joint Board vouchsafed another opinion again at variance with those of the Prime Minister when it stated with exceptional clarity: 'By themselves . . . naval and air forces seldom, if ever, win important wars. It should be recognized as an almost invariable rule that only land armies can finally win wars.' In accord with this then realistic view the U. S. Army made its estimate of the personnel required to engage the German armies on the continent of Europe itself, some 6,745,000 men exclusive of the Air Force.[37]

More specifically, under the influence of Major Albert Wedemeyer of the War Plans Division of the General Staff, the War Department in Washington had promulgated plans for putting approximately 5,000,000 men across the Channel directly into the centers of German war industry, the Saar and the Rhur.[38] This enormous force, to be organized in no less than two hundred and fifteen divisions, seemed essential in view of the Soviet defeat expected by the American planners in the near future.

Perhaps even more ambitious than this seeming reversion to the single theater strategy of the First World War — an efficient concept which the U. S. Army was always most reluctant to abandon — was the July 1943 date set for the unveiling of this impressive expression of orthodox military doctrine. As one close to General Marshall has written, the crux of this schedule was the time required to produce the necessary equipment, assuming, of course, that such equipment was produced first in the most urgently necessary priorities and that it would not be dispersed in other possible theaters of war.[39]

Despite the signature of Admiral Stark to the Joint Estimate, actually the U. S. Army was alone in its desire for a true second front in France in 1943 so far as the American military services were concerned. For example, General Marshall's nominal subordinates in the Army Air Force considered it improbable that a large-scale invasion of Europe could be made before the spring of 1944, which would prohibit such an invasion from preceding the anticipated knock-out blow of the bombers. As with the R.A.F., in all probability the real hope of the U. S. Air Force was that should an air offensive be successful, then a land assault might be unnecessary. Precisely what constituted success in the U.S.A.A.F.'s program was left unrevealed since, unlike the R.A.F., it was planning to bomb only precision targets in the Reich and had no intention of resorting to area bombing in an endeavor to break the morale of Hitler's totalitarian Reich.

In place of the Army Air Force's desire to delay any large-scale cross-Channel project, U. S. Navy planners were already offering diversion as their method of limiting the Army's grandiose scheme. The Navy asserted that the Allies should adopt a strategy which would enable them to exploit their naval and air superiority while limiting the employment of their inferior land forces to those peripheral regions where Germany could not engage them with the full strength of her army. These regions were defined in the Joint Estimate as particularly including Morocco, French West Africa, and the Azores. The principal weapon of the strongest Allied power, the Red Army, would have been nonplused by this candid naval exposition of Mr. Churchill's parallel view that offensive war should be waged for the sake of employing the heaviest investment in armaments at hand and for the sake of fighting on one's own terms rather than in pursuit of the speediest possible victory.

In a possible endeavor to divert the American Army's eyes from the large and flat plains of western Europe, the U. S. Navy could point to the interest of the former service in northwest Africa in terms of an almost immediate and essentially defensive effort against a possible German assault across the Mediterranean. Indeed, the Joint Board Estimate had declared that the prevention of any Axis entry into northwest Africa and the Atlantic islands was very important, not only for defensive purposes, but also as a possible base for a future land offensive. While action in this area might have as a motivation the recruitment of Vichy French troops in North Africa for subsequent use in Europe, in its initial stages it would necessarily be largely comprised of American soldiers. The British were considered to be too unpopular to risk using their troops in any of General Weygand's broad domains as a result of Mr. Churchill's premature attempts to induce these regions to enter the war on the Allied side.

More than a month after the Atlantic Conference the American reply to the British staff presentation of that time was prepared. In decrying the Prime Minister's mode of warfare in their statement of September 25, the United States Chiefs of Staff rather subtly chose to interpret the British position at the Atlantic Conference as diverging significantly from the strategy proposed in ABC-1 for the defeat of Germany. They declared that too much faith was being placed in the probability of success solely through bombing offensives executed to weaken the morale of the enemy. As they had with the President, so to the British the United States Chiefs affirmed that too little attention had been paid to the build-up of the large ground forces needed to defeat the German war machine, since dependence cannot be placed on winning important wars by reliance upon only naval and air forces.[40] Of the greatest significance for the future, in opposing the British view that an early American entry into the war would guarantee a swift Allied victory, the United States Chiefs wrote that the entry into the war of the American Army troops in the near future would 'at best involve a piecemeal and indecisive commitment of forces against a superior enemy under unfavorable logistic conditions.'[41]

In a statement to the President three days earlier, General Marshall had outlined his philosophy of war still more clearly. In defending the rapid expansion of the U. S. Army, Marshall stated: 'To seize and hold the initiative we must have forces available for employment at the time and place of our own choosing, not Hitler's. . . . Furthermore, sudden basic changes in policy . . . are devastating to organized effort. The "long view" is essential to our interests.' [42]

In response to this American declaration, the British Chiefs could only maintain that their review had been misunderstood. Softly they explained that their emphasis on the bomber offensive had not meant to preclude a final land offensive; but that they had been studying the problem of landing operations and had already discovered many difficulties.[43] While this last explanation was as valid in 1941 as it would be in 1942, the general British position had scarcely been misunderstood. American Army confusion was reserved hereafter only for the nature of the British Chiefs' final land offensive, a hardly encouraging conception, the emphasis of which in the upshot was to prove to be final.

The Prime Minister had also faced a fairly determined, if somewhat inchoate, series of Soviet demands for large-scale land action during this period of illuminating debate between his Chiefs of Staff and those of President Roosevelt. Stalin wrote Churchill at the beginning of September to ask for a second front either in the Balkans or France, capable of drawing thirty or forty German divisions away from Russia. While recognizing that such a message would cause Mr. Churchill dismay, it is clear that the Soviet Premier had not yet perceived that if a major effect was to be exercised upon the enemy of the kind he so urgently desired, no front in the Balkans, whether termed second or otherwise, would do.

More important, neither in 1941 nor in 1942 did the Soviet ruler ever appreciate that his only chance of winning a major invasion of France across the Channel lay in obtaining commitments from his Allies to land in the next year, by which time the requisite preparation might conceivably be made. By invariably pressing his Allies for immediate action, he merely provided Mr. Churchill with a ready means of discrediting such impossible requests. Of course, as the Prime Minister has pointed out, the Russians never understood at all the nature of amphibious warfare. In fact, it was not until 1942 that Soviet military dogma would accept the defensive as a normal aspect of combat in contemporary war,[44] let alone face the British need for landing craft

and good weather in abundance before mounting major amphibious operations.

Churchill replied to the Soviet Premier without delay. He
wrote first that the only British action possible in the West was
in the air. There was no chance of a Balkan front unless
Turkey intervened on the Allied side. Finally what the British
could do in 1942 in the way of an invasion of the Continent depended, as it always would in Winston Churchill's war doctrine,
upon 'unforeseeable' events.

Interestingly enough, the Prime Minister was already over-
pessimistic regarding the nature of the reception of his reply
in Moscow. He cabled to President Roosevelt hinting that the
Soviets might be thinking of separate terms, a fear which within
a few months would bring Mr. Churchill to the point of trying
to persuade the reluctant Americans to accept the Russian claims
to the Baltic States as a political compensation for the military
inaction of the Western Allies. To the British Ambassador in the
Soviet capital, Sir Stafford Cripps, Churchill explained that the
French coast was fortified 'to the limit' and that the Germans
still had more divisions in western Europe than the British had
in the United Kingdom.[45] Here the Prime Minister was on weak
ground; German fortifications along most of the extended coasts
of France were in their commander's own words, in large measure a 'Propaganda Wall' conjured up by the Nazis to deceive
the German people as well as the Allies. In 1944 the West would
undertake the first sixty days of their assault upon Normandy
with only thirty-five divisions against some fifty-eight to sixty
such German units nominally in the West.[46] To be sure these
thirty-five Anglo-American divisions were followed up by further reinforcements after D+60, but only for the sake of exploiting the break-out from their beachhead in Normandy rather than
simply to protect themselves or to pin the German Army down
in France.

Churchill concluded his communication to Cripps in the following vein: 'No one wants to recriminate, but it is not our fault
that Hitler was enabled to destroy Poland before turning his
forces against France, or to destroy France before turning them
against Russia.' Here one may obtain an uneasy feeling that the

Prime Minister was justifying an independent British strategy as much in the name of past Soviet errors as in terms of current British necessity. So far, it had been precisely the Prime Minister's great achievement to have partially overcome the twin bases of Hitler's rise to power: the pacifism of the democratic West and its seemingly unbridgable split with the Communists.

In no way abashed by Churchill's rebuffs, Stalin returned to his theme in a new cable on September 15. In it the Soviet ruler suggested that Great Britain could land twenty-five to thirty divisions in Archangel or alternatively send them to the Soviet Caucausus through Persia. Churchill's subsequent reaction to such a logistic fantasy is more than justified: 'It is almost incredible that the head of the Russian government with all the advice of their military experts could have committed himself to such absurdities. It seemed hopeless to argue with a man thinking in terms of utter unreality.' [47]

In October the Soviet Premier rejected a British offer to relieve Russian combat divisions in northern Persia with poorly equipped British Indian garrison divisions, although Churchill personally pledged Britain's post-war territorial and economic disinterest in this area. The trust necessary for such an elementary inter-Allied arrangement was lacking. For the present all that the British Prime Minister could offer the U.S.S.R., apart from supplies, were renewed efforts to win the active aid of what he enjoyed calling the powerful Turkish army. His own Chiefs had turned down new efforts on his part for large-scale raids on France or Norway, citing the lateness of the season and the shortage of airpower as their principal formal objections.[48]

Winston Churchill also sent the Soviet Premier a rather controversial explanation of Britain's military impotence on land in 1941. He declared that Britain could 'never hope to have an army or army munitions industries comparable to those of the great Continental military powers.' [49] This, of course, was the crux of the issue between the British and the Russians, as indeed it had been at the breaking point of the Anglo-French alliance in June 1940. In justifying the French surrender at that time, Marshal Pétain pointed out to Mr. Churchill that in the First World War Great Britain had eventually sustained a land army in France of no less than sixty divisions.[50] In addition, she then supplied her Allies with great quantities of military equipment. At that time the British commander in France, Sir Douglas Haig, had felt with some reason that his armies had won the war for the Allies, 'in spite of Lloyd George' and other British politicos; Haig had won his decisive victory in 1918 with a force which both Lloyd George and Churchill have called the largest Allied army in the world.[51] In the Second World War with almost a million men from the United Kingdom alone diverted to the R.A.F., Britain was retaining the great force of thirty-three field divisions in garrison at home in the autumn of 1941, and was organizing a total strength, including Empire units, theoretically approximating some one hundred divisions throughout the world for 1942.[52] Moreover, all of Sir Alan Brooke's stress upon the poor training and equipment of these units could hardly have impressed any Russian who was by the autumn of 1941 fighting on far worse terms.[53]

Faced with such large but seemingly passive figures there is little doubt that the Soviet dictator must have considered British inaction on the Continent, even in 1941, as deliberate. Given his Bolshevik background, Stalin may well have believed — as would so many of the politically minded — that Churchill's old hostility to the Soviets alone had created the impasse in the West.

The Soviet ruler presumably did not understand, as General Fuller would, that with bombing craft, 'in superfluity' in the British type of war, landing craft in sufficiency would not be obtainable from the production of the United Kingdom. Already Mr. Churchill's deliberate choices regarding the kind of combat he proposed were providing more and more bases for the circumstances which in 1941–42 would, as he claimed, certainly interdict any idea of launching twenty or thirty British divisions against the Continent.[54] In the future, the production rate of landing craft would be the test of the sincerity of the Western Allies' real intentions to wage serious war on land and to carry through an effective coalition strategy with the U.S.S.R.

In the autumn of 1941 that perennial political maverick and Conservative gadfly, the British Minister of Aircraft Production, Lord Beaverbrook, may have been one of the few men in Eng-

land who had surmised, contrary to Mr. Churchill's declaration
to Stalin, that British production of armaments was easily comparable to that of a great Continental military power.[55] Actually,
as a post-war American survey has shown, in aircraft, trucks,
tanks, self-propelled guns, and several other types of matériel,
British production was greater than Germany's between 1940
and 1942. Of course, had Mr. Churchill known this at the time,
he could have made it another excuse for inaction across the
Channel in 1943–44 rather than for action in the 'guns and butter'
period of the Reich's armaments production antedating the appointment of Albert Speer.[56]

In any event, the Beaver, as he was called by his old friend
and political rival,[57] Winston Churchill, now again found himself
in thoroughgoing disagreement with the Prime Minister's policy
toward Russia. In his periodicals Beaverbrook raised the first
tentative cry for a second front to relieve the Soviets, although
a cry not yet comparable to his agitation in the next year. In a
none-too-private letter, which contrasted remarkably with his
policy of stressing only sea and air warfare of some twenty
months before,[58] Beaverbrook now asserted: 'There has been no
attempt to take into account the new factor introduced by Russian resistance. There is today only one military problem — how
to help Russia. Yet on that issue the Chiefs of Staff content
themselves with saying that nothing can be done. They point
out the difficulties but make no suggestions for overcoming
them . . . For the Continent is still considered by our generals
to be out of bounds for British troops . . . We must strike before
it is too late.'[59]

In Moscow in the autumn of 1941 so ardent an imperialist as
Beaverbrook had evidently been impressed by Stalin's argument
that if the British Empire were to survive 'it must become a
land power as well as a sea power.'[60] But before the First World
War Enver Pasha had been informed by Winston Churchill that
Britain could defend herself with her navy alone and, therefore,
needed no large army. The leader of the Young Turks had re-
joined, without effect, that 'no great empire could last that did
not have both an army and a navy.'[61] After the experiences of
1916–40 it would take more than appeals to imperial glory to

make Mr. Churchill accept large-scale warfare on land in 1941 or 1942.

Indeed, Mr. Churchill would ask quite naturally under the impact of the Japanese assaults in January 1942: 'Where should we have been, I wonder, if we had yielded to the clamour . . . three or four months ago that we should invade France . . . ?' [62] So long as the British Empire was in serious danger of a major defeat anywhere, the Prime Minister would face insuperable political and military objections at home to any offensive designed to stave off the collapse of his more powerful ally. Nevertheless under the impact of this clamor, Sir John Dill ordered the formulation of a plan for the British Army to return to the Continent. [63]

If not when he uttered his criticisms, at least shortly after that, Beaverbrook may well have been aware of one difficulty which the British Chiefs of Staff showed insufficient interest in overcoming throughout the war. So late as the planning in 1943 for the Overlord attack across the Channel in 1944, General Morgan was to deplore the fact that British fighter production was 'indissolubly wedded' to the Spitfire, a fine defensive weapon but one with the terrible defect, from the point of view of offensive warfare, of a very short range. [64] It goes without saying that the R.A.F. with its vested interest in nocturnal area bombing was not at all concerned with devising a fighter of greater range, such as the U. S. Army Air Force with its old concern in daylight bombing would introduce in 1944. Of course, the U.S.A.A.F. had pioneered its long-range P-51's as a means of protecting its daylight flights over the heavily defended Reich [65] rather than to enable any Allied army to get ashore on the Continent. As a general rule the service arms of no nation would reflect much capacity of their own accord for putting the total defeat of the enemy ahead of the exaltation of their own service pride of place.

The most serious effect of the short range of the British-based fighters throughout the prolonged debate regarding the possibilities of a second front was the exceedingly limited number of beachheads in France open to a seaborne assault within the protection of air cover. In 1941 the Spitfire, as much as the

absence of landing craft, confined the area of British planning
for an amphibious attack across the Channel to the already fortified Pas-de-Calais section, a factor of great assistance to Mr.
Churchill's subsequent arguments against any such operation.[66]
As, in not giving landing craft a higher priority than bombers,
so also in permanently allowing the confinement of fighter plane
production to short-range types, the Prime Minister was per-
mitting the continuation of the conditions which he was to cite
so often hereafter as impossible barriers to initiating a kind of
war which he detested in any case. What was really missing, in
Mr. Churchill's Britain, as the chief British planner for Overlord,
General Frederick Morgan, would perceive so late as 1943, was
any determination on the part of the British Government to
undertake large-scale warfare on land.[67]

If Winston Churchill found pessimism so far as major cross-
Channel operations were concerned most expedient, his bel-
ligerence regarding the Mediterranean had been accentuated
by the German absorption with the Russian campaign. Realistically the Prime Minister's first objective was now Tripoli, the
chief Axis base in North Africa. With Tripolitania in hand, he
hoped as one possibility to invade French North Africa, both
with the British Eighth Army from Libya and through Casablanca with four British divisions sailing directly from the
United Kingdom. This old project, now code-named Gymnast,
the Prime Minister informed President Roosevelt, might produce
a profound effect upon Italy and eventually win the participation of Turkey as an active ally in the Mediterranean theater.[68]

Still anticipating a renewed German threat against northwest
Africa in the late autumn of 1941 and distinctly defeatist regarding the chances of Vichy French resistance to such a threat,
Washington was now more susceptible than ever to the continued British preoccupation with this region. Moreover, in Algiers the potentially pro-Ally General Weygand was being forced
out of his semi-independent command as a result of increasing
pressure on the part of the suspicious Germans.[69] Despite the
U. S. Army view that land forces were lacking for any such
operation, that rather indiscreet interventionist, the U. S. Secretary of the Navy, Colonel Frank Knox, had already discussed

the landing of 150,000 American troops in northwest Africa with the British Ambassador, Lord Halifax. Another emissary of the Prime Minister, Lord Louis Mountbatten, had evidently considered this plan with the President in this same period.

Joint operations in French Africa indeed would have been invaluable as a method of bringing the United States into a more active participation in the war and its peaceful occupation was probably within the military capacity of the Anglo-American forces by October 1941; Gymnast, however, was not dropped by all concerned when the Japanese attack at Pearl Harbor finally resolved the problem for the Roosevelt administration of completing the transition from peace to war. Pulling the Americans into the Mediterranean was more than a means to Mr. Churchill, it was an end in itself.

Pending active American assistance in Gymnast, the Prime Minister was still depending upon the acquiescence of the French proconsuls in North Africa, and by this period he had few, if any, illusions of the likelihood of their response to a limited and all-British invasion. Consequently, after the eagerly anticipated conquest of Tripolitania he was already contemplating Operation Whipcord, a new project for an assault upon Sicily as an alternative to the occupation of northwest Africa. This action, felt the Prime Minister, would constitute 'the only possible "Second Front" in Europe' while Britain was still alone in the West.[70] A good case can be made out for this audacious desire in 1941; on the other hand in 1943 when the strength of Britain and her now belligerent ally, the United States, had waxed manyfold and that of the Axis had waned considerably, Churchill's successful advocacy of the invasion of Sicily would merit Ralph Ingersoll's outraged cry: 'The mountain of headlines that Casablanca had become labored mightily and six months later brought forth the Sicilian mouse.' [71]

Luckily for the birth of Sir Alan Brooke's Sicilian project in 1943, in late 1941 the harassed and overburdened British commanders in the Middle East did not consider the invasion of Sicily either practical or necessary. Greece had soured the Middle East Command upon another trans-Mediterranean venture at this stage. Failing a British movement into the Caucausus to support the chilly and distrustful Russians, Cairo preferred the occupation of Tunisia in French North Africa. Although he again emphasized the perhaps decisive benefits of the bombing of Italy from Sicilian and Sardinian airfields, the Prime Minister accepted the indefinite postponement of Operation Whipcord with unusual grace.[72] He was also very fond of Gymnast.

On November 5, 1941, a memorandum on over-all strategy submitted to the President by General Marshall and Admiral Stark summarized the dominant American strategic opinion in the month before Pearl Harbor. The Chief of Staff of the Army and the Chief of Naval Operations wrote: 'The basic military policies and strategy agreed to in the United States — British Staff conversations remain sound. The primary objective of the two nations is the defeat of Germany. If Japan be defeated and Germany remain undefeated, decision will still have not been reached. In any case, an unlimited offensive war should be not undertaken against Japan, since such a war would greatly weaken the combined effort in the Atlantic against Germany, the most dangerous enemy.'[73]

The American decision had gone beyond any simple reaffirmation of basic strategy in the event of war. By December 1941, Samuel Morison has observed, the U. S. Navy had been so deployed from the Pacific to the North Atlantic that no responsible military authority could have advised a return to the prewar isolationist conceptions of defense. Rainbow No. 5 was on the ways ready to take automatic effect when the Japanese unveiled their equivalent basic war plan, the appropriately named 'East Wind Rain.'[74]

When on December 7, United States time, Admiral Yamamoto's preventive war coup materialized at Pearl Harbor, it was already possible that a long campaign lay ahead for the German armies in the Soviet Union. In the dark and demoralizing February of 1942 Winston Churchill was to sum it all up when he emphasized that the entry of the United States and the halting of Hitler in Russia were the basic causes which in the end would make victory possible for the Allies 'in a form never possible before.'[75]

More recently Mr. Churchill's memoirs have recognized the true turning point of the Second World War. 'So,' the British war leader has written with candor, 'we had won after all! Yes, after Dunkirk; after the fall of France . . . after seventeen months of lonely fighting . . . we had won the war . . . Hitler's fate was sealed. Mussolini's fate was sealed. As for the Japanese, they would be ground to powder. All the rest was merely the proper application of overwhelming force.' [76]

On the night after Pearl Harbor, exhausted with emotion, the Prime Minister went to bed to enjoy the sleep of the reprieved and the grateful. Britain was finally cast in a more certain and familiar mode of warfare, that of the fulcrum of a great coalition. Circumstance had wrought for the Duke of Marlborough's brilliant descendant another grand alliance; now he would have to use it.

5

ARCADIAN IDYLL

AN AFRICAN CONCEPTION

December 7, 1941–January 13, 1942

'. . . . if I could afford, or the British Government or nation would allow of my being as prodigal of men as every French general is. They forget, however, that we have but one army . . . and that if I am to preserve that army I must proceed with caution.' [1] — The Duke of Wellington

'British strategy seems to be guided by the most persuasive talker, Winston, for instance! The cause of this is the obliteration of the general staff . . . It must be . . . allowed to function.' [2] — Sir Douglas Haig in March 1918

'Therefore, there will be no infantry except escorts in cars; tank followers.' [3] — Sir Ian Hamilton

'In this war the tendencies are far more important than the episodes. Without winning any sensational victories we may win the war . . . It is not necessary for us, in order to win the war, to push the German lines back over all the territory they have absorbed, or to pierce them.' [4] — Winston Churchill in 1915 and reiterated in February 1942

ON December 12, 1941, one day after his declaration of war on the United States, a declaration accompanied by assurances to his personal staff that the American soldiers were 'nothing but a bunch of rowdies' who, lacking ideals, would not stick in a crisis,[5] Adolf Hitler asked Grand Admiral Raeder two extremely pertinent questions. First, the Fuehrer inquired whether his C-in-C, Navy, believed that the Allies would occupy the Azores, the Cape Verde Islands, and perhaps attack Dakar again to win back some of the prestige that they had lost in the Pacific. Secondly, Hitler now desired to know if there was any chance that the British and Americans would abandon eastern Asia for a time in order to attack Germany when her forces in

Western Europe were being denuded for the Russian campaign. Raeder informed his Fuehrer that, in his opinion, Allied steps against Dakar and the Atlantic islands were not imminent. The Grand Admiral explained that his assurances that the chances of major Allied operations against France were also decreasing — were based upon the belief that such an Anglo-American operation in the West would leave India almost defenseless before a Japanese attack and that the United States could not withdraw her fleet from the Pacific so long as the Japanese were advancing.[6]

By January Hitler appeared to have been convinced that his Naval Commander was correct concerning the improbability of a landing across the Channel and he began worrying about the possibility of an Allied attack on northern Norway. Like Winston Churchill, the Fuehrer was convinced that Norway would be a 'zone of destiny' in the war.[7] Unlike the British Prime Minister,[8] however, Hitler had no failure to be vindicated in this Ultima Thule.

Nevertheless, Hitler was not so certain now as he had been in the spring of 1941 that in a war involving the entire Axis coalition the Americans would necessarily put the great weight of their effort against Japan; he had recently been informed by the American isolationist press of the emphasis embodied in the basic American war plan, Rainbow No. 5.[9] Although rejecting a new effort of Raeder and Goering to cut back his Russian campaign in order to favor the Mediterranean, in War Directive No. 40 Hitler attempted to lay down certain organizational bases upon which his forces in western Europe might resist invasion. In March he persuaded Marshal von Rundstedt to take over what the latter's Chief of Staff has described as a 'muddle-headed' command at Saint Germain near Paris. From the beginning, Rundstedt was not given control over the German Air Force or Navy in his theater and at this time still had only one tank batallion and a few concrete fortifications on his long Atlantic coastline.[10]

Fortunately for Hitler the British and Americans had not yet fully grasped the fact that they would soon have the chance to seize the initiative and, consequently, in this period their war

plans were to veer as uncertainly as the new fears of the Fuehrer
between contemplation of a true offensive, as in France, and
consideration of peripheral operations in such regions as Norway
or northwest Africa.

Indeed, Mr. Churchill in drawing up his basic plan for the
war while en route to Washington within a week of Pearl Harbor
suffered keen anxiety lest his hopes and dreams of winning
American support for his defensive type of operations in Europe
and Africa be thwarted by an overenthusiastic American response
to Hitler's Japanese diversion.[11] He was to inform the House of
Commons later in the year that upon his arrival in Washington:
'We were relieved to find that these simple but classical conceptions of war, although vehemently opposed by the powerful
isolationist faction, were earnestly and spontaneously shared by
the government and dominant forces in the United States.' [12]
Ironically, it was Winston Churchill's own subsequent successes
in violating the simple and classical conceptions of war upheld
by the U. S. War Department which would accentuate the
American emphasis in 1942 and 1943 upon the Pacific theater.

Nevertheless, in the harassed weeks following Pearl Harbor
the Roosevelt administration remained firmly resolved to concentrate upon winning victory in Europe before undertaking
offensive action against Japan. The promise of Mr. Roosevelt to
Congress on January 6, 1942, that the United States would not
fight 'isolated wars — each nation going its own way,' [13] constituted a reaffirmation of Rainbow No. 5, organically growing
from his supra-nationalist foreign policy since 1937–38.

The President recognized, as one of the U. S. Army's ablest
planners, Brigadier General Dwight Eisenhower, put it, that
'the European Axis was the only one of our two separated
enemies that could be attacked simultaneously by the three
powerful members of the Allied nations . . . The United States
was the only one of the coalition free to choose which of its
enemies to attack first. Further, and vitally important, it was
not known at the time how long Russia could hold out . . . No
effort against Japan could possibly help Russia stay in the war.' [14]
Nor, as Eisenhower frequently affirmed hereafter, would any
effort against Italy have any serious effect upon the basic con-

flict of the war from 1941 until 1944, that is, between Germany
and the Soviet Union.

At the first meeting of the Anglo-American military staffs at
the Arcadia Conference convening in Washington on December
22, General Marshall and Admiral Stark formally accepted an
agenda suggested by the British, an agenda which put emphasis
upon action in the West rather than in the East.[15] But in reaffirming the previously accepted principles of ABC-1, the United
States Chiefs used their own language, language which as it
developed proved incompatible with Mr. Churchill's concept of
ABC-1 and Rainbow No. 5. They declared: 'Much has happened
since February last, but notwithstanding the entry of Japan into
the war, our view remains that Germany is still the prime enemy
and her defeat is the key to victory. Once Germany is defeated,
the collapse of Italy and the defeat of Japan must follow.'[16]

While on his eight-day voyage aboard the *Duke of York* on
his way to the Arcadia Conference in Washington, Winston
Churchill had formulated his 'Proposed Plan and Sequence of the
War' in three papers. Essentially this plan was as much a reiteration of the defensive Anglo-French basic war plan of 1939 [17] as
it was of Mr. Churchill's earlier views from the First World War.
In addition, it was in accord with the strongly held opinion of
his new C.I.G.S., Sir Alan Brooke, that, above all, Britain must
now concentrate upon the opening of the Mediterranean in order
to gain shipping. In his post-war explanation Brooke has maintained that it was necessary to obtain this shipping before undertaking larger operations across the Channel,[18] a claim in harmony
with the customary position taken by the British since the war.

Thus, in the first of his papers, the Prime Minister declared
that the main Allied objective in the West in 1942 should involve
the occupation of the whole north coast of Africa. Boiled down,
this general expression of a Mediterranean rather than Atlantic
emphasis meant that Mr. Churchill wished, subject to French
acquiescence, to ship 55,000 British troops into Tunisia and Algeria as soon as possible. The Americans were to co-operate with
this revival of the British Gymnast plan by sending at least
150,000 men during the next six months into northwest Africa
through the French Moroccan ports on the Atlantic. Finally, the

early convoying of four American divisions to Northern Ireland (Operation Magnet) would enable three additional British divisions based upon the United Kingdom to reinforce Gymnast.

Of his third paper — his second concerned the Pacific — Mr. Churchill maintained after the war that it was his earnest desire that the Allies should cross the Channel and liberate France in the summer of 1943. But his post-Pearl Harbor concept of this cross-Channel invasion reveals little change from the invasion views he had upheld earlier in 1941.

In the first place, it must be reiterated, Winston Churchill's concept of Roundup involved the launching of several relatively minor offensives from diverse points in the Mediterranean basin as well as from the British Isles, an idea which if honestly accepted at the Arcadia Conference was to turn out as the most unlikely sort of chimera by the summer and fall of 1942. The landing craft shortage alone would necessarily interdict any such numerous invasions against hostile shores.

In the second place, despite Mr. Churchill's interpretative text in 1950 to the contrary, in the Prime Minister's paper of 1941 it is stated clearly enough: 'It need not be assumed that great numbers of men are required,' that is, required for the type of invasion, whether across the Channel or the Mediterranean, actually envisaged by the Prime Minister at that time. Once these elite Anglo-American armored troops were ashore, the local population were still relied upon to supply, in the words employed by the Prime Minister in 1941, 'the corpus of the liberating offensive.'

In fact, Mr. Churchill's second paper specifically decried the creation of a vast United States Army of ten millions and suggested preventing any such force from materializing by diverting the Americans with 'secondary overseas operations.' [19] Ten million American soldiers would necessarily mean a real cross-Channel invasion, as the Prime Minister could well foresee, and neither the Pacific nor the Mediterranean theaters together could hope to employ land forces on such a scale. British staff pessimism in 1941 had also led to the conclusion that even with United States aid Britain could 'never hope to build up a very large force on the Continent.' [20]

The only manner in which Mr. Churchill's conception of 1943 Roundup can be understood is by stressing that to the Prime Minister, until the end of the Second World War any operations in the Mediterranean were to remain on at least as important a plane as those in western Europe. Consequently an assault upon Sicily in 1943, for example, could be considered as an integral part of his circular view of Roundup of 1941; the Prime Minister had never committed himself to giving an operation against the northern coast of France any priority, in timing, at least, over those he contemplated against Norway or Italy.

In addition to this rather nautical ring [21] concept of Roundup, as opposed to the United States War Department's idea of a single concentrated invasion utilizing all arms and on as large as possible a scale, the determination of the Prime Minister to employ the native populations of Europe as infantry presumably reflects his continued faith or simulated faith in area bombing as a means of making the enemy's morale crack. Only with a serious deterioration of the German will-to-fight could Mr. Churchill's widely dispersed armored forces ever hope to get ashore where German troops were guarding the beaches, as on the northern coasts of France.

Furthermore, in general, until the Badoglio Government destroyed this main base for Mr. Churchill's strategy in September 1943 by surrendering, the most promising Mediterranean invasion beaches were guarded by the Italian military forces when they were not watched by the even more demoralized Vichy French. Here, above all, the Prime Minister could hope to stage his numerous weak assaults and thereafter to enlist the considerable but poorly armed manpower of Turkey and the Balkans before essaying the circuitous and mountainous route toward Budapest and Vienna.

Fortunately, before the nature and area of the strategic disagreement between Mr. Churchill and the United States War Department had become too clear-cut, the grave problem of an organization for a unified Anglo-American command was conclusively settled at the Arcadia Conference soon after that conference opened in Washington in late December 1941. Of the previous war in a classic passage Lloyd George had written:

'The real weakness of Allied strategy was that it never existed;
instead of one great war with a united front, there were at least
six separate and distinct wars with a separate, distinct and independent strategy for each. There was some pretence at timing
the desperate blows with a rough approach to simultaneity. The
calendar was the sole foundation of inter-Allied strategy . . .
There was no real unity of conception . . . Before 1917 no
general that mattered in the East had ever met a military leader
who counted in the West. The two-day conferences of great
generals . . . were an elaborate handshaking reunion. They had
all of them come to the meeting with their plans in their pockets.
There was nothing to discuss. It was essential that a body should
be set up for common thinking . . .' [22]

The body set up at the Arcadia Conference was to become
famous as the Combined Chiefs of Staff or C.C.S. Foreshadowed
in the ABC-1 Staff Agreement of early 1941, the C.C.S. immediately transcended the simple planning role originally conceived for it by the British Government. Indeed, as time passed,
the Combined Chiefs gradually assumed the bulk of the strategic
conduct of war for the Allies. In this process the C.C.S. was
developed, under the acknowledged leadership of General Marshall, into an instrument, through which in the latter part of
1943 and thereafter, Mr. Churchill was progressively removed
from the direct and personal control of Anglo-American strategy
in the West, a process hastened by the increasingly well-defined
areas of strategic disagreement between General Marshall and
the Prime Minister. In the final judgment of Henry Stimson,
both Mr. Roosevelt and Mr. Churchill were men whose great
talents required 'the balancing restraint of carefully organized
staff advice.' [23]

The new body was strengthened in several ways. First, what
the candid Hopkins called 'everybody and his grandmother,' e.g.
the lesser Allies, were realistically and effectively excluded from
participation. The Combined Chiefs might, as has been asserted,
suffer from the faults inherent in committee rule, but notwithstanding the theoretical possibility of a liberum veto by a single
member in such a set-up, they certainly would not resemble a
Polish Diet in size and general unwieldiness.

Secondly, the Combined Chiefs were to meet continuously rather than periodically and were to be served by several subordinate and permanent staff sections such as the Combined Planning Staff, the Combined Intelligence Committee, the Combined Military Transport Committee, and, especially, the Munitions Assignments Board. To win control by the C.C.S. of this latter board, a board jointly headed, it must be noted, by two of Mr. Churchill's more determined opponents in strategy, Beaverbrook and Hopkins, General Marshall had to threaten resignation as his only alternative. The U. S. Army Chief advanced the argument that no Chief of Staff could plan operations and carry them through if some other and independent authority could refuse to assign the matériel required for such operations.[24]

It can be seen why Henry Stimson declared that 'it was Marshall who insisted that the combined Chiefs should, in fact, be Chiefs, and not merely elders of the Council.' A military historian has written that the minutes of the Arcadia meeting show why the U. S. Army Chief won such ascendancy among both the Joint and Combined Chiefs of Staff.[25] Ultimately, as his great admirer President Truman has said, General Marshall would attain a predominant influence in the strategy of the Second World War.[26]

If certain essential bases for a working coalition strategy had been settled early in the Arcadia meeting, specific action had also to be taken on Mr. Churchill's proposals for action in the year 1942. These extremely tentative and provisional decisions were made against a background which in November and early December 1941 was in certain ways still as alarming with respect to the potentialities of a Spanish intervention as those of the Japanese.

The precursors of the American O.S.S. organization in Washington now estimated that the French North African forces were only supposed to have enough ammunition for ten days of combat, while at the same time London concluded that fourteen German divisions could reach French Morocco within six weeks after crossing the Pyrenees, notwithstanding any possible Spanish resistance to their passage. Colonel Donovan wrote the President in similar tones on December 13 and again on the 27th,

stating on the latter date: 'Immediate reinforcements of North
Africa army by American air and ground troops seems the only
possible move which could retrieve the situation. Double thrust
at Africa under present circumstances would almost surely succeed.' [27] The President does not, however, seem to have taken
these warnings any too seriously at the time he made his decision for the African operation.[28]

The double thrust mentioned above in this most inaccurate
intelligence analysis by the future chief of O.S.S. referred to
the fact that the British Middle Eastern forces were again advancing upon Tripoli and thence, in conjunction with an Allied
seaborne assault from the Atlantic, they might again also hope
to approach French North Africa from two sides. One of
the great possible advantages of a British attack westward in
Libya from the point of view of Mr. Churchill may have lain in
the fact that the retiring Axis troops would probably be forced
to occupy and employ Tunisian ports in their retreat to Sicily.
Then Mr. Churchill could enter northwest Africa in his eagerly
desired role of the protector of French colonies. Simultaneously,
he could frighten the susceptible administration in Washington
into supporting this role by finally being able to show some concrete evidence to substantiate his old picture of an Axis offensive
ultimately leading to Morocco and Dakar.

Similarly, between the two leading partners in the European
Axis the principal reason given for an Axis intervention in northwest Africa was preventive in nature. But, like the Americans,
the Germans would ultimately be taken in by Il Duce's tardy
appeals for the physical occupation of Tunisia, although for the
moment Hitler still did not want to commit himself further in
this region than he thought was essential. Both the Fuehrer and
his Army General Staff normally gave priority to serious land
warfare in Europe in preference to indecisive campaigns conducted across seas which sooner or later were apt to be dominated
by the British. On the other hand, like the British Prime Minister,
Benito Mussolini had rather less altruistic motives for entering
Tunisia than those which he formally presented to his Ally at this
time.[29]

On December 21, before the arrival in Washington of Mr.

Churchill and his Chiefs of Staff, General H. H. Arnold of the U. S. Army Air Force was called to the White House for a preparatory briefing between the President and his military advisers concerning operations planned for the immediate future. After some discussion by Mr. Roosevelt regarding the needs of the Pacific, the President brought up the subject of taking over the Azores and, perhaps, Dakar and the Cape Verde Islands. Supported by Secretary Stimson, General Arnold then advocated the occupation of the Azores and Dakar, both of which he believed to be essential bases on the aerial ferry routes across the Atlantic.[30] The ground was well laid for the conference in Washington between Winston Churchill and his American Ally, a conference which, in retrospect, must have seemed truly Arcadian to the British leader with respect to the facility with which he obtained his way in matters strategic.

Not surprisingly, therefore, at an informal meeting with the President on the day of his arrival in the American capital, December 22, Mr. Churchill found himself pretty well in agreement with his new full-fledged Ally so far as the general area of the proposed operations was concerned. Since the debate with the Americans over Africa had so pleasantly turned out to be not whether but how, Winston Churchill immediately broached his Gymnast plan, an operation involving the invasion of northwest Africa rather than West Africa.[31] As he had previously intended, the Prime Minister boldly desired to put British forces into a seaborne invasion of Algeria and Tunisia while the Americans were to be induced to land in Morocco as far north and east from Dakar as possible.

The essential incompatibility of the U. S. Joint Planning Board's original plan for a limited operation against Dakar — which led nowhere — and the fundamentally different British Tunisian concept — which, if initially defensive, could also lead to an ever-widening attack, first upon Sicily and thereafter by geographic necessity to the mainland of Italy — would later in 1942 reveal itself again in the planning for and aftermath of the actual invasion of North Africa with consequences of a serious order. For the present, however, a synthesis between Mr. Churchill's plan and the American concept was embodied into a

plan known as Super-Gymnast.[32] To effect this somewhat awkward weld both sides shifted grounds, the British moving west
from Tunisia into Algeria and the Americans north from Dakar
to Casablanca.

Super-Gymnast was contemplated on a scale large enough to
alarm profoundly the U. S. War Department and especially the
irate general chosen to command the three American divisions
contemplated for the project — Vinegar Joe Stilwell.[33] By decision of the President and Prime Minister, Super-Gymnast was
scheduled to materialize before May 25, and earlier if the French
proved friendly.[34] Nevertheless, that Super-Gymnast still remained a fairly speculative operation in the opinion of the
United States armed services can be seen by the fact that it
continued to retain only a fourth priority rating in the U. S.
Air Force's list as late as January 15.[35] So ardent an enthusiast
for African action as Sir Alan Brooke also felt that Super-
Gymnast was premature, although he blamed this on the Americans rather than on the Prime Minister.[36]

Mr. Churchill's momentary triumph in strategy was recognized
in theory as well as in practice at the Arcadia Conference. The
old British emphasis upon putting the defensive needs of a
gigantic geographic ring around the Axis ahead of offensive
action was now formally endorsed. In reality, this strategy involved committing the Americans to giving precedence to the
British desire to prevent the supposed threat of German erup-
tions across the Mediterranean over the infinitely more important
defense of the U.S.S.R., a power which could be effectively aided
only by a major (i.e. a cross-Channel) offensive in the West.

Several other operations planned at Arcadia for 1942 likewise
fitted snugly in with the Prime Minister's concept of war, i.e.
bombing, blockade, supplying Russia, and inspiring a spirit of
revolt among the occupied peoples. Only in 1943 was frankly
offensive action contemplated and even then, as usual, the accepted phraseology offered no clear-cut priority to a cross-Channel assault, reading as follows: 'In 1943 the way may be clear for
a return to the Continent, across the Mediterranean, from Turkey
into the Balkans, or by landings in Western Europe.' [37] Just to
padlock the door, in the British estimates the larger American

army was envisaged as handling the presumably larger and evidently more important trans-Mediterranean assaults, while the smaller British Army was to deliver its necessarily weaker blow in the West.

With characteristic political innocence, General Joseph Stilwell now wrote of his Commander-in-Chief: 'Besides being a rank amateur in all military matters, F. D. R. is apt to act on sudden impulses . . . We'll do this, we'll do that, we'll do the other. Blow hot, blow cold. And the Limeys have his ear while we have the hind tit. Events are crowding us into ill-advised and ill-considered projects.' In conversation with the President Stilwell quoted the former as declaring, 'a 28,000 mile front is my conception . . . The real strategy is to fight them all,' an attitude which this uninhibited general considered 'just a lot of wind.' More temperately, Vinegar Joe concluded: 'The plain truth is we can do one thing and not several and we'll have to pick it out.' It would take others than the President a long time to perceive this fundamental fact of war.

Another American general involved in the Arcadia Conference opposed the President's and Prime Minister's North African plans directly, although according to Stilwell's contemporary record not so bluntly as one might gather today.[38] In his own story General H. H. Arnold informed Roosevelt and Churchill that the way to win the war was simply to hit Germany 'where it hurts most, where she is strongest — right across the Channel from England, using the shortest and most direct road to Berlin.' [39] In this outlook Arnold was backed by Secretary of War Stimson and apparently every ground force general concerned in the city of Washington, but it goes without saying that there was considerable opposition from the British. On this occasion, however, Mr. Churchill preferred not to oppose a cross-Channel attack on principle; his current objections to a great operation across the Channel into the heart of Hitler's Reich, as usual in the forthcoming two years, were outwardly based upon purely practical considerations.

Like Joseph Stilwell, Dwight Eisenhower was called to Washington as a result of Pearl Harbor. In his new post at a desk in the War Plans Division he speedily reached conclusions essentially similar to those of Stilwell and Hap Arnold. All three of these officers disliked 'sideshows' in the European theater in general, and Super-Gymnast in particular, not only because they feared the consequences of a Spanish intervention on behalf of Hitler in the event of an Allied landing in northwest Africa, but also because they failed to find adequate visible reasons for such an operation at all. To Stilwell's request for an explanation of the motives for this initial phase of Mr. Churchill's concept of offensive warfare, his unenthusiastic superior, General Marshall had recourse to the argument that the opening of the Mediterranean route to the Allied mercantile marine would save a great deal of shipping; [40] to Eisenhower the sole and feeble justification for Super-Gymnast was 'the mere denial' of French West Africa to Germany as a submarine base.[41]

Evidently to these devoted practitioners of Clausewitz, a German assault across the Iberian Peninsula into Morocco would look hardly like an unmitigated disaster so long as the Allies were not there to meet them. To these strong proponents of large-scale and concentrated land warfare a further Nazi involvement in North Africa would have the great advantage of making the Germans weaker where they felt that this would really count, namely in France. Certainly Marshall's senior adviser on strategy, General Embick, considered Churchill's course as 'persuasive rather than rational' and motivated by political rather than military considerations. Embick had concluded that North Africa constituted a theater of war far better suited to the Germans than the Allies.[42]

At his first meeting with President Roosevelt at the Arcadia Conference, Prime Minister Churchill had brought up another project, contemplated in the ABC-1 Agreement, and known hereafter as Magnet. This generally misunderstood war plan, conceived a year previously as a method of implementing a strategic emphasis upon the European theater and especially upon Germany, was to undergo a remarkable transformation as a consequence of the mischances of war.

Briefly, the Prime Minister proposed sending a much larger force than envisaged in the ABC-1 discussions, specifically some three or four American divisions, to Northern Ireland to relieve the United Kingdom troops stationed there for duty elsewhere. Churchill has been frank enough today in admitting that his primary purpose in advocating Magnet at the same time as Super-Gymnast, notwithstanding the serious shortage of shipping for either operation, was because he saw Magnet as complementing rather than competing with the larger northwest Africa project. In his conception the British troops released by Magnet from Ireland were to be sent to the Middle East. There they would reinforce the British Eighth Army's drive upon Tripolitania and Tunisia from its base in Egypt.[43]

As it turned out, and Mr. Churchill could not have anticipated this development, the British divisions tediously conveyed around the Cape to the Middle East as a result of Magnet would simply compensate for the Australian divisions withdrawn from the Middle East for the defense of their Australian homeland against a supposed Japanese assault. And, instead of serving the avowed purpose of the President, namely to focus American interest upon an offensive in Europe rather than on a stronger defensive position in the Pacific,[44] a defensive against Japan was precisely what Magnet, in effect, would become, and at much greater cost in shipping than had the American Magnet divisions been shipped directly to Australia instead of to Ireland.

Toward the end of the Arcadia Conference it became apparent that Mr. Churchill's hope of seizing the port of Tripoli, the main Axis base in Africa, was running foul of Erwin Rommel's brilliant evasive tactics and, therefore, that one of Super-Gymnast's basic prerequisites might well not be fulfilled.[45] To the dauntless British Prime Minister these new circumstances meant only that the Western Allies would now be able to consider Super-Gymnast more thoroughly, and instead push Magnet ahead with the utmost speed.

Consequently on January 11, the Combined Chiefs formally accepted Magnet, although they were not to reflect Mr. Churchill's enthusiastic view that it was 'a most necessary war measure, which nothing should be allowed to prevent.'[46] Nevertheless Super-Gymnast was far from abandoned. On January 12 President Roosevelt, who understandably had never showed much awareness of what Magnet was all about, stressed: 'We will make Beaverbrook and Hopkins find ships and will work on Super-Gymnast at the earliest possible date.' [47] Despite the grave misgivings of all his advisers, the President still wanted Super-Gymnast as impatiently as Mr. Churchill now desired Magnet. Super-Gymnast at least offered him the eagerly desired possibility of fighting the German ground forces 'face to face as soon as possible!' The President added that he wanted immediate action against the European Axis to raise American morale and to have the opposite effect on the enemy.[48]

On January 13, the Combined Chiefs of Staff accepted Super-Gymnast as 'the project of first strategic importance in the Atlantic area, consonant with that part of the combined basic strategy which aimed to close and tighten the ring around Germany.' Henceforth Super-Gymnast was called simply Gymnast, the name of one of its original components. The mating of British and American war plans regarding Africa was complete well before their differing concepts of a cross-Channel assault had ever begun to conflict.[49]

6

ROUNDUP — AMERICAN STYLE

MARSHALL, EISENHOWER, AND ABSOLUTE WAR

January 13, 1942–April 14, 1942

'This present [movement] is not out of choice on our part, but of some kind of necessity; and it's to be hoped will have the like issue . . .' [1] — Oliver Cromwell

'There is . . . but one response possible from us: Force Force to the utmost, Force without stint or limit, the righteous and triumphant Force which shall make Right the law of the world . . .' [2] — Woodrow Wilson

'Bonaparte never acted otherwise. The shortest high road from Army to Army; from one capital to another, was always the way he loved best.' [3] — Carl von Clausewitz

'The reader will observe how low the art of war had sunk. In its supreme expression at this melancholy and degraded epoch it represents little but the massing of gigantic agencies for the slaughter of men by machinery. It is reduced to a business like the stockyards of Chicago . . . But the scale and the mechanism of the enterprise were the very features which captivated Ludendorff. These were the calculations on which he had spent his life. This was the quintessence of all he had learned and wrought.' [4] — Winston Churchill

THE Arcadia Conference did not, however, finally settle Allied strategy either in theory or in practice. For example, on January 22, General Eisenhower, slated to become chief of the Army's War Plans Division within three weeks, wrote: 'Everybody is too much engaged with small things of his own. We've got to go to Europe and fight — and we've got to quit wasting resources all over the world — and still worse — wasting time. If we're to keep Russia in, save the Middle East, India and Burma; we've got to begin slugging with air at West Europe; to be followed by a land attack as soon as possible.'[5] On the next day at their first formal meeting subsequent to the Arcadia Conference, the Combined Chiefs of Staff canvassed all conceivable objectives along the coasts of Europe from Norway to Biarritz, and in Africa from Tunis to Dakar. The President urged again the new Allied version of the Gymnast plan (i.e. Super-Gymnast) for simultaneous landings in Morocco and Algeria.[6] Obviously, neither the hopes of Mr. Roosevelt nor those of Mr. Churchill were definitely set.

Apart from the ever-increasing Japanese threat in the Far East, a new factor now arose to render more uncertain the still unsettled war plans of London and Washington, namely renewed concern for the Soviet Union. The Red Army's winter offensive before Moscow, paced by the Siberian divisions released by Japan's assault on the United States, had come to a halt and Stalin had again begun to inquire as to the prospects of a second front in Europe. After being informed by the British that the Western Allies were contemplating measures leading to an attack upon Italy, the Soviet dictator declared that he expected a German attack in the spring with greatly superior strength in tanks. Moreover, he also expected a Japanese attack on the Soviet Union before the spring. If the Japanese did not attack, Russia would gain enough time to restore her forces in the Far East to full strength.[7] But, as yet, it could not reasonably be accepted that the inadequacy of Axis coalition strategy would grant the Allies time and still more time on the Amur River front until the Soviet Far Eastern Forces were ready to open up a second front of their own in 1945.

The search by the Western Allies for means of aiding the Russians more directly than the most successful North African operation might aspire to do led to the appointment in February 1942 of Sir Arthur Harris as Chief of the R.A.F. Bomber Command.[8] Unlike his predecessors in the Royal Air Force, Sir Arthur considered area bombing as more than a temporary expedient; he regarded it as the most effective possible type of assault. While distrusting the possibilities of lowering German war production through strategic bombing of any type, Harris and his assistants would succeed in initiating an offensive against

German civilian morale so early as the spring of 1942. Notwithstanding ultimately negative results, this British offensive was to
continue relentlessly until April 1944. Only in this last named
month, and then only after an epic struggle, would General
Eisenhower succeed in subordinating these furious exponents
of Douhet into a larger and infinitely more rewarding pattern of
offensive warfare.[9] But in February 1942 Sir Arthur and Mr.
Churchill were still preparing to profit by what an American
Air Force observer in Britain called the erroneous belief, entertained by the British public and fostered by Royal Air Force
publicity, that Germany could be defeated by intensive bombing
alone.[10]

Also, by February 1942, in United States Army circles theories
of offensive warfare were moving in a markedly different direction from those so generally manifested at Arcadia. Secretary
of War Stimson had begun to feel that the absence of any
strategic plan for the use of Great Britain as a base for offensive
operations on land constituted a serious weakness; without it
Stimson believed there would be 'no firm commitment that could
prevent a series of diversionary shipments of troops and supplies
to other areas more immediately threatened.'[11]

A War Plans Division study at the end of February reiterated
the Army Secretary's theme in language which goes to the heart
of the problem of how to conduct war. Affirmed W.P.D.: 'We
must differentiate sharply and definitely between those things
whose current accomplishment in the several theaters over the
world is *necessary* to the ultimate defeat of the Axis, as opposed
to those which are merely *desirable* because of their effect in
facilitating such a defeat.' This study then asserted that since the
British Isles offered the only point from which effective land and
air operations against Germany could be attempted and that
since in any event the United Kingdom had the highest priority
on defensive needs, a definite plan should be made with the
British for the employment of Allied land troops across the
Channel by the summer of 1943.[12]

Another force influencing the War Department toward large-
scale offensive land action in Europe at this time was the fact

that American and British military leaders were not hopeful regarding the ability of the Russians to resist a new German assault in the summer of 1942. General Eisenhower wrote: *'Russia's problem is to sustain herself during the coming summer,* and she must not be permitted to reach such a precarious position that she will accept a negotiated peace, no matter how unfavorable to herself, in preference to continuation of the fight.' Eisenhower was not alone in his anxiety in this era regarding the possibility of a Russo-German truce; an Anglo-American intelligence appraisal had already discussed this henceforth permanent threat to the Western Allies in a serious enough tone.[13] Nor was the new Chief of Army War Plans lacking in justification for his fears concerning a Russian defeat in the forthcoming years. The moderate Soviet recovery in the winter of 1941–42 had not fundamentally altered the situation in which the Germans had occupied an area comprising 40 per cent of the population and almost two-thirds of the coal, steel, and pig iron resources of the U.S.S.R.[14]

In his concern over the possible consequences of another drastic Soviet retreat, General Eisenhower now advocated an attack across the Channel in the summer of 1942 into the area of Dieppe, should circumstances in Russia render it necessary. Such an operation would necessarily be largely British, although by mid-September of this year it could be supported by some three and one-half American divisions. Even in W.P.D. itself, however, a strong faction opposed Eisenhower's bold recommendation, preferring instead to stress a 1943 cross-Channel invasion as a method of keeping the concept of such an assault to the fore.[15] It is not surprising that the British planners would consider any 1942 attack upon France only as something of a glorified Commando raid for the purpose of intimidating the Germans and provoking a fight with the Luftwaffe, but hardly as a means of opening a second front in the West. For this slim and indecisive type of operation, Prime Minister Churchill now coined the overweening code-name of Sledgehammer.[16]

By March 3 these American proposals for action across the English Channel were elevated to the ranks of living possi-

bilities through the practical abandonment of the Gymnast operation on the American side. The Combined Staff planners in
Washington termed the planning for Gymnast simply an aca-
demic study and recommended that no forces be held in readiness
for a North African expedition.[17] To Mr. Churchill the cause for
what he evidently considered only a delay in his Mediterranean
program would appear to rest in considerable measure upon the
failure of the British offensive against Rommel in Libya in the
beginning of 1942.[18] Moreover, what Allied shipping and naval
strength allocated to Gymnast was not diverted to the Pacific by
the Japanese advance in those regions was now being consumed
by the rapidly increasing losses of Allied merchant ships resulting from the new German submarine campaign off the east
coast of the United States. At the end of January Marshal
Pétain had warned Admiral Leahy in Vichy that there would
be French resistance in North Africa against all comers 'including Americans.' With this final *sine qua non* of Operation
Gymnast — the expectation of no serious French opposition to
a weak Allied landing — thus removed, the African project was
certainly moribund regardless of the desires of both the President
and Prime Minister.[19]

On March 5 a long and gloomy cable from Prime Minister
Churchill took cognizance of the seriousness of the general Allied
position and, in effect, recognized the impracticality of seizing the
initiative for the moment. To gain additional American air support for Australia, Burma, India, and Egypt the Prime Minister
was now prepared to postpone Magnet, Gymnast, and the growth
of the American Air Force in England.[20] With his suspicions of
the British disinclination toward concentration thus so amply
confirmed, on the same day at the White House Henry Stimson
argued against any such dispersion of strength and pressed upon
the President instead the sending of an overwhelming force to
Great Britain to bring about an attack on the Germans in France.
Stimson reaffirmed that a policy of concentration was 'the proper
and orthodox line of our help in the war . . . and that it would
now have the effect of giving Hitler two fronts to fight on if it
could be done in time while the Russians were still in.' On the

following day, March 6, Stimson's position was concurred in by all the President's advisers and, especially, by the Army's War Plans Division.[21]

In the three weeks which followed this revindication of Rainbow No. 5 and the principle of Germany first, the War Plans Division was given the exceedingly palatable task of setting up the detailed plans for the cross-Channel assault which it had so successfully advocated. In the course of this elaborate preparation, and as part of a general reorganization of the American Army, W.P.D. itself was given the new title of the Operations Division or O.P.D. Just as the reorganization of the wartime Army finally and reluctantly recognized the need not for one overseas theater, but for a great many, so the Operations Division was now given the duty of reconciling the needs of these new and different theaters with over-all strategy.[22]

Hereafter, as the Operations Division grew into an effective command post for the Chief of Staff, its duties more and more involved combatting what General Marshall called 'localitis.' The symptoms of this characteristic disease of theater or army commanders included, above all, the view of such commanders that their front was needlessly subject to a lower priority in both supplies and strategic significance than could be justified on any rational grounds. With this point of departure, it became all too easy for such a commander to advocate an offensive on a shoestring as a fairly effective method of extorting more men and supplies, once his weak offensive had committed national prestige.

General Eisenhower was appointed the first Chief of the new Operations Division in pursuance of General Marshall's policy of replacing officers who were growing stale from overwork. The Chief of Staff did not like to keep any man at a post so long that his subordinates' ideas went no further than his own.[23] As a consequence of this appointment General Eisenhower was given the unusual opportunity to propound the strategic concept which he was subsequently to execute, although for a later date than he was then postulating.

During the formulation of the basic W.P.D. or O.P.D. plan for the cross-Channel invasion of France two developments favorable to this plan made themselves felt in the United States. On March 14 Harry Hopkins wrote the President that he believed in General Arnold's proposal to concentrate all the forces originally scheduled for Magnet and Gymnast in Great Britain in order to support an assault across the Channel as soon as possible in 1942.[24] But, like Roosevelt, Hopkins was much more of an enthusiast for immediate action than a reasoned advocate of an invasion where it counted. The President had already written Mr. Churchill on March 9 saying: 'I am becoming more and more interested in the establishment of a new front this summer.' Secondly, on March 16, the United States Joint Chiefs of Staff accepted the possibility that with the United Kingdom given highest priorities for a cross-Channel invasion, the Southwest Pacific might well be lost.

In Great Britain at the same time another apparent trend toward cross-Channel took shape which requires interpretation in the revealing, if often misleading, light of future events. On March 16 Lord Mountbatten's Combined Operations Planners in Norfolk House proposed a tentative operation in the region of Le Havre and Dieppe in the early summer of 1943, but only if Germany rather than Russia was greatly weakened.[25] This last qualification reflected a fundamental conclusion of David Lloyd George from the First World War [26] and would eventually constitute the most important difference between the concept of Roundup upheld by the British and that of the U. S. War Department. To the U. S. Army, of course, the whole point of Roundup was that it would create this severe deterioration among the Germans rather than merely take advantage of it.

On March 25, in order to grease the ways for a Presidential acceptance of the O.P.D.'s preference for a concentration in the United Kingdom at the expense of all other theaters of war, Henry Stimson, Harry Hopkins, and the U. S. Chiefs of Staff met with Mr. Roosevelt at the White House. There, at first, Stimson was staggered by what looked like the wildest kind of 'dispersion debauch' on the part of the President, but after the latter had toyed a while with the charms of the Mediterranean basin, General Marshall managed to make a fervent plea on behalf of the North Atlantic. When Mr. Roosevelt urged that the whole subject be turned over to the Combined Chiefs, Harry Hopkins took up the ball and argued that it should not go to the official body for the co-ordination of Allied strategy, for there it would be quickly destroyed. Instead Hopkins recommended by-passing the C.C.S. and handling the American cross-Channel proposals directly with the Prime Minister and his Chiefs of Staff in Britain as a means of obtaining action immediately.[27]

Two days after this meeting, with the warm approval of Hopkins and Marshall, Stimson sent the President a letter designed to persuade him to take a firm and final position with respect to over-all strategy. Wrote Stimson:

March 27, 1942

Dear Mr. President:

John Sherman said in 1877, 'The only way to resume specie payments is to resume.' Similarly, the only way to get the initiative in the war is to take it.

My advice is: As soon as your Chiefs of Staff have completed the plans for the northern offensive to your satisfaction, you should send them by a most trusted messenger and advocate to Churchill and his War Council as the American plan which you propose . . . You should not submit it to the secondary British Chiefs of Staff here for amendment . . . And then having done that, you should lean with all your strength on the ruthless rearrangement of shipping allotments and the preparation of landing gear for the ultimate invasion. That latter work is now going on at a rather dilettante pace. It should be pushed with the fever of war action, aimed at a definite date of completion not later than September. The rate of construction of a number of landing barges should not be allowed to lose the crisis of the World War. And yet that is the only objection to the offensive that, after talks with British critics here, I have heard made.

If such decisive action is once taken by you, further successful dispersion of our strength will automatically be terminated. We shall have an affirmative answer against which to measure all such demands; while, on the other hand, so long as we remain without our own plan of offensive, our forces will inevitably be dispersed and wasted.

Faithfully yours,
Henry L. Stimson [28]

O.P.D.'s plan for *Operations in Northwest Europe*, which with its supporting segments and technical papers would soon become better known as the *Marshall Memorandum,* was presented for approval by the U. S. Joint Chiefs on March 27, the same day on which Stimson dispatched his preparatory letter to the President. This fundamental American war plan, shortly to receive the code name of Roundup from its decidedly different British counterpart, may be properly considered the first true predecessor of Overlord, the actual assault upon France which took place in 1944.

O.P.D. had frankly rejected the Mediterranean areas suggested by the President on the grounds that a commitment of American troops there would be strategically defensive.[29] Instead the Operations Division had scheduled a major assault across the English Channel from Britain into the region most favored by the British planners in this period, that of the Somme Valley of France. This operation, set for April 1, 1943 at the earliest, was to embrace some thirty American and eighteen British divisions, only nine of which were to be armored.[30] Such a proposal was, indeed, a far cry from Mr. Churchill's plans of a few months previous for a forty division elite armored Army, to be launched from all sides of the periphery of the European Axis in 1943, relying thereafter upon the liberated populations for the bulk of their infantry.[31]

The main purpose of O.P.D.'s plan in this era of uncertainty was to establish a strategic conception so firmly that the production, training, and movement of men and matériel could be coordinated to a single end. An immediate decision was necessary since under the existing production schedules only 10 per cent of the tank landing craft required would be available.[32] So strongly did O.P.D. feel the need of having a target on which to fix its sights that on March 25 it had declared: 'Unless this plan is adopted as the eventual aim of all our efforts, we must turn our *backs* upon the Eastern Atlantic and go, full out, as quickly as possible, against Japan!' Like the elusive landing craft, this posing of the threat of an American concentration in the Pacific was to be a perennial theme in subsequent U. S. Army memoranda. If the Combined British and American Planning Staff were confident of success for Roundup in the spring of 1943, their optimism did not extend to the additional American suggestion for a much smaller attack across the Channel in mid-September 1942. This proposal, termed Sledgehammer, was now contemplated only if absolutely necessary to prevent a Soviet collapse or to take advantage of a sudden deterioration in German morale in the West.[33] Because Sledgehammer in 1942 was a dangerously weak operation — it included only three and one-half American divisions — it was not planned as a permanent bridgehead on the Continent. Moreover, O.P.D. now adopted the British condition for a 1943 operation, a grave weakening in the German resistance, as an American condition for any assault in 1942.[34]

Leaving aside any such project of desperation as Sledgehammer, the arguments employed by O.P.D. in the *Marshall Memorandum* on behalf of a cross-Channel operation in 1943 rather than a Mediterranean approach were impressive and diverse. In the opinion of General Eisenhower the first disadvantage of Mr. Churchill's route to the European Axis was the distance of North Africa from Germany. After the war Eisenhower stated: 'While conceivably Italy might readily be eliminated as an enemy, the heart of the opposition was Germany — an Italian collapse would not be decisive. The difficulty of attacking Germany through the mountainous areas on her southern and southwestern flanks was obvious . . .' [35] With respect to this last essentially insuperable objection to what Mr. Churchill may have already called 'the soft underbelly' of the Axis, General Marshall has also had his say. In 1945 the U. S. Army Chief of Staff pointed out that no seriously opposed crossing of the Alps has ever been achieved,[36] a fact of which so experienced a military historian as Mr. Churchill can hardly have been unaware.

Secondly, to O.P.D. the British Isles were the only place where air superiority over the enemy before a major attack could be achieved by the Western Allies. This was a consequence both of the numerous airfields in England and of the presence of most of the Royal Air Force on these fields. Similarly, of course, the major part of the British Army was based on the British Isles and could be employed only in an offensive close to Britain in view of the shortage of shipping and the defensive needs of this most vital base.[37]

In the autumn of 1941 the British Prime Minister had emphasized this factor when he pointed out that he could not allow the defensive forces in Great Britain to fall below a strength of some thirty-odd divisions. To Mr. Churchill, at that time the maximum number of divisions thus available, above these defensive units, for expeditionary forces overseas would be some six or seven divisions, a force obviously too small to land in western Europe.[38] Mr. Churchill had, therefore, already neatly dodged the obvious conclusion that only in France could the full strength of the British Army be employed.

The fourth point in the *Marshall Memorandum* was closely related to the third. This was that the United States could convoy and employ larger forces in western Europe than elsewhere as a consequence both of the comparative proximity of Britain and of her incomparable facilities for the mounting of a major invasion. Furthermore, as General Eisenhower brought out in stressing this fourth point, the choice of Great Britain as the Allied base would save shipping in another way. The submarines then concentrating upon the North Atlantic could best be destroyed by strong naval convoys, convoys essential in any event to supply the defensive and productive needs of the British Isles. Of course, to the Prime Minister the tremendous efficiency and economy of force of this basic American plan may have been its chief fault; it saved in shipping, it may have seemed to Mr. Churchill, in order to spend in lives.

The arguments in the *Marshall Memorandum* for Roundup, American style, concluded with an orthodox but valuable resumé of the principles of successful coalition warfare. Declared O.P.D.: 'The bulk of the combat forces of the United States, United Kingdom and Russia can be applied simultaneously only against Germany . . . We cannot concentrate against Japan. Successful attack in this area [France] will afford the maximum of support to the Russian front.[39] The Operations Division again stressed that the continued participation of the U.S.S.R. in the war was essential to the defeat of Germany.[40]

All of the reasons for action in France listed above by O.P.D. were, to its Chief, Dwight Eisenhower, so obvious as to be 'axiomatic.' But thereafter O.P.D. was to be troubled by the conviction, held by some American military men, that the fortified coast of western Europe could not be successfully attacked. General Eisenhower found that at first only a few American officers took an optimistic view. These officers, including such key figures as Generals Marshall, McNarney, Spaatz, and Handy, held that with air and naval supremacy and with adequate numbers of escort and landing vessels, an assault across the Channel would lead to the defeat of Germany. Furthermore, these officers maintained that 'no other operation could do more than peck at the outer perimeter of the German defense; that unless this particular campaign were undertaken the prospect of defeating Germany on land was completely black.' [41]

The acceptance by General Marshall of the O.P.D. plan was a foregone conclusion, a plan which, according to one unofficial source, Marshall considered the logical implement of his often-repeated objective 'to win the war as quickly and as economically as possible.' [42] But the approval of the President and that of the U. S. Navy was by no means an automatic matter.

Appropriately at a general meeting held at the White House on April 1, President Roosevelt, although still in favor of the North African operation, was finally induced by Stimson, Marshall, and Hopkins to agree to the idea of a new front on the European continent. Apart from his increasing desire for early action against Germany, a decisive influence in this change of front by the President was his recognition of the political importance of a second front with relation to Russia. [43] Another influence may be found in his extraordinary faith that Germany could not withstand another year of fighting in the U.S.S.R. [44] At this same meeting Harry Hopkins, who had particularly feared intransigence on the part of the U. S. Navy, asked Admiral King point-blank whether he saw any reason why Roundup could not be carried out. The new Chief of Naval Operations, who was more Pacific-minded than his predecessor, Harold Stark, replied that he did not. [45]

On April 4 the two most influential American proponents of a cross-Channel operation, Harry Hopkins and General Marshall, left the United States to win over the British in London to what the President now proposed to call 'the plan of the United Nations.' [46] On this same day the President raised landing craft from tenth to a more urgent category on the Navy's Shipbuilding Precedence List. Action was now seriously desired in Washington at any rate and the essential U. S. Navy program for the production of destroyer-escorts to protect the North Atlantic shipping routes would necessarily suffer the consequences.[47]

At the first meeting held with the British on April 8, according to Hopkins, while Winston Churchill made it clear that he did not treat the United States' concept of Roundup as seriously as the Americans wanted, he was still prepared to accede to their proposals. General Marshall, in fact, had expected a great deal more resistance than he encountered from the Prime Minister, but was unfavorably impressed by Churchill's new C.I.G.S., Sir Alan Brooke. Of the latter, who had immediately expressed many misgivings concerning the boldness of American plans, the U. S. Army Chief of Staff thought that he lacked the brains of his predecessor, Sir John Dill. Certainly Brooke was more in accord with the Prime Minister's views on strategy than Sir John had been and perhaps for that reason had doubts of his own regarding General Marshall's intelligence. Of his American opposite number Brooke felt that he was 'in many respects . . . a very dangerous man' who, if charming, was deficient in strategic ability.[48] The ground had been prepared for disagreement and misunderstanding between the British and American armies.

On the next day, April 9, Hopkins attempted to make very clear to the Prime Minister that the Americans were all for a cross-Channel assault and for only such an assault. The President's personal representative stressed that Mr. Churchill should not agree to his Allies' proposal on any assumption that the Americans did not mean business. Hopkins took care to add that the United States' view of business involved the use of ground forces as soon as possible, since it was politically impossible to immobilize large numbers of American troops indefinitely. Here Hopkins was, as usual henceforth, pushing the insistence of the President upon immediate action in Europe rather than accurately emphasizing the strictly military conclusion of the O.P.D. in favor of an invasion of France in 1943. In any event Hopkins now believed that the Prime Minister took the American case seriously for the first time.[49]

On the same day General Marshall informed the British Chiefs of Staff that the reason for his visit was to decide what the principal effort of the Western Allies should be and where and when it should be carried out. The Americans subsequently emphasized that their desire to aid the Red Army was, indeed, their 'main objective,' although the need of the U. S. Army for combat experience was also of the greatest importance. But they were forced to concede that because of heavy commitments in the Pacific, the United States could not build up a great force in England before the spring of 1943.[50] To this extent, then, Hitler's encouragement of the Japanese diversion was effective in protecting his own interests.

As on his next visit to London in July 1942, General Marshall now argued for Sledgehammer, the proposed emergency attack across the Channel in the autumn of 1942, chiefly because he did not want operations on the Continent reduced to the position of a 'residuary legatee' for whom nothing was left. Unlike Hopkins, Marshall had no impulse for a desperate assault across the Channel on a shoestring per se; he was responsible for the readiness of his army alone rather than for the state of domestic American morale and political opinion.

In reply to the presentation of the American Chief of Staff, Sir Alan Brooke employed his fears of a new German attack upon Egypt as an indirect method of opposing Sledgehammer. Among themselves, however, the British Chiefs had already decided that the establishment of a permanent bridgehead on the Continent would probably be impossible in 1942. As the British had done previously, Sir Alan reversed the American idea of Sledgehammer by maintaining that the Western Allies should land in France only in the event that the Russians proved unexpectedly strong instead of in a state of semi-collapse as in the American proposal.[51]

If to some Brooke's interpretation of this most fundamental postulate of Sledgehammer may appear surprising, in this case, at least, it would seem far more logical than the American view; should the Soviet Union be on the point of defeat the British desire to seize and hold at least all of North Africa before the

Germans could make up for their laxity in 1940–41 would represent perfectly tenable reasoning.

Notwithstanding their grave and natural doubts concerning Sledgehammer in 1942, so far as Roundup was concerned, on April 14 Winston Churchill and the British Chiefs of Staff accepted what the Prime Minister called this 'momentous proposal,' a proposal he generously added, whose underlying concept 'accorded with the classic principles of war — namely concentration against the main enemy.' The Prime Minister's sole proviso with respect to the 1943 cross-Channel operation was a reflection of Brooke's overt objection, namely that the Japanese and the Germans must be prevented from joining up in the Middle East. So strongly, however, did Mr. Churchill feel on this issue, that after the war was over such a disaster would have still ranked in his mind with the loss of all European Russia or, in fact, with a separate Soviet peace with Hitler. Of course, having just surrendered the British Empire in the Far East to Japan to some extent for the sake of sending war matériel to Russia, it is not surprising that the Prime Minister was unwilling to sacrifice the Middle East or India in order to aid the surly Soviets again.[52] Should he have made further such sacrifices, the Red Army might more surely have stayed in the field, but Mr. Churchill could hardly have hoped to have stayed in office.

Since the war, the Prime Minister has made clear that he accepted Sledgehammer at this time only as a temporary proposal in order to secure harmony with his 'cherished Ally without whose aid nothing but ruin faced the world.' In reality, for 1942, he still desired action in either Norway or northwest Africa, preferably the latter. More important yet, although accepting Roundup as the basic Anglo-American war plan for 1943, Churchill also considered Allied action in the West essential before that date. Subsequently he claimed: 'The main armies [e.g. those for Roundup] simply could not be preparing all that time.' [53] Yet unless these armies prepared uninterruptedly all this time, actually only about a year, they could not hope to invade France in the spring of 1943.

The new American commitment to convey thirty divisions, including one million men, to the United Kingdom during the remainder of 1942 and in 1943 under the Bolero plan, the immense build-up necessary for a major cross-Channel assault, won from one enthusiastic British expert, the Chief of Combined Operations, Lord Louis Mountbatten, the admission that the delivery of American troops on such a scale altered the whole problem of combined operations against the Continent. Now, stated Lord Mountbatten, 'we should be enabled to plan that real return to the Continent, without which we could not hope to bring the war to a successful conclusion.' [54] Mountbatten's reference to the idea of a real return to the Continent of Europe as the only means of winning the war illuminates some of the frustrating conditions which he had already faced in his Norfolk House planning for a cross-Channel invasion in 1941–42, conditions referred to so mildly by his successor in that disheartening task, General Sir Frederick Morgan.[55]

Harry Hopkins now stated with great conviction that once the decision was taken to go ahead with the trans-Channel Operation 'it could not be reversed, for the United States would consider this the major war effort. He said that of course the United States was fighting in its own interests, and the British were doing the same, but now the interests of the two nations coincided and they must fight together.' [56] In agreeing to the American plan Mr. Churchill glowingly reiterated the pleasanter part of Harry Hopkins' theme, saying that the 'two nations would march ahead together in a noble brotherhood of arms.' [57]

With such an apparently unstinted British acceptance of Roundup the whole atmosphere in Washington changed. In the War Department at this moment of success Henry Stimson was overjoyed, while General Eisenhower said: 'At long last . . . we are all definitely committed to one concept of fighting . . . and we won't just be thrashing around in the dark.' [58] But as Clausewitz has written: 'That the conduct of War is very difficult is a matter of no doubt; but the difficulty is not that special learning is required to comprehend the true principles of conducting War — The great difficulty is to adhere steadfastly to the principles we have adopted.' [59]

7

'STRATEGIC NATURAL SELECTION'[1]

A NAUTICAL LIAISON

April 14, 1942–June 30, 1942

'To have the initiative is an immense advantage; at the same time it is a heavy and exacting responsibility. Left to itself, opportunity may easily lead to divergency.' [2] — Winston Churchill

'Now I have always thought . . . that the power of public opinion is almost equal to that of arms.' [3] — Lord Palmerston

'Wilson, I'm a damned sight smarter man than Grant . . . but I'll tell you where he beats me and where he beats the world. He don't care a damn for what the enemy does out of his sight but it scares me like hell. I'm more nervous than he is. I am more likely to change my orders or to countermand my command than he is. He uses such information as he has according to his best judgment; he issues his orders and does his level best to carry them out without much reference to what is going on about him.' [4] — General William Sherman

'Success at that [the decisive] point will compensate for all defeats at secondary points.' [5] — Carl von Clausewitz

ALTOGETHER it appeared in mid-April 1942 that, after a hard struggle, the long-range and over-all strategic attitudes embodied in the American Roundup plan had triumphed before irredeemable damage was done. But already many factors, certain of which were to be found on the enemy side, were acting to push Gymnast, Roundup's older African rival, again to the fore.

With the opening of the year 1942, possibly in order to divert attention from his failure to defeat the Russians in 1941, Adolf Hitler was willing to consider action in the Mediterranean once again. In any event he received Admiral Raeder in an expansive

mood, in part because his conference with the Admiral followed
close upon the spectacular German naval coup of February 11,
the escape of the battleships Scharnhorst and Gneisenau up the
Channel from the harbor of Brest.

The German Grand Admiral had approached the Fuehrer to
inform him of the exceptionally favorable naval possibilities for
the launching of an attack on Suez in order to make contact with
the Japanese. In the single month after November 25, 1941, the
Allies had lost the use of one-third of their capital ships in all
oceans. 'Such an undertaking, if successful,' declared the German
naval chief, 'would completely solve all our Mediterranean problems.' The Oriental ally, Raeder went on to claim, had a similar
perception of 'the decisive significance' this would have on the
outcome of the war and was planning to co-operate with the
Reich by capturing Ceylon. As Mr. Churchill was also well aware,
Japanese naval domination of the whole Indian Ocean would
soon starve out the British forces in the Middle East.[6]

Fortunately for the British, in order to attack India the Japanese would have been compelled to discard a limited war in favor
of an all-out effort. They would have had to curtail their absolute
conception of national sovereignty in order to co-operate effectively with their Axis partners in a unified strategy. To be sure,
in January 1942 the Japanese Navy did briefly consider an assault upon Ceylon before the Russia-minded Japanese Army
halted such planning.[7] But for the moment the picture which
Raeder drew of the collapse of the British Empire and of a link
with Japan made an immediate appeal to Hitler. He consented
to the preparation of what subsequently became known as the
Great Plan.

Of course, the Fuehrer's consent was given a year too late, but
if the Axis could not act together over the plains and forests of
the Soviet Union, by aiding Rommel's advance on Egypt Hitler
might have some hope of evoking a complementary Japanese
thrust into India.[8] Furthermore, although unlike Napoleon he
did not seek India for himself, the oil fields of the Middle East
were as valuable as those in the Caucasus. On the other hand,
the reaction of the already hard-pressed German Army against

the glib 'dreaming in terms of continents' so characteristic of the German Navy would seem amply justified.[9]

Profiting from previous sad experience with the consequences of an enervated supply line to Africa, the first objective of the Great Plan was the seizure of that 'linchpin' [10] of the campaign in the Mediterranean, British-held Malta. This operation was code-named Hercules. Only then was the second stage of the Great Plan, the land offensive of the Afrika Korps against Egypt, to be launched. The actual occupation of Malta was now finally recognized as essential if the Axis convoy routes were to be adequately protected. At the end of 1941 only one-third of the supplies sent to Rommel had reached him; on the other hand, for a brief period in January and February 1942, during concentrated Luftwaffe attacks on Malta, approximately three-fourths of the Axis supply ships reached Libya.[11]

It is worthy of note that in 1941 Hitler could plan three separate attacks in both the Mediterranean and Russian theaters; in 1942 he was reduced to a single assault in each region. Both of these later attacks, that on Egypt and that in southern Russia, were planned with the idea of joining in the Middle East, prior to meeting with Japan.[12] Both assaults led to disaster before the year was out.

Hitler's enthusiasm for invading islands, slight, even before the chastening experience at Crete in 1941, induced him to procrastinate on the Malta operation. Then in the middle of May the Germans were informed that the next Japanese offensive would be in the Pacific and not against a largely defenseless India.[13] On the 26th of May, Erwin Rommel launched the opening phase of the Great Plan in Cyrenaica. The dramatic and unexpected capture of Tobruk — a conquest with such important repercussions on the Allied side — persuaded Hitler by June 29 that the seizure of Malta was unnecessary. Two days later Hitler, in turn, convinced Mussolini to send the troops reserved for Malta to reinforce the attack on Egypt. Malta, the Fuehrer decided, could be taken after the fall of Alexandria. Finally, the Luftwaffe squadrons assigned to attack Malta were also withdrawn for the Russian campaign and what Field Marshal Kesselring has called the decisive factor in the African campaign, the capture of Malta, hereafter was no longer possible.[14]

By the end of August the Germans in Africa again were losing a large part of their supplies to Malta-based British submarines and Admiral Raeder was again emphasizing his naval view that an attempt of the British and Americans to occupy northwest Africa with French acquiescence would constitute 'a very great danger to the whole German war effort. They would attack Italy from there and endanger our position in Northeast Africa.'[15] Raeder reiterated that the seizure of Gibraltar would be the best Axis counter to this continuing threat.

Garbled rumors of the Great Plan had reached the Western Powers, accentuating their already grave anxieties on the score of Africa. Laval's return to power at Vichy in April brought matters to another artificial crisis. For example, O.S.S. cabled Washington on April 15: 'If Malta falls, Germans plan to enter Tunisia with or without Spanish zone attack on Morocco.' Admiral Leahy, as usual, added to the pressure by reporting the hope expressed in all Vichy quarters for the appearance of an Allied expeditionary force in either Europe or North Africa.

The Joint Chiefs of Staff kept their heads despite the alarm; African mirages were by now almost a two-year-old story to them. Their Joint Intelligence Committee had concluded that it was impossible to prevent a forcible Axis occupation of North Africa in the near future.[16] This opinion, reached on the same day, April 20, as the complementary decision in London in favor of Roundup, was almost immediately accepted by the United States Joint Chiefs of Staff.

Nevertheless, both the State Department and the O.S.S., influential forces working for American action in North Africa, continued to line up potential French military opposition to the Axis. General Weygand, when approached, however, was still strongly opposed to the idea of Allied landings anywhere in North Africa on the grounds of poor French morale, the danger of a Franco-American clash, and the general deterioration of the French military administration in this region. Perhaps not altogether altruistically, Weygand urged that any such military intervention as the Allies contemplated should be undertaken in continental France, preferably in the north and the sooner the better. General Henri Giraud, already high in the favor of the U. S. Department of State as a potential non-de Gaullist French leader, expressed the belief that North Africa should serve only as a base of operations for an American landing on the Mediterranean coast of France, a landing to take place in the spring of 1943.[17] Like their professional U. S. Army colleagues, the French generals were not dazzled by the African enthusiasms of the O.S.S. and of the State Department.

To return from this sensitive periphery to the seats of power, in a cable to the President on May 28 the Prime Minister announced the imminent arrival in Washington of Lord Louis Mountbatten, who was coming to inform the President and the Joint Chiefs of Staff about certain difficulties that had arisen in the cross-Channel planning and to present a new plan, codenamed Jupiter, for the seizure of northern Norway. The Prime Minister's message concluded ominously: 'We must never let Gymnast pass from our minds.' [18]

Notwithstanding this final exhortation on the part of Winston Churchill, by now there was little chance of Gymnast passing from the minds of the United States Joint Chiefs for already, especially under the not always military influence of General MacArthur, President Roosevelt was wavering about Roundup. He expressed his impatience with continued inactivity and he was troubled by the objections the American and British navies had to operations in the European theater before 1943. Here was emerging in unmistakable outline the growing conflict between the political needs of the President and the long-range strategy which he had accepted.

Simultaneous with the introduction of this political complication, the U. S. Navy had been growing lukewarm about Roundup as the realization of the consequences to its own bailiwick of the tremendous Army plan grew upon it. Admiral King declared with his customary bluntness: 'The mounting of Bolero [the immense American logistic build-up in Britain for the Roundup invasion] should not be allowed to interfere with Pacific plans.' The new Chief of Naval Operations intended further to reinforce the United States garrisons in Australia regardless of the consequences elsewhere. Under these circumstances General Marshall deemed it necessary to remind the President 'that sustaining Russia, not holding the Japanese, was the basic strategy.' Momentarily Roosevelt retreated, declaring, 'I do not want Bolero slowed down.' But the President concluded: 'The necessities of the case call for action in 1942 — not 1943.'[19] Inquiry can be made concerning the necessities of what case he meant — certainly not the military case for war strategy.

At this not particularly auspicious moment, while on his way to Washington in response to an invitation of the President, Soviet Foreign Minister Molotov descended upon London to discover more regarding the plans of the West toward a second front. Mr. Roosevelt had whetted Soviet interest by specifically designating the second front as one designed 'to relieve' Russia in the near future.[20] Statesmen so dextrous and determined as Mr. Churchill and Mr. Eden found no difficulty in escaping any positive commitments on this score,[21] but the President, perhaps intentionally, was not to be as discreet. It goes without saying that the relentless Soviet Foreign Minister was not to make evasion easy for the President; nevertheless the latter was no innocent child in the gentle art of procrastination when put to it.

Within a day of his arrival in Washington on May 29, Molotov requested a straight answer to a Soviet desire for an Anglo-American landing on a large enough scale to draw off forty German divisions from the Russian front. In 1943 General Morgan's cautious planners for the Overlord operation must have been amused to read of this hopeful Soviet aspiration in the previous year. The Soviet Foreign Minister also advanced the distinctly provocative view that while the question of a second front was 'both military and political, it was predominantly political.'

General Marshall endeavored to meet such stimulating candor, if it were so intended, somewhat more optimistically than would seem wise. For operations in 1942, Marshall asserted, the United States had adequately trained men and a sufficiency in matériel. It was in transport and, above all, in lack of airpower that he felt his difficulties lay. In this period it is probable that Marshall did not yet appreciate that what frigates were to Nelson, landing craft would be to the Allies in the Second World War. Further-more, the Soviets, accustomed to fighting Germany in 1941–42 with a very serious degree of inferiority in the air, were, no doubt, not unduly impressed by the tremendous emphasis which the still untested Americans placed upon aerial superiority. In any event, Molotov remained extremely persistent, asking re-peatedly in various ways for the answer of the President about the second front.[22]

Eventually the embarrassed Chief Executive took a dangerous step, in part because he believed that Sledgehammer was still possible for the late summer of 1942, a belief shared by others than the President at this time. Moreover, weakened in domestic politics at home, Mr. Roosevelt eagerly sought a dramatic offen-sive action in the West before the Congressional elections in November. His urgent desire may have led him to issue his famous statement, a statement to be publicized by the Soviets as a binding promise to the Russian people, regarding his discus-sions with Molotov. This declaration read: 'In the course of the conversations full understanding was reached with regard to the urgent tasks of creating a Second Front in Europe in 1942.' [23]

Although General Marshall, presumably foreseeing some of the dangers of this step, protested vigorously concerning the employ-ment in this statement of the fateful date — 1942 — the coinci-dence of the President's personal inclinations with the military requirements of the Russians proved too powerful and the Chief of Staff was overruled.[24] It is often overlooked that in the future the President would choose to retain the weaker part of his statement — the date — but only at the price of discarding the point — Europe. To many Americans, as is repeatedly evident from 1939 to 1943, Europe and Africa were parts of the same Atlantic theater. To neither the Red Army nor to the Wehrmacht did these semantic escapes apply, and not even a modest number of German divisions would leave Russia in 1942 or, for that mat-ter, in 1943.

Post-war propaganda employment of the Roosevelt statement by the Soviets has remained remarkably consistent with their line during 1942. For example, in 1948 a release issued by the U.S.S.R. maintained: 'Everybody knows that in the . . . communiqués of June 1942, the British and Americans assumed the obligation of opening the Second Front in Europe as early as 1942. This was a solemn promise, a vow, if you will, which should have been fulfilled on time . . . It is also well known, however, that this promise was not fulfilled either in 1942 or in 1943, despite the fact that the Soviet government declared on several occasions that the Soviet Union would not reconcile itself to the postponement of the Second Front.' [25] Without doubt, regardless of whatever promises the West may have made, in 1942 the Soviet Government had felt it necessary to convince its own people that a second front was imminent. It is significant of the climate of opinion in Russia at that time that the intensely anti-Communist American Ambassador in Moscow, Admiral Standley, was convinced that the West had broken its promises to Stalin.[26]

Mr. Churchill, however, would appear to have the final word on at least the British end of this supposed Western promise. He has cited an *aide-mémoire* which he gave to Molotov during the latter's passage through London on his return from Washington, an *aide-mémoire* which specifically declared that Great Britain could give no promise to invade France in 1942. But for 1943 the Prime Minister had indeed offered the Soviet Foreign Minister assurances that the then current plans of the Western Allies contemplated 'the landing of a force of up to a million and a half United States–British troops on the Continent.' [27] The Anglo-American invasion of southern Italy in late 1943 can hardly fit this unmistakable description of Roundup. On the other hand, if Churchill was deliberately simply stringing his Russian ally along on the Second Front at this time, he was not treating Moscow any worse than Washington.

To the United States the British reluctance regarding any cross-Channel prospect in 1942 at any rate was now becoming clearer day by day. In April and again in July the British proposed, as a partial substitute for the second front, an increase of their bomber raids over Germany.[28] To be sure, to employ Mr. Churchill's own adjective, such 'dramatic' activity might prove futile enough in Germany. But then, as General Arnold himself has admitted, the target of these immense British raids — such as that upon Cologne on the night of May 30 — was 'as much public opinion as Cologne, with a special eye on opinion in America.' [29] Evidently this gigantic *coup de théâtre*, fraudulent even to its facile figure of one thousand bombers, stole a British Army code name for a second front, Millennium. The reality was not to be so easily obtained.

In this same period popular if perilously misleading publications such as Seversky's best-selling *Victory Through Airpower* or Ziff's *The Coming Battle of Germany* [30] provided invaluable assistance for Air Marshal Harris' campaign to capture greater American support, however much Seversky, for example, might disagree with R.A.F. tactics. Closely reasoned arguments in favor of a 1943 land offensive in Europe, such as those brought out somewhat later in Max Werner's *Attack Can Win in 1943*, would rarely catch the public eye, if only because of suspicions of Werner's political bias. What did meet with public favor, like Colonel Kernan's *Defense Will Not Win The War*, while it might demolish the passion for the Pacific of the now sublimated American isolationists, it would still accept the bombing panacea. [31] Even more significant was the fact that both Kernan and Hanson Baldwin's *Strategy for Victory* at this time stressed a Mediterranean approach to the Reich. [32] Yet both of these last-named men were military authorities of long standing.

Kernan, in fact, refuting the purpose of his text, remarked: 'Alas. It should now be evident to anybody with the simplest knowledge of strategy that the way to defend Suez, as well as Dakar, is by the . . . possession of Italy.' [33] The only fault with this theory is that offense, not defense, was needed to win the war and the conquest of Italy for defensive purposes hardly constituted an effective offensive toward the seat of Axis power. Nevertheless the equating of a defensive Mediterranean strategy with a true offensive affected many able minds in power in 1942, equally with those of the more or less popular critics.

In the United States, in apparent accord with the President, Harry Hopkins epitomized the public attitude toward land assaults, crying: 'A second front? Yes, and if necessary a third and fourth front, to pen the German Army in a ring of our offensive steel.' [34] Others would reiterate with great political effect this grandiloquent expression of the British contracting-ring theory, but such strategic innocence on the part of Hopkins was of little aid to General Marshall in his great debate with the British in 1942.

On the other hand, General Dwight Eisenhower in London in May on his first wartime visit, as befitted so prominent a member of the Operations Division, was advocating a concentrated, single-front assault across the Channel in 1943, conducted in its initial stages by British troops supported by approximately ten or twelve American divisions.[35] Eisenhower had been sent to Great Britain, accompanied by Generals Arnold, Clark, and Somervell, to see what progress was being made on Bolero. He was impelled to report to General Marshall that it was 'necessary to get a punch behind the job or we'll never be ready by spring 1943,' a possibility of which the Chief of Staff of the American Army was already painfully cognizant. In the next month he would appoint Eisenhower as Commanding General of the U. S. Army in Europe to provide Roundup with the necessary punch.[36]

As Eisenhower had discovered, both Lord Mountbatten and his subordinates in Norfolk House had decided against a cross-Channel attack upon the heavily defended if temptingly close Pas-de-Calais sector. At Mr. Churchill's suggestion, Mountbatten was considering the possibilities of an operation in Norway as an alternative to one in France.[37] To emphasize these conclusions by means of direct and personal contact with the President, Mountbatten visited Washington in the middle of June. Presumably, like General Marshall, Winston Churchill desired to have one of his own men deliver his case and report home on the President's attitude. At any rate after hearing the President dilate on the possible need for a sacrifice landing in France in order to bring immediate help to Russia, the British Chief of Combined Operations evidently took pains to emphasize the difficulties of a cross-Channel project in 1943, let alone in 1942.[38]

The U. S. War Department, very much alone, consoled itself with the hardly heartening impression that Mountbatten was expounding the views of the British Chiefs of Staff rather than his own.[39] The Chief of Combined Operations himself reported that in his conversation with the President he had pointed out that because of the shortage of landing craft the Allies could not hope to mount a cross-Channel assault large enough to attract any new German troops from Russia.[40] On the other hand, given the limited resources available, the desire of the Prime Minister in this period to raise Roundup to a more adequate 'scale and spirit,'[41] of course, would serve equally well to inhibit or perhaps to block entirely this ambitious operation.

Mountbatten also reported that Roosevelt disliked the British sending divisions out of Britain to the Middle East while the Americans simultaneously were sending them into the United Kingdom (under Magnet and Bolero). According to Mountbatten's account the President now suggested that six American divisions should be sent to fight in North Africa, either around the Cape or through French Morocco, instead of allowing the British to do all of the land fighting in the West in 1942 as prescribed by the professional war planners. Of course, killing Bolero would conveniently dispose of Roundup as well as Sledgehammer, as so experienced a figure as Lord Louis, if not the President, must have known.

Mountbatten concluded as shrewdly as he had argued previously. He pointed out that this new Presidential revival of the Gymnast plan would mean that the Allies would obtain Dakar without having to fight for it. Roosevelt must have weakened under that blandishment indeed! After two weeks of such sensitive treatment at the skillful hands of the British Chief of Combined Operations it is only natural that Hopkins was to write: 'I am somewhat discouraged about our getting into the war in a manner that I think our military strength deserves.'[42]

Henry Stimson has written more strongly and with a less tolerant understanding of the sorely tempted President. According to the diary of the U. S. Secretary of War, by June 17, before Churchill's arrival, Roosevelt wanted to take up Gymnast again, under the impression this would help the Soviets. Anxiety concerning Russia may conceivably have played as great a role in the mind of President Roosevelt as anxiety concerning his domestic problems in determining his desire in Stimson's phrase 'to jump the traces' and imperil the whole previously accepted strategy of Bolero-Roundup. Like Stimson, General Marshall, who had anticipated what was coming, energetically opposed the wavering of the President. The U. S. Navy was less specific and a good deal weaker in resisting the President than Stimson had hoped.

In the next few days, with the complete approval of General Marshall and his staff, the Secretary of War prepared his brief on behalf of the cross-Channel operation. In this statement submitted to the President on June 19 Stimson reiterated his profound conviction that 'the one thing Hitler rightly dreaded was a Second Front. In establishing such a front lay the best hope of keeping the Russian Army in the war and thus ultimately defeating Hitler.' The Secretary concluded: 'Thus German success against Russia, whether fast or slow, would seem to requisite not a diversion from Bolero but an increase in Bolero as rapidly as possible.' [43] In effect, Stimson was attempting to bid the Presidential preoccupation with Russia against the Mountbatten offer of supposed aid to Russia, with Dakar tossed in as gravy.

At an informal meeting of the Combined Chiefs of Staff on June 19 it was decided to support the April decision in favor of Roundup without reservations. The C.C.S. reached the same conclusions as had the Secretary of War, namely that Bolero should be pushed, that Gymnast should not be adopted, and that planning for Sledgehammer should be continued.[44] Gymnast was rejected because it depended upon an uncertain political situation and because, by opening another front, it would spread thinner the already attenuated Allied resources. But, as a result of a conference with the President on June 21, it was enjoined that a most careful study of Gymnast must be made as an alternative to operations on the mainland of Europe.[45] Mr. Roosevelt was already fond of his embryonic African baby and had no intention of killing it at the moment of the arrival of its proud, though still discreetly modest, father, Winston Churchill.[46]

Nevertheless, hereafter the President must have had an increased feeling of awkwardness before his military advisers, an embarrassment not eased by a declaration in Moscow on June 18 by Soviet Foreign Minister Molotov before an extraordinary session of the Supreme Soviet. Technically Molotov had expressed only hope for a second front. But in Russia this front was popularly represented as an irrevocable symbol of Allied sympathy and assistance.[47] Such persistent and intense U. S. War Department and Soviet intransigence did not pass, of course, without an effect. Roundup could not be scuttled swiftly and silently in June; a more tactful and tedious process had become necessary.

Preceded by such numerous harbingers of the future, the letter the Prime Minister wrote President Roosevelt on the day of his arrival at Hyde Park June 19 scarcely came as a great shock. Churchill's attack on Roundup proceeded obliquely; at first it was simply that the British considered Sledgehammer, the 1942 operation, impossible.[48] They could present an excellent case for this position and few Americans attempted to refute it. But in view of the always rather obvious impracticability of Sledgehammer, the Prime Minister demanded whether the Allies could afford to stand idle in the Atlantic theater during the whole of that year. Churchill knew very well that the President, at any rate, could not; the Prime Minister had come to the United States because he had been alarmed by reports from Admiral Mountbatten that the President was pressing for a 1942 operation. Here was the American Achilles heel and Churchill did not hesitate to strike at it as hard as possible.

Although certain authorities have suggested that the preference of the Prime Minister for a Mediterranean approach was caused by a conscious desire to anticipate the Soviet arrival in eastern Europe, there is little evidence for any such expectation on the part of Mr. Churchill in 1941–42. Indeed at this time the chief Western fears regarding Russia revolved about her all-too-likely collapse. Rather, it seemed to the U. S. Chiefs of Staff not merely that Churchill wished to reassert his basic strategic values of the First World War — values only emphasized in the Prime Minister's mind through the failure of his campaign in the Dardanelles — but also that his motive for limited operations in the Mediterranean had resulted from his desire to reduce the casualties supposedly implicit in large-scale land warfare. Not until 1944 can it be said with any certitude that British policy was deliberately aimed at the thwarting of Communist ends in central or eastern Europe.[49]

The American Chiefs of Staff presumably had based some of their conclusions regarding the judgments of Winston Churchill upon his memoir of the First World War. In *The World Crisis,* Churchill had propounded his strategic conception of a more desirable form of war, a conception which remained essentially unaltered at least until the spring of 1944. He wrote that in January 1915 the war was still not 'unmanageable,' that Europe could still have escaped injuries which might prove fatal to the civilization. 'Victory was [yet] to be bought so dear as to be almost indistinguishable from defeat' through the generals' land war in France. To Churchill, in retrospect, 'no plan could be more unpromising than the plan of frontal attack . . . no war is so sanguinary as the war of exhaustion. . . . It is a tale of the torture, mutilation, or extinction of millions of men, and of the sacrifice of all that was best and noblest in an entire generation . . . [But] there were regions where flanks could have been turned; there were devices by which fronts could have been pierced.'

To this descendant of John Churchill and tender analyst of the great duke's swift and sudden marches: 'Battles are won by slaughter and manoeuvre. The greater the general, the more he contributes in manoeuvre, the less he demands in slaughter. . . . There is required for the composition of a great Commander not only massive common sense and reasoning power, not only imagination, but also an element of legerdemain, an original and sinister touch which leaves the enemy puzzled as well as beaten.' [50] To O.P.D. practitioners of a less subtle logic, Gymnast might leave the enemy puzzled; it certainly would not leave him beaten in any decisive sense.

In fact, in explaining the victories of the man considered by Sir John Fortescue the greatest British soldier of all time, Mr. Churchill himself has admitted: 'In this action Marlborough used the one method which he afterwards, with modifications, pursued at Blenheim and at Ramillies. He thrust a mass of English infantry, . . . soon to be dreaded for their prowess, upon what the enemy felt was the key of their position; and he pressed these attacks with a disregard of human life unusual in those prolonged and stately wars. By this means he attracted disproportionate forces of the enemy to the threatened point, and strove with might and main to crash through them. Success here meant victory.' [51]

Likewise of the Boer War Mr. Churchill has written: 'All the generals at this time had received the most severe warnings against incurring casualties. Frontal attacks were virtually prohibited. Everything was to be done by kindness and manoeuvre, instructions admirable in theory, paralysing in effect.' [52]

In the second year of the First World War Winston Churchill had considered that the basic facts of the war situation were: 'First, the deadlock in France, the main and central theatre; secondly, the urgent need of relieving that deadlock before Russia was overwhelmed; and thirdly, the possibility of relieving it by great amphibious and political-strategic operations on either flank.' All in all, an adequate summary of the Allied strategic problem in 1942. To be sure, an operation in Norway (Jupiter) had replaced Borkum as Admiral Fisher's northern flank alternative to the deadlock on the main front. But, as in 1915, and for many of the same reasons, the southern flank approach most appealed to the former First Lord of the Admiralty. 'It did not require the use of any intrinsically vital [53] element in our resources: Neither by sea nor by land was the same formidable German resistance to be expected. No supreme battle need be fought: afloat or ashore. It was essentially a subsidiary operation. But it was an operation from which consequences of first magnitude might flow.' [54] As the Secretary of State for War, Sir James Grigg, put it in 1942, as soon as Gymnast had been completed the Allies should have a jumping off place for attacking the enemy 'in his weakest spot.' [55]

The weakest-spot theory, likewise, stemmed from Winston Churchill and his experiences in the First World War. As a well-known 'Easterner,' Churchill had then belonged to the school of thought which argued that it was foolish to strike where the enemy was strongest; instead this school advocated the lopping off of Germany's Balkan limbs before attacking her trunk.[56] But in 1942 the U. S. War Department could not escape the thought that if the Allies dissipated their strength on the limbs, they might never be able to attack the trunk. By 1943

Washington was to be reasonably certain that Mr. Churchill was fully aware of this possibility as well.

Yet so persuasive an advocate was Mr. Churchill that as strong an Anglophobe as Admiral King confessed at the Casablanca Conference that he might have given the Prime Minister his cherished watch had the latter asked for it.[57] Or, in the words of Admiral Fisher: 'I am sure I am right, I am sure I am right, but he is always convincing me against my will. I hear him talk and he seems to make difficulties vanish. . . .' [58] In a still more explicit reference to the Dardanelles, Fisher had complained of the 'Miasma,' which, when Mr. Churchill and those who agreed with him were present, 'imperceptibly' floated down upon the British War Councils, a 'Miasma' (sic) which 'with rare subtle dialectical skill . . . proved so incontestibly that cutting off the enemy's big toe in the East was better than stabbing him in the heart in the West.' [59] Such were the deep-seated prejudices and such was the tremendous personality of the man whom Franklin Roosevelt took with him on June 20 from Hyde Park to Washington for the sake of his influencing the American Chiefs of Staff as he had already moved their more malleable Commander-in-Chief.

Upon the already too numerous war fronts, except for the Pacific, the news was bad. The much-dreaded German summer campaign in Russia was under way, Malta was on the verge of starvation, and in Africa Tobruk fell on June 21, the opening day of the formal conversations with the Prime Minister in Washington.[60] To Winston Churchill the news concerning Tobruk was at first so surprising that he could not believe it. Subsequently he has written harshly: 'Defeat is one thing; disgrace is another.' [61]

Without doubt Tobruk's fall came as a painful and unexpected blow to the Allies and it could not have come at a moment more inopportune for Roundup. Churchill was to be forced to defend himself with his usual vigor before a shocked Commons after he hastened his return to England later in this same week.[62] Of course Winston Churchill did not consider resigning his post on the eve of his greatest strategic victory; no longer for Lord Randolph's son was the *hubris* that had mortified his own and had wrecked his father's career. But there is little doubt that following the fall of Singapore and a series of embarrassments for the Royal Navy in early 1942 the Prime Minister did have some justification for his claim that the capture of Tobruk made him the unhappiest Englishman in North America since that somewhat more self-conscious tragedian, General John Burgoyne.[63]

Far more for General Marshall, however, the threatened collapse of the Middle East afforded 'a very black hour.'[64] The U. S. Army Chief could well anticipate that strategic folly might be realized under the demoralizing shock of tactical disaster. As that tireless opponent of David Lloyd George in the First World War, Sir William Robertson, had put it, in war 'prestige . . . is apt to become a bogey, and to scare away the timid from doing what is clearly the right thing to do, or what may prove to be worse, frighten them into a dissipation of strength in the vain effort to be safe everywhere at the same time.'[65]

Although doubtless unhappy, the Prime Minister was not rendered speechless on the day in which he received the news of Tobruk. On the contrary, his energies were redoubled and, in Henry Stimson's indicative phrase, he promptly took up Gymnast, knowing full well that it was the President's 'great secret baby.' As Stimson had expected, Churchill opened the conversations with a terrific attack on Roundup, but Mr. Roosevelt reassured his Secretary of War by standing up to this assault fairly well. The efforts of the Prime Minister on this occasion may not have been enhanced by his customary lurid depictions of the Channel as a river of Allied blood;[66] the President wanted action anywhere in the West, so long as it was before winter.

As the leading advocate of the opposing thesis, the U. S. Army was now called upon to defend the cross-Channel project. General Marshall made a very fervent exposition for Roundup himself and in the evening session of this meeting called upon Colonel Albert Wedemeyer of O.P.D. to buttress his position with more facts and figures. Earlier in the year Wedemeyer had helped prepare Roundup and may have already angered Churchill in fighting for its adoption in London in April. Unawed by the frowns of the Prime Minister, the young colonel offered detailed evidence to support the contention of the U. S. War Department that logistic and geographic factors would prevent an offensive from the Mediterranean from driving very far into eastern Europe.[67] In winding up his argument, the Army's representative expounded the basic principle of the Operations Division, that by limiting the war in the Pacific and elsewhere the Western Allies would have enough shipping, manpower, and matériel to invade France in 1943.

Among the military members of the Combined Chiefs of Staff, the course of debate foreshadowed the future much less frankly. On June 19, the Chief of the Imperial General Staff, Sir Alan Brooke, broached again that old Churchill favorite, Jupiter, the proposed invasion of northern Norway. To the great relief of Marshall and King, he agreed that no African invasion should be attempted under the prevailing circumstances, although the next day Brooke qualified to the extent of saying that it would be necessary to seek an alternative to a major offensive on the Continent in 1943 if Russia failed to hold out. The C.I.G.S. favored pushing Bolero as rapidly as possible, presumably because in any event it would build up strength in Great Britain for some action in the West. And, as Sir Alan did not add, an increase in Bolero would also lessen the chances of a major American offensive in the Pacific. According to Brooke the American Chiefs now accepted the British position that since preparations for a cross-Channel operation in 1942 would have a delaying effect upon a more serious invasion in 1943, such an operation in 1942 should be undertaken only out of necessity or because of an exceptional opportunity.

In view of the benefits eventually brought by Gymnast to the U. S. Navy for its Pacific campaign, it is worthy of note that Admiral King had shown himself entirely opposed to any limited operation in Africa in 1942 on the grounds that it would open another front. He considered it better to concentrate the maximum on one front, as in France, even at the cost of taking extensive risks in the Pacific.[68] It goes without saying that General Marshall agreed there was no other logical course than that advocated by his naval opposite number.

Although the President and Prime Minister formally accepted the recommendation of the Combined Chiefs on behalf of

Roundup on June 21, the day of the receipt of the news of Tobruk, they insisted upon what must be called an escape clause.[69] General Marshall was informed that he must prepare an alternative to operations in northern France, an alternative which would be ready in 1942. To the Prime Minister, as to the President, while operations in western Europe would, if successful, yield greater rewards than operations in any other theater, it was still essential that the United States and Great Britain should take the offensive in 1942. Lest there be any misunderstanding Marshall was told that plans for a revivified Gymnast must be explored 'carefully and conscientiously' and be completed in detail as soon as possible.[70]

Notwithstanding such an explicit warning, both Marshall and his civilian superior, Henry Stimson, were under the impression that Bolero-Roundup had remained the primary strategic plan contemplated by the Allies in the West. To be sure, Stimson had been told of a reconsideration of the situation scheduled for September 1, but by then it would be dangerously late for any amphibious operation, except, as the Secretary of War may have overlooked, for one in the Mediterranean.[71] On the other hand, upon the return of Winston Churchill to London at the end of June, in informed circles there it was generally accepted that there would be no invasion of France that year.[72] The Prime Minister had had to content himself with disposing of the most immediate threat to his strategy, Sledgehammer; but only if forced by the insistence of the President was he prepared to go through with an invasion of France in 1943.

Since the war Mr. Churchill has written that the loss of British prestige resulting from the fall of Tobruk had made it impossible for him to push through his African project, a project on the express behalf of which he had made his trip to Washington in June 1942.[73] Yet, as we have seen, on June 19, two days prior to the news of Tobruk, Sir Alan Brooke had reaffirmed Roundup to the evident exclusion of Gymnast. Still more curiously, at the end of 1942 President Roosevelt declared that in the June conferences there had been general agreement as to the need for the African venture in the same year, a view upheld by Mr. Churchill himself in 1943.[74] In retrospect, at least, it is clear that the U. S. War Department had been pushed into a most delicate position — though one to become familiar enough in the forthcoming year — that of fundamental defeat with some of the trappings of victory.

8

TORCH

THE OFFICIAL CONSUMMATION

July 1942

'But, on the whole, in a modern war of peoples a new truth is becoming apparent — that defence is the best attack.' [1] — Captain Liddell Hart

'The soldiers think each of his own front, and the politicians think of the exigencies of the moment.' [2] — Lord Esher in 1915

'Not merely the Tory Party, but on the whole the bulk of English opinion, preferred . . . an expedition to Spain to the grim ding-dong in Flanders. To Parliament Spain seemed the easy and clever road. It was, in fact, an additional detour on a journey already only too long.' [3] — Winston Churchill

'Now, the way to end this war is to kill Germans and not Turks. . . . All history shows that operations in a secondary and inffectual theatre have no bearing on major operations — except to weaken the forces there engaged. History, no doubt, will repeat her lesson once more for our benefit.' [4] — Field Marshal Sir Henry Wilson in 1915

WITH the advent of July the simultaneous crises on the African and Russian fronts and in the Battle of the Atlantic had become so serious that a showdown on Roundup or Gymnast would soon be forced. On June 30 Marshall informed the President that Rommel might reach Cairo in one or two weeks. The seemingly successful German drive toward the Volga and Caucasus was to gain ever-greater impetus throughout this month. It should be recalled that, so far, in warm weather the Germans had not been stopped in the U.S.S.R. Finally, the rate of sinking in the Atlantic, according to a cable Churchill sent to Roosevelt on July 14, had attained the highest point of either the First or the Second World Wars. At this rate sinkings were exceeding the rate of ship construction by two and one-half to one.[5]

The problem of merchant shipping as a causative factor on behalf of Gymnast is not as clear-cut an issue as might be thought. The opening of the Mediterranean was, of course, one of the greatest, if not the greatest point in favor of an African landing; for example, the supply of the Middle East via the Mediterranean used less than half as much shipping as did the lengthy passage around the Cape.

How great a burden this African route had been may be seen by the fact that between Italy's entry, in June 1940, and June 1942, the Allies had sent one million men, six thousand planes, and forty-five hundred tanks around the Cape.[6] While both Mr. Churchill [7] and British public opinion were to be constantly distressed by how little had been accomplished so far with such an enormous but still inadequately equipped force, it was obvious that with their military strength growing, the Allies must shorten their supply lines as much as possible. Only in defensive warfare with inadequate equipment could 12,000-mile supply lines be tolerated, since a war conducted south of the Mediterranean tended to limit Germany's qualitative and quantitative superiority on land. Once the Allies had assumed the offensive, a greater economy of shipping became much more essential, for now they had to convoy still larger quantities of men and matériel, and convoy them on a scale more and more comparable to that of the major land forces of the European Axis.

There is another side to the argument regarding Gymnast as a saver of shipping. As one interested party put it bitterly enough: 'So the troops that it was not practical to transport twenty miles across the Channel [from Britain for Roundup] were loaded in transports and taken one thousand miles across the open sea to land in Africa.' [8] Later they or their equivalent had to be carried back to Britain to stage the major attack (Overlord) from the original point. On the other hand, the President believed that North Africa represented the shortest shipping route to invasion. Actually, while Casablanca and Liverpool were about the same distance from the United States, Liverpool led to Cherbourg, about the same distance from New York as the British port, while Casablanca led to Tunis and Naples, both decidedly greater distances from the United States.[9]

In justifying Gymnast on the basis of a saving of a million deadweight tons in shipping, Sir Alan Brooke ignores the fact that in the long run the loss in shipping incurred as a result of sustaining his new Mediterranean campaigns must have greatly outweighed what was gained in opening up the sea. Furthermore, with the Mediterranean once open, there was no longer nearly so serious a need for it as a route, because the Middle East theater, the principal front which the Mediterranean passage could supply, and at the greatest economy in shipping, would necessarily be wound up through a victorious campaign to open the inland sea. In short, as General Marshall would become well aware, in spite of what Brooke has liked to consider the American Chief's ignorance of logistics, an operation to clear the Mediterranean was self-defeating so far as a net profit in shipping was concerned.[10]

Indeed, in the First World War what the Germans were prone to call their greatest internment camp for Allied troops — the long-stalled front at Salonika — when added to the Middle East had absorbed six times the tonnage in shipping required for the main theater in France. In 1917–18, as in 1943–44, the consequences of limited British offensives in the Mediterranean would interfere seriously with the allocation of ships to transport the American armies to the decisive theater — western Europe.[11] It is apparent why Mr. Churchill has made as his first principle of how to wage war the only too often unreal distinction between the main and the decisive theaters of war.[12]

At the beginning of July under the impact of the fall of Tobruk, Mr. Churchill had to face probably the most painful debate he would encounter as Prime Minister in the House of Commons. Although few members followed Sir John Wardlaw-Milne and Lord Winterton in actually voting against Mr. Churchill's control of the central direction of the war, an earlier suggestion that there should be a Minister of Defence, separate from the Prime Minister and less liable to dominate the Chiefs of Staff, was repeatedly brought up.[13]

But the opposition was confused and disunited, the Prime Minister adamant regarding the maintenance of his authority over the direction of the war and too obviously irreplaceable as a war leader. Even among those who opposed Mr. Churchill openly, the more influential, such as his old admirer, Admiral of the Fleet Sir Roger Keyes, did so only in order to advocate more vigorous amphibious operations in the Mediterranean. In calling for 'a quick and complete reversal of our fortunes,' the former Secretary of State for War, Leslie Hore-Belisha, reiterated his earlier pleas for an assault on southern Italy. Mr. Hore-Belisha also took pains to disassociate himself from the Communist cries for an immediate second front in France.[14]

Mr. Aneurin Bevan's suggestion that the Prime Minister sometimes conceived of the war in medieval terms, treating it as if it were 'a tourney,' could, of course, easily be dismissed as the normal carping of a Left Socialist who had opposed conscription so late as 1938.[15] Yet here Bevan was reflecting the old suspicions of the Left that Winston Churchill deplored not the immorality of war, per se, but merely its impersonality in modern times [16] — an impersonality deliberately sought by the Pacifist Left as a feeble compensation for what was to it the inherent evil of external violence of any sort.

Now in charge of the U. S. Army in Britain, but perhaps oblivious to the trend of opinion in Parliament, General Dwight Eisenhower still felt that if he were ordered to conduct an offensive in 1942, he would prefer to cross the Channel rather than to open a new front in North Africa which he believed would 'not materially assist the Russians in time to save them.' [17] The new American Commanding General, however, was already subject to the full force of Mr. Churchill's personality. Eisenhower was quickly impressed by the fact that the Prime Minister believed that any Allied assault across the Channel would result in a 'slaughter' because of Allied weakness. At last Eisenhower was learning something of the real motives for the coming Allied strategy. Although the Prime Minister feared heavy losses in France — which he so generally referred to as deaths in the Channel — he manifested full confidence about the northwest

Africa operation, a confidence which General Eisenhower did
not share.

Nevertheless, as a result of a more prolonged exposure to the
climate of his new post, Eisenhower was coming to reflect a less
optimistic attitude toward the problem of disposing of Germany. Regarding the O.P.D. concept of a major cross-Channel
invasion in 1943, Eisenhower was now informed that the Royal
Air Force was not equipped to carry out the initial softening up
supposedly essential to a successful invasion. Secondly, the Royal
Navy could not provide the direct support considered desirable
by the British for successful landings. On land, matters were apparently no better; the British Army could not obtain more than
fifteen divisions for such an invasion, while landing craft, stores,
and so forth, were so short that it became more and more uncertain whether a major attack could be launched at all in the spring
of 1943. In fact, a large-scale invasion might not be possible before 1944. To Eisenhower, to the Chiefs of Staff, and to the
heads of state this was 'a bitter possibility' to contemplate.

If Eisenhower still professed to favor an invasion of France for
that same year, 1942, in his post-war account it now appears that
his 'only real reason for favoring it was the fear of becoming so
deeply involved elsewhere that the major cross-Channel attack
would be indefinitely postponed, possibly even canceled. Almost
certainly any 1942 operation in the Mediterranean would eliminate the possibility of a major cross-Channel venture in 1943.' [18]
Henceforth this would be the true cause for the American Army
desire for Sledgehammer, namely, its invaluable utility as a de-
vice to keep attention and priorities focused upon a cross-Channel operation to be conducted from the British Isles, regardless
of date.

Following the distressing debate of July 1–2 on his direction
of the war, Mr. Churchill evidently decided that it would be
easier to face the U. S. Army again rather than the House of
Commons. Natural selection was not achieving his goal rapidly
enough. Instead Sir Alan Brooke noted that the Prime Minister
was now no longer able to control the War Cabinet, where in
Brooke's phrase there was 'a dreadful exhibition of amateur

strategy' following the debate in Commons. The anxious C.I.G.S. was discovering that other civilian ministers besides Mr. Churchill were capable of wild and dangerous ideas.[19]

On July 6 the Prime Minister presided over a meeting of his own Chiefs where it was agreed by all that Sledgehammer offered no hope of success and merely would 'ruin all prospects of Roundup in 1943.' [20] In a communication addressed to President Roosevelt on July 8, enunciating this absolute British refusal to accept Sledgehammer, the Prime Minister carefully reiterated that Sledgehammer would mar and perhaps ruin all possibilities of mounting a large-scale operation in 1943. As yet, Churchill was obviously in no manner ready to admit that the acceptance of his African project would mar the chances of a large-scale attack upon France in 1943 far more effectively than could any earlier such attack in 1942, however unsuccessful. The trouble with Gymnast from the real American Army point of view may have been that it was only too apt to succeed and consequently to tie down the bulk of the Western Allies' limited offensive power in the Mediterranean, leaving only points in that sea, such as Italy, as available objectives in 1943. Sledgehammer, on the other hand, could fail completely in 1942 and yet be tried again in northern France in 1943 in the unlikely event that the British and Americans had the will to do so.

In winding up his argument in this letter of the 8th, the Prime Minister did not fail to assure the President that Gymnast rather than Sledgehammer constituted his 'true second front of 1942' and that it would offer 'by far the best chance for effecting relief to the Russian front in 1942.' [21] That the Prime Minister had his doubts concerning the chances of a Soviet acceptance of this view, however, may be seen in his additional injunction to Sir John Dill, an injunction which read: 'Naturally we are not as yet telling the Russians that there is no possibility of Sledgehammer.' [22]

The leader of another Continental power, Adolf Hitler, also disagreed with Mr. Churchill. On July 9 he asserted that unless Britain opened a second front in the West, the resistance to which he planned to lead in person, Russia would soon collapse.[23] In London the day before Hitler's testimony to the value of a

second front, General Eisenhower had been informed that Sledgehammer was out of the question because of the lack of suitable
landing craft; there were only enough for one division. His
Majesty's Government was afraid in reaching this decision that
General Marshall would feel that he had been let down. Politely
the British Chiefs added that no other officer commanded such
universal respect and confidence as the Chief of Staff of the U. S.
Army.[24]

Mr. Churchill was about to discover that soft words, if effi-
cacious elsewhere, would win no favor with General Marshall.
On July 10, very much disturbed and weary of decisions which
did not 'stay made,' Marshall had proposed a showdown to his
superior, Henry Stimson.[25] With the cordial endorsement of the
Secretary of War, Marshall and King then sent a joint memorandum to the President stating that even if Gymnast were found
practicable it would be 'indecisive,' that it would kill Sledgehammer, and would jeopardize the American naval position in the
Pacific. In addition, the U. S. Chiefs declared Gymnast would
limit if not make impossible the execution of Roundup in the
spring of 1943. The Joint Chiefs also were careful to point out
that dropping Sledgehammer would involve a repudiation of an
American commitment to Russia, an issue on which the President
was especially sensitive in view of his public statements regarding the creation of a second front in May. Marshall and King
wound up with another reference to their Pacific threat. They
wrote: 'If the United States is to engage in any other operation
than forceful, unswerving adherence to full Bolero plans, we are
definitely of the opinion that we should turn to the Pacific and
strike decisively against Japan.' [26]

Five days later Marshall suggested as an alternative to Bolero-
Roundup a great expansion of an offensive proposed by Admiral
King in the Solomon Islands. This plan, authorized following the
practical demise of Sledgehammer during Mr. Churchill's visit in
June, ultimately contemplated a landing on the coast of Asia
sometime in 1943.[27] Nobody could accuse the Army Chief of
Staff of lacking the courage of his convictions; the previous day
the President had informed him that he did not approve of the
Pacific proposal. On July 15 Roosevelt reiterated this opinion,

calling Marshall's desperate attempt 'something of a red herring.'
The President made it perfectly clear that he did not even like
the appearance that the United States had proposed to abandon
the British.[28]

Sir John Dill of the C.C.S. took Marshall's red herring seriously enough to warn the Prime Minister on this same day that
unless he could convince the American Army Chief of Britain's
unswerving devotion to the cross-Channel concept, everything
pointed to a complete change in the already accepted Allied
strategy, with the Americans withdrawing to a war of their own
in the Pacific.[29] It should be noted that in this period General
MacArthur was already urging the creation of what the Pacific
commander termed a second front in the East, purportedly
to relieve Russia from a Japanese threat. Such a front Mac-
Arthur had written Marshall so early as May 1942 would have
'the enthusiastic psychological support of the entire American
Nation.' One can understand why Mr. Churchill found it wise
to treat the United States military as tactfully as possible at this
time, although subsequently he would find it desirable to aver
that it was not before 1944 that he ever disagreed with his American ally on a major strategic matter.[30]

Like the Prime Minister, the President now realized that he
must have the matter of strategy, in 1942 at any rate, settled
finally and immediately. Unlike the much more experienced
Prime Minister, the President had little idea of the consequences
of his position or of what type of strategy or action would ensue
from a Mediterranean approach. On July 15 he cabled Churchill
that Marshall, King, and Hopkins were leaving for London at
once.

On the evening of the fifteenth, Roosevelt had a long conversation with his friend and intimate, Harry Hopkins, in which he
declared especially for the benefit of his personal emissary:

*But my main point is that I do not believe we can wait until 1943
to strike at Germany. If we cannot strike at Sledgehammer, then we
must take the second best — and that is not the Pacific. . . . If
Sledgehammer cannot be launched then I wish a determination to be
made while you are in London as to a specific and definite theater
where our ground and sea forces can operate against the German*

ground forces in 1942. The theaters to be considered are North Africa and the Middle East. Gymnast has the great advantage of being a purely American enterprise, it would secure West Africa . . . it would offer the beginning of what should be the ultimate control of the Mediterranean — it is the shortest route to supply. . . . Under any circumstances I wish Bolero and Roundup to remain an essential objective even though it must be interrupted. I am prepared to consider in the event Sledgehammer is not mounted — an appropriate transfer of air and landing craft to the Southwest Pacific.[31]

Gymnast, of course, was no longer purely American, nor did it ultimately represent the shortest route to supply, but the damage was done and MacArthur and the Navy Department would gladly accept the President's offer of priceless landing craft for the southwest Pacific. Mr. Churchill's two-year educational campaign with respect to North Africa was paying off.

The more formal instructions of the President to Hopkins, Marshall, and King, dated July 16, are not quite so candid. As so often with the conclusions of President Roosevelt, when their dichotomies could not be resolved by the great political magician himself, they were left to circumstance. For example, instruction 3(b) 'We should concentrate our efforts and avoid dispersion' is followed by instruction 3(e) 'It is of the highest importance that U. S. ground troops be brought into action against the enemy in 1942.' Both of these declarations are consistent with each other only through the highly problematic Sledgehammer. To be sure in these instructions, instructions subject to the scrutiny of many, the President wrote: 'Sledgehammer is of such grave importance that every reason calls for the accomplishment of it. . . . In the event Russian collapse becomes probable Sledgehammer becomes not merely advisable but imperative.' Nonetheless Mr. Roosevelt had not forgotten his point. 'If Sledgehammer is finally and definitely out of the picture, I want you to . . . determine upon another place for U. S. Troops to fight in 1942.'

Despite his determination for 1942 through motives of a seemingly unmilitary nature, the President still accepted the basic war principle of placing Germany ahead of Japan. This is best witnessed by his clear and always relevant instruction: 'It is of the utmost importance that we appreciate that defeat of Japan does not defeat Germany. . . . Defeat of Germany means the defeat of Japan, probably without firing a shot or losing a life.' [32] Unhappily this last aspiration was not to be possible if powerful service and nationalist pressures in the United States and South Pacific were to be appeased and a future policy of more or less unconditional surrender was to be actually carried through.

In London awaiting these important visitors was an Eisenhower ever more concerned over the Russian position, a position which he now considered 'desperate.' On the other hand, by July 20 there were some grounds for assurance that Rommel had been halted in Egypt.[33] The Americans also noted that the British military had been promised a sixty-day warning by the Prime Minister before the start of an invasion and that the last date on which the weather would permit a Channel crossing was September 15, only fifty-nine days off. In reality Sledgehammer was dead even before the arrival of the second Hopkins-Marshall mission in Britain on July 18.[34] It was Roundup which was being groomed for slaughter.

The United States Chiefs of Staff on this occasion offended Mr. Churchill by refusing to stop at Chequers, the Prime Minister's official estate in the country, to see him before going on to London. Contrary to the express desire of Mr. Churchill, King and Marshall wanted to open their talks with Stark and Eisenhower and with the British Chiefs before facing the redoubtable Prime Minister himself. According to Eisenhower's official diarist, upon hearing of this evasion the suspicious and indignant Prime Minister raised 'holy hell' and declared in most vigorous language that 'he was the man to see first, that he was the man America should deal with, and that the British Army-Navy Staffs were under his command.' To emphasize his authority to his visitors Mr. Churchill read from the British military code and 'as he read each page, tore it from the book and threw it on the floor!' [35] To employ his own term, Churchill had had plenty of cause in the past for anxiety concerning a military 'frame-up' against him behind his back.[36]

In the First World War Lord Beaverbrook observed that if any man other than his friend, Winston Churchill, had used as 'outrageous language' on him, Beaverbrook would never have forgiven him. The Beaver had then decided 'Churchill on the top of the wave has in him the stuff of which tyrants are made.' [37] Here, again, Mr. Churchill did not resemble his infinitely patient ancestor, the first Duke of Marlborough.[38]

Churchill would have been even more annoyed had he known that in his absence from London on the first day of the still exclusively American staff talks, opinion had hardened in favor of an attack on the Cherbourg peninsula. The Americans found it expedient again to resurrect Sledgehammer for tactical purposes, a resurrection facilitated by the nature of their instructions from the President. Consequently, Eisenhower spent the next day, July 19, drafting the official American proposal to the British, a proposal in which there was advocated a second front in France by October.[39] Whatever he may have thought privately or in retrospect concerning this operation, at that time Eisenhower was, along with General Spaatz of the Air Force, outwardly eager to go ahead with Sledgehammer. Among the Americans in London only Admiral Stark was observably half-hearted.[40]

Sledgehammer in its final appearance had a new look and a more rational purpose; it was transformed from an emergency sacrifice into a contemplated permanent occupation of the Cotentin Peninsula of Normandy, an area thereafter to be used as a base for greater offensive operations in 1943. Yet it remained an operation of such a forlorn nature that in his cautious post-war account Eisenhower could safely conclude that Sledgehammer was unwise and, at best, would have been very costly.[41]

On July 20, Winston Churchill, again firmly ensconced in his busy capital, underlined two points for the Americans to consider as essential prerequisites for a continued contemplation of Roundup. First the Prime Minister emphasized that heavy and prolonged air action was required against German communication lines between eastern and western Europe. Secondly the enemy submarine menace must be solved. It goes without saying that any such program would further delay decisive land operations against the Reich. The Prime Minister was pained to discover, however, that so far only Mr. Roosevelt appeared to have been influenced by his arguments.[42]

The American Army effort to prop up the corpse of Sledgehammer for the sake of shielding Roundup soon failed, and its
formal obsequies were held on July 22. The British officially
turned down Sledgehammer on the grounds both that it could
not be maintained as a permanent force in France until 1943
and that it would not relieve the Red Army. Perhaps smelling
a rat, on July 23 in a bitter cable Stalin said that he could not
accept the postponement of a second front in Europe until
1943.[43]

More convincingly, the British stated that they did not wish
to risk a disaster both because of the superior German strength
in the West and because of the lateness of the season. The shortage of landing craft and the German threat to North Africa and
the Middle East were also adduced as reasons for inaction in
France in 1942.[44] While none of these important considerations
would apply to Roundup nearly so much, they were to kill that
pride and joy of the U. S. General Staff quite as dead as Sledgehammer.

General Bedell Smith expressed the U. S. Army position perfectly when he maintained: 'We should carry out Roundup if
we have to wait three years.' Eisenhower said at dinner on the
evening of July 22: 'Napoleon had written that the most difficult
thing for a commanding general is, after making a plan like
Roundup . . . to await the development of the plan and not
allow himself to become impatient and diverted from the main
plan by starting inconsequential side shows.' Bitterly anticipating the future, he thought this moment might well be called 'the
blackest day in history.'[45]

Hopkins, likewise, felt 'damn depressed' by this more or less
automatic decision on Sledgehammer, and the Anglo-American
discussions had apparently reached a complete stalemate. Worthy
of note, the U. S. Navy officers participating in the discussion
had been more impressed by the British position than were their
Army colleagues. Given the British unanimity in opposition, any
doubts on the American side would not help the case for Sledgehammer.[46] As Eisenhower has made clear, Sledgehammer had
embodied more elements of bluff than of real practicality and
the British, knowing this, had called the bluff successfully. An

additional explanation for the British victory lies in the fact that the American position was weaker because in 1942 they could not carry a large part of an invasion of France themselves.[47]

The next day the Americans assembled again to face the wreckage of their plans and to confront two questions posed by Mr. Churchill. The Prime Minister first wanted to know, with Sledgehammer eliminated, what was to be done prior to Roundup? In the event that the Americans claimed that the exclusion of Sledgehammer had also destroyed Roundup, what should be done anyway? The Prime Minister made it clear that in his opinion the Allies should act on Gymnast.[48]

When General Marshall reported the finale of Sledgehammer to the President, the latter asked for a study of Gymnast as the next most desirable operation, although offensives in Norway, Egypt, and Persia were still retained as alternative possibilities. Mr. Roosevelt also pressed for speed in reaching a decision; [49] in addition to his own needs he may have anticipated an attempt at stalling by his reluctant Chief of Staff of the Army. In fact, Marshall was to attempt to do exactly that.

Meanwhile in Washington on July 24 Henry Stimson tried to help his embattled Army Chief resist the revival of Gymnast. Already the North African operation, as befitted one rising so rapidly to the position of hegemony, had received from Winston Churchill himself a stirring symbol, Torch, as its new code name.[50] In his own words, the United States Secretary of War pushed his disagreement with the President to the limits prescribed by loyalty and offered to wager Mr. Roosevelt regarding the wisdom of any operation in Africa. Stimson's utter disapproval of Torch was in full accord with the whole War Department staff.[51] It was all in vain.

In the British capital, at the same time that Stimson was working so futilely upon the now fully resolved President, General Marshall's dilatory tactics took the form of a new proposal from the American Joint Chiefs to their British opposite numbers. There was to be no avoidable reduction in the preparation for Roundup so long as there remained any possibility of carrying out the operation before July 1943. If by mid-September the condition of the Soviets should warrant it, the decision was to be made to undertake an operation against North Africa as soon as possible before December 1942.

The United States Chiefs of Staff were, of course, clutching at straws, but it is rather significant that the British were willing to tolerate this continued American evasion of an immediate decision. In accepting the placing of Torch on a par with Roundup, the American military carefully insisted that the British agree to a formal statement that a commitment to Gymnast made it 'impracticable' to execute Roundup successfully in 1943 and involved the acceptance of 'a defensive encircling line of action' in Europe except for air operations.[52] Mr. Churchill may have had difficulty in reconciling his regrets of the fall of 1942, regrets which he would show over the supposedly hitherto unimagined possibility of the demise of Roundup, with his acceptance of this American proviso in July. Nowhere else has the contracting ring strategy of which the British were so enamored been labeled so clearly for what it was — a defensive rather than offensive strategy.

On July 25 Harry Hopkins dropped a wrench into the well-greased wheels of General Marshall's plans to hang on to Roundup a little longer. With the intention of vindicating the role of the presidential intimate, Robert Sherwood has let the cat out of the bag. It was Mr. Hopkins who on July 25 cabled Roosevelt to tell him of General Marshall's 'procrastinations' and to urge him to set a date for Gymnast before October 30, 1942, avowedly because the situation in Russia was so serious that any delay would be dangerous.[53]

What Mr. Sherwood does not illuminate so clearly is that a military amateur, but very practical politician, was frustrating the Fabian tactics of the U. S. Army for his own purposes. In the last analysis, Hopkins was loyal to the President and to his political needs (hence, presumably, the date October 30) and not to the American military. He might mask his concern for the next election under the guise of another then more acceptable preoccupation of the President, the fate of the Soviet Union, but there was no way of knowing in July that the Red Army would be in especially mortal danger in the first week of November 1942. In fact, if 1941 were any criterion, once the Soviets had survived that long, the winter would tide them over for several months thereafter. Then, unlike Gymnast, Roundup, scheduled for the spring of 1943, could really hope to relieve them.

If it may be difficult to say just when the official commitment on Torch was made, the reply which President Roosevelt sent on July 25 to his delegates in London, following upon Hopkins' warning, clearly stands out as the *coup de grâce* for Roundup, and conversely, as the date of the real decision in favor of North Africa. In Washington the President called in Secretary Stimson and without further ado announced his decision to go ahead on Torch. Mr. Roosevelt saw no reason why the withdrawal of a few troops to the Mediterranean would prevent Roundup in 1943.[54] He wanted action now.

The President's cable to Hopkins requested this faithful servant to inform Winston Churchill as follows: 'Tell Prime Minister I am delighted that decision is made.' For General Marshall and Admiral King, in the President's own words, orders for Torch were now 'full speed ahead.' [55] This presidential stress upon speed can particularly be understood in view of Captain Butcher's remark that originally it had been calculated that Torch could not be mounted before December 1.[56]

The Chief of Staff of the U. S. Army was left, for once, without much to say. By nightfall of the twenty-fifth Hopkins was able to send the President a cable which may be cited as a model of triumphant brevity. It consisted of the single word, 'Africa.' 'Thank God!' was President Roosevelt's scarcely more verbose reply.[57] Two days later Mr. Churchill informed the President: 'I doubt if success would have been achieved without Harry's invaluable aid.' [58]

9

A SECOND FRONT?

THE CRISIS IN UNITED NATIONS STRATEGY

August–December 1942

'Power, when wielded by abnormal energy, is the most serious of facts and all [Theodore] Roosevelt's friends knew that his restless and combative energy was more than abnormal. Roosevelt, more than any other man living within the range of notoriety, showed the singular primitive quality that belongs to the ultimate matter — the quality that medieval theology assigned to God. He was pure act.' [1] — Henry Adams

'In other words, to define the direction of the basic blow means to predetermine the nature of operations in the whole period of war, to determine nine-tenths of the fate of the whole war. In this is the task of strategy.' [2] — Joseph Stalin

'Mr. Lloyd George and several of his colleagues held the general view of preventing vain slaughters on the Western Front before the arrival of the American armies, and he looked for an operation in the Italian Theatre, which might be more fruitful, which would fill in time, and which would definitely be minor.' [3] — Winston Churchill in 1939

'Anything done in a great hurry is always done the best.' [4] — Admiral Fisher

IT is surprising that it is still necessary to construct the story of the final decision for Mr. Churchill's current conception of a second front from such a variety of authoritative and official sources. Perhaps the best case that one can put forth on behalf of the intentions of President Roosevelt on this issue is that, assuming his rejection of Torch in 1942, had the British then still refused to go through with a cross-Channel invasion in 1943, it would have been impossible for any American President

149

to have resisted the popular cry to make the principal American offensive effort in the Pacific. Militarily it took four years for the United States to prepare for Overlord on the scale on which it was undertaken in June 1944; psychologically Franklin Roosevelt and a democracy so bold and restless as the United States would not wait that long to repair the consequences of the severe distinction between war and peace taken for granted in America before June 1940.

Following this great strategic decision Eisenhower's war diarist noted that the British did not accept the American view that Torch had ruled out Roundup. When sincere, this most expedient belief may have whetted British appetites for further Mediterranean operations at the time of the Casablanca Conference six months later in order to kill Roundup for good. In any event, for the present Roundup was left, in Eisenhower's aeronautical phrase, 'ticking without a load.'[5] Hereafter, its principal *raison d'être*, apart from face-saving purposes for the U. S. Army, was deception.[6] The mighty war plan, formulated by the U. S. Army General Staff to win the war in the West, had fallen to the level of a cover plan, a plan designed to cover the acceptance of a strategy of expediency on the part of the British and Americans.

For the fully mobilized British, the strategic vacuum following the July decision was not too serious. Although in both World Wars Chiefs of the Imperial General Staff complained of the evil consequences of frequent changes of plans,[7] after 1939 Mr. Churchill's Britain was held ready to take advantage of the turn of military events. Furthermore, the British were quite capable of using the bulk of their more limited resources in a Mediterranean push — a push which for that reason made good sense without an American entry into the war. But for the Americans the expansion of the U. S. Army was less than half complete and the increasing production of American matériel had to be planned and allocated over a year ahead in accord with a basic strategy now quite unknown.[8]

Even before the final decision for Torch, on July 24 the U. S. Army Air Force had recognized that this operation would conflict with another program popular in the highest circles, the strategic bombing of Germany. Air Marshal Sir Charles Portal had broached the issue by asking whether American air support for Torch would be taken from the forces assigned to Roundup. As would also turn out with the U. S. Army divisions originally reserved for Roundup, of course there was no other source to tap.

Another unfortunate consequence of Torch can be found in the new necessity for feeding American Air Force heavy bombers into action piecemeal with the Luftwaffe over western Europe. American equipment and combat methods would thereby be revealed without any serious injury being sustained by the enemy in return. General Arnold concluded sadly, 'we were dispersing our military power, even before we really had it.' [9]

Nor was Torch the only diversion from Europe. On July 24 the Combined Chiefs had already agreed to grant the Pacific theater fifteen combat groups allocated to Roundup, notwithstanding the most strenuous opposition on the part of General Arnold. To the Air Force Commander the southwest Pacific afforded a more deadly threat to his proposed offensive against Germany than did the Mediterranean. The Army Air Force had at least opposed Pacific diversions in principle, but now the U. S. Navy began to seize upon the eclipse of Roundup as a vindication of its deep-seated desire for an all-out offensive against Japan.[10] The Pacific 'bluff' was returning with a vengeance.

Although Admiral Sir Bertram Ramsey had objected to raids on the French coast as liable to warn the Germans of their weak spots, on July 25 Mr. Churchill reapproved a previously discarded plan to raid Dieppe as partial substitute for a second front. Lord Mountbatten explained to Admiral Ramsey that 'political reasons' [11] had evoked this revival of the proposed attack on Dieppe on the day that Roundup, a real cross-Channel invasion, had been liquidated.

The wide variety of explanations for this profound modification of Allied strategy already offers rich fare and richer problems to the military historian. In Secretary Stimson's brief conclusion, by all odds the best statement thus far on the subject, the Torch decision was 'the result of two absolutely definite and final rulings, one by the British and the other by the President. Mr. Churchill and his advisers categorically refused to accept the notion of a cross-Channel invasion in 1942. Mr. Roosevelt categorically insisted that there must be *some* operation in 1942. The only operation that satisfied both of these conditions was Torch.' [12]

In his lean and uninformative report General Marshall has declared with notable reserve that the only operation that could be undertaken with a fair prospect of success in 1942 was Torch. The Chief of Staff forbore to state publicly why an operation had to be undertaken at all in 1942, but like Stimson he elucidated Torch's most deadly consequence, the destruction not merely of any possibility of crossing the Channel in 1942, but also of any such assault in 1943. As an operation in execution Torch would obtain most of the Allied resources in the Atlantic.[13]

With such a record of discretion it is not too surprising that Ralph Ingersoll could write that Marshall, although purportedly the only Allied general who could talk to Churchill as an equal, still often got pushed around. According to Ingersoll, the U. S. Army Chief was only mildly irritated at the policy of Mediterranean diversions, because he was too 'literal-minded' and somewhat naïve.[14] In truth, on this matter above all, Marshall certainly was neither too literal nor naïve; as for his supposed mild irritation, both Sherwood and Stimson have recorded often enough keen indignation in the Chief of Staff so far as Torch was concerned,[15] leaving aside entirely his reactions to the forthcoming imbroglio in Italy. The fact was that on the American side President Roosevelt alone bore the responsibility for Torch and he had had to override his Chief of Staff on the occasion of the African decision as on one other occasion during the war.[16] Indeed, General Marshall evidently had opposed Torch at one point to the verge of resignation,[17] an action recommended by Napoleon as the correct course for generals in his position.

Three years after the appearance of Mr. Ingersoll's book General Marshall unburdened himself in a public speech. Even so, it is necessary to know the past in some detail to appreciate the weight of these markedly generalized observations. The wartime Chief of Staff told his audience that there was one consideration which he did not remember having seen mentioned in connection with the last war, and that was 'the political necessity for

action. The public demands it. They must have action. The party
opponents utilize the lack of it to attack those in power. It presented a difficult business. The military staff planners, as a rule,
do not fully appreciate this phase of the matter, if at all.' [18]

Eisenhower has expounded some of the reasons against Torch
in his post-war memoirs at considerable length. Initially he made
clear that with Torch instead of Roundup he had weeks in which
to prepare instead of months, that he would lack airpower and,
in view of the lack of bases other than Gibraltar, that an immediate success would have to be achieved in exploiting the landings in North Africa.[19]

According to his decidedly less guarded and less reflective
war diary, in 1942 Eisenhower felt that he was undertaking an
operation of a 'quite desperate nature' whose unfavorable potentialities included the serious risk of bringing both France and
Spain into the war against the Allies.[20] Likewise pessimistic,
General Marshall reported that important Army officers in Washington believed that Torch had only a fifty-fifty chance of success. Later General Douglas MacArthur, Sir Alan Brooke's paragon
among American strategists, evidently expressed Marshall's own
views when he termed the African venture 'absolutely useless.' [21]

On the other hand, the only gains which General Eisenhower
expected from Torch were the permanent denial of northwest
Africa as a possible submarine and aircraft base for the Axis,
the relief of Malta, and the opening of the Mediterranean to
Allied convoys,[22] all rather too nautical objectives to appeal
much to an Army commander. But in all probability the U. S.
Army was more sincere in its inability to see the gains of a
Mediterranean push than in any professions of fear regarding
the dangers of disaster in such a campaign.

A more interesting as well as more relevant influence involved
in the American Army's enforced acceptance of Torch may be
found in the remarkably opposed views of different Americans
on the fundamental matter of Russia's chances of surviving the
German summer campaigns of 1942 and 1943. While Roosevelt
and Hopkins, quite sincerely, conceived of Torch as serving the
needs of the U.S.S.R. as well as those of the West, to as rigorous
and experienced military logicians as Eisenhower and Marshall,

Torch was tolerable chiefly because Russia might be defeated in the near future. Eisenhower noted in 1942 that Torch was 'strategically unsound as an operation either to support Roundup or to render prompt assistance to the Russians. Its execution now may be a logical alternative to 1943 Roundup, but it is not a logical operation to insure execution of Roundup. If undertaken now, *it should be done on the theory that the Russian Army is certain to be defeated* and that, consequently, we should take advantage of the relatively favorable situation now existing to improve the defensive position that will be forced upon us in Europe and western Asia by a Russian defeat.'[23]

Here speaks a rational if not a favorable voice on behalf of Torch. In fact, in 1942 Eisenhower was so unguarded or bitter as to declare to his official diarist that the decision for Torch had been made on the assumption that Russia might not hold out, a view in which General Bradley has concurred.[24] Naturally, we hear practically nothing of this excellent argument for Torch since the conclusion of the Second World War. On the other hand, General Bedell Smith has said that in 1942 the American Army did believe that the U.S.S.R. would pull through and that policy was based upon this belief. Since the war Mr. Churchill has maintained that he felt then that there was an even chance that the Russians would hold, although Sir Alan Brooke did not.[25] But at the time Brooke evidently agreed with the American generals that a Russian collapse was the best justification of Torch.[26]

To General Marshall, also, the decision for Torch meant the acceptance of a probable Soviet defeat which would prevent an Allied assault against Normandy. He felt that since it was 'too much to hope that the Russians can continue fighting unaided all through 1943,' the final result would be the abandonment of a cross-Channel operation in 1944.[27] If this postulate was a principle reason for the passionate desire of the U. S. Army for an invasion of France in 1943, President Roosevelt, who may have accepted the opinion of Harry Hopkins so early as August 1941 that the Soviets would survive,[28] was more willing to take the gamble on an African operation. Moreover, the President still did not appear to recognize that Torch automatically ruled out

Roundup — in mid-1942 he still relied upon the pleasing thesis of Mr. Churchill that Torch was an essential precursor to any cross-Channel invasion in 1943.

Eisenhower has not stressed what some observers have considered a primary benefit of Torch. This was the invaluable and essential opportunity it gave the untried American Army in the European theater to practice realistic and large-scale maneuvers at no great cost in English and American lives, at least. The U. S. Army badly needed large-unit training [29] and Africa was a relatively safe place in which to prolong this preparation for a more serious affair, while at the same time keeping the emphasis upon the European Axis and satisfying the public demand for action. Tactical theories and equipment could be proved or disproved, logistic discoveries made, and commanders and staffs tested in the course of what turned out to be something more than a brief romp over the site of ancient Carthage.

Since Mr. Churchill disclosed privately in 1944 that he would 'personally assume responsibility before God for the decision to do Torch,' his views on this subject would seem fundamental.[30] During the war,[31] as after it, the Prime Minister gave the shortage of landing craft as the primary reason for the impossibility of an invasion across the Channel in 1942. This is, at best, no more than an explanation why Sledgehammer was not carried out, and hardly an explanation for its replacement by Torch. Only subsequent to the war has Mr. Churchill stressed that there were still not enough landing craft for a cross-Channel invasion so late as 1943.[32] At the end of 1942, when landing craft production was so drastically cut back, the shortage of such craft could hardly have been employed as a serious argument against Roundup. As many recognized after the invasion of North Africa, the presence of Torch had ruled out Roundup regardless of the number of landing craft available; the Mediterranean had then consumed almost everything else needed for a cross-Channel operation in 1943 down to the very planning staffs assigned to Roundup.[33]

At the end of July Mr. Churchill tactfully cabled the President to ask him for General Marshall as the Supreme Commander of Roundup. As always, the Prime Minister was maintaining in this period, at least as much through wishful thinking as from a desire to spare the feelings of his Allies, that Roundup was still possible in spite of Torch.[34] It might be thought that it would have been extremely awkward for Churchill had Roosevelt actually given his outstanding Chief of Staff such a nominal command post, but it must be recalled that Mr. Churchill's concept of Roundup was undated and could have perfectly well covered a cross-Channel attack in 1944 or even 1945.

Truly the American military authorities required British tact; they had not fully accepted the fact that the basic Allied strategy had been fundamentally altered without their approval. On July 30 Admiral Leahy told the Combined Chiefs in Washington that the President and Prime Minister 'believed' Torch was on.[35] On the same day, however, the United States Joint Chiefs recommended turning down the North African project. As a result the President was forced to summon them to the White House and insist that preparations for the landings be pushed through with speed and determination.[36] On August 1, Mr. Roosevelt declared that Torch was now the principal United States objective with precedence over all other operations. Thus the end of July may also be taken as the date on which a serious cross-Channel invasion was — to employ the phraseology of the Combined Chiefs — 'in all probability' put off until 1944.[37]

Nevertheless, so late as mid-August Admiral Cunningham of the Royal Navy observed that the American military did not appear to be getting down to preparing for Torch and were only paying lip service to it. He noted that Admiral King, in particular, was 'dead set against it' and that his opinion was generally shared by other U. S. Navy officers.[38] General Marshall's resistance also had not been completely worn down. He still maintained that it was a 'big issue' whether the principal United States effort should be in the Pacific or in the European theater.[39] At the same time General Eisenhower, facing profound doubts concerning the logistic difficulties of Torch among his staff in Britain, had to inform them repeatedly that the African operation was an order from the President that had to be carried out whether they liked it or not. Eisenhower asserted that he was going to land in North Africa 'if I have to go alone in a row-boat.' [40]

The basic disagreement between the British and Americans over the strategic conception of Torch continued through the planning for its execution and thereafter to its consequences. So far as the conflict over the execution was concerned, the British had a new ally in Eisenhower. In retrospect, it is clear that the British and Eisenhower (and Henry Stimson) were the more prescient; for whatever reasons, President Roosevelt and his Army Chief of Staff, George Marshall, proved less so.

The new conflict came up over the location of Torch's landing areas in North Africa; to the British the essence of the operation was to occupy Tunisia within twenty-eight days — this being the time they estimated necessary for the Germans to move in troops and equipment to resist the invasion. The time required for the Allies to reach Tunisia also involved the already unreal argument over whether Roundup would still be possible in 1943.

On the grounds that they feared a German invasion through Spain, the United States Joint Chiefs insisted upon landings near Casablanca in the Atlantic. This would, of course, delay the approach to Tunisia and consequently, in theory at any rate, would postpone Roundup as well. On the other hand the British preferred to land so far east on the Algerian coast as Philippeville or Bône, the Prime Minister himself maintaining that the speedy conquest of Tunis was necessary to make the campaign 'a strategic success.' [41] What really constituted success to Mr. Churchill was defined rather explicitly in his communication of August 27 to President Roosevelt, a communication in which he wrote that 'the movement towards Tunis and Bizerte is an indispensable part of the attack on Italy . . .' [42]

Eisenhower and his planners in London agreed with the British that by limiting the range of the initial landings the Allies would give up before the start 'in the race against time and the Germans to capture Tunisia' and, therefore, that the American emphasis upon security would defeat its own purpose. [43] Nevertheless Eisenhower cheerfully accepted the decision on behalf of the Atlantic coast landings because, in his opinion, 'the governing considerations were political more than tactical, and political estimates are the functions of governments, not of soldiers.' Although the vicissitudes of the Malta convoys had given the United States War Department some basis for its anxieties concerning amphibious operations close to Sicily or Sardinia,[44] the probabilities are that other than purely tactical considerations had influenced Washington in favor of Morocco. But officially, as always, the American military separated the political aspects of war from the military with Puritan precision; [45] Mr. Churchill was willing to take more obvious risks here since his conception of war was, if anything, more political than military.[46]

Churchill himself clearly manifested very considerable political foresight on this amphibious operation. As he had tried to do at Constantinople in 1915, but had so far achieved only in fantasy in his romantic novel *Savrola*,[47] he was at last able to predict correctly that an amphibious assault on Algiers would be aimed at the political focal point where any reaction would be most decisive through North Africa.[48] Algiers was thus finally added, as an American compromise from their cautious and purely military proposals for assaults directed against Oran and Casablanca. But Bône and Philippeville, so much nearer to Tunis, were still excluded from the initial Allied landings.

Before this issue was settled the Prime Minister had come to suspect that the American Chiefs of Staff were attempting to sabotage his African scheme by means of a new and last-minute insistence upon landings near Casablanca. Churchill temporarily considered sending a personal letter to the President, a letter which was to read in the following subtle but revealing vein: 'Frankly I do not understand what is back of all this. I thought that there was agreement with Marshall and that King had been paid off with what he needed for his Pacific war. But now it seems that there is a bad come-back from the professional circles in the American Army and I have a deep and growing fear that the whole of the President's enterprise may be wrecked bit by bit . . .' [49]

It is one of the more interesting commentaries on Torch that the American error in its execution accentuated the British error in its conception so far as prolonging the course of the war was concerned; in each instance the side with the poorer case won out, though neither British nor American observers tend to point out the responsibility of their own side for misjudgment. Yet, despite any delays in the execution of Torch which may have resulted from the opposition on the part of the American military, in his post-war record at least one well-informed Briton has written that even had Torch been carried out in one or two months, it still would have been too late for a cross-Channel invasion in 1943.[50] It can now hardly be considered a matter of dispute that in the latter part of 1942 the Allies were committed to the Mediterranean throughout the whole year 1943, long before they knew of the delay in the execution of Torch which would result from Hitler's decision to intervene on a large scale in Tunisia.

In the upshot it turned out from this German intervention, as Mr. Churchill has freely conceded, that 'the unexpected came to the aid of the design and multiplied the results' achieved in Tunisia.[51] In short, the Allies had not expected the principal benefit of the Tunisian campaign, the destruction in that French African protectorate in 1943 of more Axis divisions than were in Africa in 1942. But the Allies, or at least the American Ally, had certainly anticipated the chief fault of Torch, the destruction of Roundup. In 1943 Hitler may well have congratulated himself that he had purchased — although this asset was actually offered free of any charge — a year's immunity in the West at the cost of only one hundred and twenty-five thousand German soldiers.[52] Roundup could very well have cost him far more and without giving him an additional lease on life.

In 1704 the Rock of Gibraltar had been seized as a compensation for the failure of a British amphibious assault in the Mediterranean designed by the Duke of Marlborough to assist his more decisive operations in northern Europe.[53] In the eighteenth century the greater logistic advantages of sea power in comparison with today sometimes permitted simultaneous and complementary thrusts in widely separated regions against land power then too slow to stop both thrusts in time.

Gibraltar had affected the Allied debate on the position of the

African landings because it was essential as the only available field for the staging of the land-based air support for Torch; at the same time both its harbor and air field lay in full view of General Franco's Spanish artillery, scarcely a point in favor of the whole operation in North Africa. The American Chiefs of Staff hoped to intimidate Spain with their landings in French Morocco, since a German invasion across the Straits of Gibraltar might otherwise trap the Allies by land.[54] Before the unanticipated German defeat at Stalingrad such an action would have been the logical German countermove to an enterprise such as Torch; far more sensible, indeed, than reinforcing Tunisia across the much wider central Mediterranean while leaving the Allied supply lines to Algiers and Casablanca intact.

During the Anglo-American debate over the execution of Torch, Winston Churchill very properly drew the duty of going to Moscow and breaking the news of the African expedition to Stalin. The Prime Minister had no illusions concerning the nature of his reception in the Soviet capital; at the time he wrote President Roosevelt that his was 'a somewhat raw job,' and subsequently he has recalled that his trip was rather 'like carrying a large lump of ice to the North Pole.'

In Moscow in uncomfortable explanations beginning August 12, the Prime Minister went over the difficulties of Sledgehammer and the reasons for its postponement. He was careful, however, only to inform Stalin of the impossibility of any cross-Channel invasion during 1942. For 1943 Churchill still offered the Soviet dictator positive assurances that the Allies were preparing for 'a very great operation,' involving the dispatch of some twenty-seven American divisions as well as twenty-one British across the Channel.[55] One can well understand the Prime Minister's desire to minimize the shock of the loss of Sledgehammer by not mentioning the possible loss of Roundup to boot. As usual, Stalin co-operated in damaging his own interests by not showing concern for a cross-Channel operation a year ahead,[56] possibly under the apprehension that to do so would further jeopardize the likelihood of such an invasion in the current year. But the eventual bitterness of the Russians regarding the sincerity of the promises of the Western Allies concerning a second front in 1943 seems amply justified by the facts of Mr. Churchill's own case.

After a more amicable discussion regarding the bombing of the Reich, in which Stalin democratically advocated the destruction of the homes of the German proletariat as well as their means of production, Churchill sprang the idea of an Allied landing in North Africa in 1942. More informally and effectively to illustrate his thesis before the stubborn master of the Politburo the Prime Minister fell back upon another of his arts. He drew a picture, that of a crocodile, and then expressed the appealing sentiment that the soft underbelly of the beast in the Mediterranean was a better place to strike than its more formidable snout which he located in France. Stalin did not take immediate offense at this famous and ultimately unfortunate analogy, although he undoubtedly believed that Russia rather than the United Kingdom faced the German snout.[57]

In fact, perhaps hoping for no more than such a project at best, but more likely not understanding at once the probable effect of such a landing upon a cross-Channel operation in 1943, Stalin now showed some enthusiasm and urged that Torch be launched as soon as possible. President Roosevelt must have been pleased when he learned of this particular point. Churchill has noted that the turning point in this conversation came when he declared that if North Africa were conquered in 1942 the Western Allies could make a 'deadly' attack upon Hitler in France in 1943.[58]

Stalin listed as advantages of Torch the following: 'It would take the German enemy in the rear. It would provoke French and Germans to fight each other. It would put Italy out of action. It would make it all the more advisable for Spain to stay neutral.' The British themselves had not claimed the last attribute for Torch — far from it. Soon enough Stalin was to have second thoughts regarding what region constituted the rear of the German enemy, thoughts which, like those of the U. S. Army, centered in France. But in this mood the former Orthodox seminarian was willing to invoke the Deity to help Mr. Churchill's enterprise succeed.

Evidently the Soviet ruler was briefed by his military advisers, because on the next day, August 13, the agreeable atmosphere of the previous meeting was no more. Stalin now made it very apparent that he and his colleagues were quite uninterested in the North African operation. Molotov described Torch as 'ambiguous' and Stalin submitted an official Soviet *aide-mémoire* which declared in strict accord with the future Soviet position:

> *As is well known, the organization of a second front in Europe in 1942 was pre-decided during the sojourn of Molotov in London . . . It will be easily understood that the Soviet Command built their plan of summer and autumn operations calculating on the creation of a second front in Europe in 1942. It is easy to grasp that the refusal of the Government of Great Britain to create a second front in 1942 in Europe inflicts a moral blow to the whole of the Soviet public opinion . . . It appears to me and to my colleagues that the most favorable conditions exist in 1942 for the creation of a second front in Europe, inasmuch as almost all the forces of the German Army, and the best forces to boot, have been withdrawn to the Eastern front, leaving in Europe an inconsiderable amount of forces and these of inferior quality. It is unknown whether the year 1943 will offer conditions for the creation of a second front as favorable as 1942.*

Stalin and his military experts still had not grasped the fact that Roundup offered them their only hope; by reverting to Sledgehammer they would certainly receive neither it nor Roundup.

Stalin reinforced his *aide-mémoire* with exaggerated figures to the effect that since supposedly there were two hundred and eighty German divisions on the Eastern front, it should not be too difficult for the Allies to land six or eight divisions in France. Like their British equivalents, Stalin's intelligence agencies seem to have known how to arrive at estimates useful for their superiors. In reply, Churchill was forced to strum once again that favorite theme, the dangers of any operation across the English Channel.[59] Stalin remained unmoved, observing, in fact, that if 'the British infantry would only fight the Germans as the Russians had done . . . it would not be so frightened of them.' On the anniversary of the battle of Blenheim, Churchill answered with dignity: 'I pardon that remark only on account of the bravery of the Russian troops.'[60] Not until three years later at

Yalta could a victorious Stalin afford to toast Winston Churchill's courage in fighting alone in 1940.[61]

Mr. Churchill has added to these revealing encounters himself, saying that Stalin suggested that in view of the British fears he was willing to send several Russian corps to Great Britain for an invasion of France. Using a rather literal evasion of this deliberately provocative remark, the Prime Minister wrote: 'It was not in my power, through lack of shipping and other physical facts, to take him at his word.' [62]

Yet Stalin's attitude can be understood only too well. If the British lost a few score thousand men in France in a failure in 1942, let them try again in 1943; the U.S.S.R. lost that number almost every month. But despite the Soviet dictator's invocation of Russian public opinion, he faced much less difficulty in that respect than did a medium-sized democracy in decreeing a blood bath.

A description of Stalin on this occasion, given by so naturally unsympathetic an observer as Sir Alan Brooke, is striking. Noted Brooke: 'Stalin is a realist if ever there was one; facts only count with him. Plans, hypotheses, future possibilities, mean nothing to him, but he is ready to face facts, even when unpleasant. Winston, on the other hand, never seems anxious to face an unpleasantness until forced to do so. He appealed to sentiments in Stalin which do not, I think, exist . . . [Stalin] has a quick brain and a real grasp of the essentials of war.' [63]

On August 14 Churchill replied to the Soviet *aide-mémoire* by asserting that 'the best second front in 1942 and the only large-scale operation possible from the Atlantic is Torch.' Sledgehammer, reiterated the Prime Minister, would use up 'wastefully and wantonly the key men and the landing craft required for real action in 1943.' [64] Whatever might be maintained after the war, it is obvious that in 1942, to the British, as to their Allies, real action meant action only in France. When in a somber mood on August 15 Churchill went to take his farewell he was again surprised — for good will was again present and the Russians seemed to have accepted what they called the British decision that there would be no operation across the Channel in 1942.[65] Nevertheless, in retrospect, it would appear almost certain that Stalin had not changed his mind. Coalition policy has its requirements in politeness when the most brutal possible language has failed.

After his return to Great Britain, on September 8 the Prime Minister informed the House of Commons that the Russians had shown difficulty in appreciating the efforts of the United Kingdom, but the fact which remained outstanding to Mr. Churchill was that while the Russians were, most assuredly, 'land animals,' the British remained 'sea animals.' [66] Mr. Churchill had perhaps forgotten a reminder which Lloyd George had given him to the effect that 'most of us live on land.' [67] Later Churchill declared that Stalin, evidently during one of his friendly days, had termed Torch militarily correct. On the other hand, the disturbing possibilities of the Soviet reaction when Moscow would finally realize that as a result of Torch there could be no second front in 1943 would constitute henceforth a persistent anxiety for the Prime Minister.[68]

In any event the Prime Minister came back from Russia in no way less enthusiastic for Torch. On the contrary, rather than forgo the African project, now in logistic and planning difficulties, he would 'hop on a plane and see the President . . . to keep Torch lit.' With the nervous impatience observed so often in both world wars, Mr. Churchill now urged President Roosevelt to undertake the North African assault regardless of grave inadequacies of equipment so early as the middle of October.[69] The Prime Minister added that he was prepared to take 'any amount of responsibility for running the political risks and being proved wrong about the political assumptions' of a campaign which was 'primarily political in its foundations.' [70] Nobody could be bolder than Winston Churchill — inside the Mediterranean. On August 30 Roosevelt replied: 'It is my earnest desire to start the attack at the earliest possible moment. Time is of the essence . . .' [71]

The Prime Minister had recognized that it was now or never for Torch. As had happened in 1915 with his Dardanelles shortcut to victory, now he was encountering a growing pessimism concerning the African 'adventure' even among the British military.[72] General Mark Clark in London at this time concluded that only Churchill himself was all for Torch, the latter, however, feeling so determined that he told Clark that Torch was 'the one thing that is going to win the war.' [73] Yet it can be seen why in a *cri de coeur* in September, according to Sir Alan Brooke, Churchill said that 'this machine of war with Russia at one end and America at the other was too cumbersome to run any war with. It was so much easier to do nothing. He could so easily sit and wait for work to come to him.' [74] Only Churchill's last assertion may provoke incredulity.

It was under these circumstances that the landing areas imbroglio was finally settled by the personal intervention of the President and Prime Minister. In Henry Stimson's sadly impersonal reflections Torch now had what Bolero had never had, 'the enthusiastic support of the highest authorities, and it was therefore possible to give it priorities and exclusive rights with the kind of ruthlessness that Stimson had so ardently and fruitlessly urged for Bolero.' Hereafter the United States Secretary of War confined himself to obtaining a promise from Marshall that he would make another stand against the final execution of Torch, if at any time it seemed headed for an obvious disaster. In retrospect, so far as his previous views on Torch were concerned, Stimson could only argue that if he were again faced with the problems of 1942, he would follow the same course as he had then.[75]

The landing craft bugbear was the first to be cracked under the impetus of the new drive and determination at the top. For example, on August 17, General Clark, who was engaged in the harassed planning end of the American preparations for Torch, had complained rather bitterly of the shortage of landing craft. 'Only eighteen of one type and about eighty of another, which he thought was a pitiful trickle from the much-ballyhooed American production. Both he and Ike wondered where all this production is going.' [76] This thought would reoccur to Clark and Eisenhower frequently enough again in 1943–44, so far as landing craft were concerned.

In this same month American production was diverted to the hitherto lowly landing craft. President Roosevelt now declared that they were so important that they should override any other program if necessary. As a result, in the last six months of 1942 there was produced twenty times the deadweight tonnage of LC's and LST's as in January to June of 1942. Thereafter the production of this key item was drastically cut back.[77] The landing craft shortage, so often to be represented as a cause for Mr. Churchill's strategy, was actually in large measure a reflection of it.

The heavily competitive naval escort shortage was also faced in the autumn of 1942. By October 1942, with the new production of escort vessels and the institution of convoys in American waters and with aerial patrols and radar, Admiral King considered German submarines under sufficient control to make possible the North African expedition, although King himself may well have been chiefly responsible for delaying Torch in view of his preoccupation with the Pacific theater.[78] After December 1942 merchant tonnage losses were cut in half from the terrible levels of February–November 1942.[79] But this new tonnage was immediately consumed by the new campaign which officially was designed to create new tonnage.

In August of this year the spectacular Canadian raid on Dieppe had stressed among other things the necessity for a rapid build-up if future and permanent landings were to be exploited; again the answer was landing craft. In fact Dieppe had been planned in part to test the nearly developed LCT, landing craft tank, in landing tanks across beaches and to find out whether it would be possible to take a port by direct frontal assault.[80] But like the elder Pitt's unhappy 'conjunct expeditions' to alarm the coasts of France,[81] the losses at Dieppe convinced the Allies that an assault of this kind against a defended port was not practical. Although this first amphibious attack since Gallipoli was not encouraging, particularly to the British who would remain pessimistic on this score until 1943, the Allied planners would return to Admiral Fisher's Baltic beetles [82] and design still more specialized craft for landing on open beaches. For example, within ninety days of their landing in Normandy in June 1944, the Americans would send in three times as many supplies over the Utah and Omaha beaches as went through the quickly captured but shattered port of Cherbourg.[83]

In Marshall Rundstedt's command in western Europe, Dieppe had important repercussions. In September, in an analysis of the raid, Hitler declared: 'I must freely admit . . . that a major landing of the enemy in the West would bring us to a generally critical position.' The Fuehrer believed that Dieppe had been a major attack that failed and that the British had no alternative but to try again. He thereupon ordered that an Atlantic Wall should be completed by May 1, 1943, the precise date scheduled by the U. S. Army for the launching of Roundup against this same coast. Fortunately for the Allies, with the supposed lessons of Dieppe in mind, Hitler directed that first priority in building fortifications should be given to the ports and the lowest priority to the open beaches of the kind Dieppe had persuaded the Allies to employ.

Organization Todt, however, thought that it would be lucky if 40 per cent of these fortifications were finished by the date laid down for completion by the Fuehrer. Furthermore, in 1942–43, as in 1944 with so much greater effect, the emphasis of the Germans, both in fortifications and in troops, was placed upon the sector of the Channel ports rather than south of the Seine in western Normandy. During 1942 three times as many troops and four times as much concrete were allotted to the more northerly region than to the area against which Overlord was finally launched.[84] In 1943–44 the location of the V-1 propelled missile bases in the northern sector would accentuate this important German bias with beneficial results for the execution of the Overlord invasion.[85]

Hitler's orders for the serious diversion of the Reich's resources inherent in even the partial creation of a West Wall during the height of a general war did not result from a simple mood of impulsive reaction to the prematurely posed Allied threat in the West. Contrary to what British Intelligence maintained, throughout 1942 and 1943 the German Army in the West was always desperately pressed for manpower. Whether Stalin had learned this from his uniquely magnificent intelligence sources or simply had said so anyway from self-interest when he had argued so futilely with Churchill in August 1942, the fact remains that by the autumn of that year the point was reached in Rundstedt's command in which the troops available for Attila, the possible emergency seizure of the French Unoccupied Zone, were insufficient for this modest task. At Moscow Churchill had asserted that there were nine first-line German divisions in France in contradiction to Stalin's claim that there was at this time 'not a single German division in France of any value.' [86] Since the war a U. S. Army historian has concluded from evidence drawn from enemy sources that by 1942 the German Army had already recognized that the campaign in Russia usually precluded the stationing of first-rate troops in the West.[87]

By September 7, with Torch definitely set, in London Captain Butcher noted that Eisenhower and Bedell Smith were both already concerned with the need for 'crystallizing the direction of the grand military strategy the U.S. and G.B. will take, once the Torch operation is completed. A meeting of minds of the President, the P.M. and the Staffs at an early date is essential. In democracies plans are frequently changed to meet the strong current of political opinion; these must be weighed against the greater value of understanding and pursuit of a clear-cut objective towards which all effort would be unremittingly applied.' [88] Eisenhower and Smith keenly appreciated what General Marshall was up against in Washington.

In this month Winston Churchill was likewise visibly considering the prospects of action subsequent to North Africa. Roundup, he now apparently recognized for the first time, might be wiped out by what Eisenhower explained to him were 'the inescapable costs of Torch,' [89] but there would still remain the possibility of a limited face-saving operation across the Channel in 1943. That is, an emergency operation along the lines of the subsequent British Rankin plans, to be undertaken only in event of a serious German weakening or collapse. With high enthusiasm the Prime Minister tried to talk Sir Alan Brooke into an attack on Norway in January 1943, saying that he had promised Stalin something of the kind. Brooke pointed out that the lack of shipping alone would make such a scheme impossible at the same time as Torch.[90] As the C.I.G.S. had remarked after an earlier scene with Churchill: 'This meeting with Winston was typical of many others when all difficulties were brushed aside, and many unpleasant realities, such as resources available, were scrupulously avoided.' [91]

On September 9 Eisenhower notified Churchill that Torch would be postponed until November 8. The Prime Minister was disappointed; his anxiety over the early appearance of Torch was as great as that of the President, although unlike the President he faced no Congressional election on November 3. But Mr. Churchill undoubtedly had little desire for the President to be deprived of, perhaps, his principal interest in Torch—and Gallipoli had shown the Prime Minister how much could go wrong in two months of argument.

It was not until September 22 that Eisenhower made the final decision that the date of the African invasion had to be postponed to November 8. Following this decision the Prime Minister also imparted the less unwelcome news to the President that the shipping needs of Torch would probably require the suspension for a time of Jupiter, the plan to seize northern Norway.[92] One of the Prime Minister's favorite diversions had canceled out another.

Sherwood, Eisenhower, and Marshall all have testified to how gallantly the President took the great blow to his hopes of an early date for Torch. In 1943 the President confided to General Eisenhower what a disappointment it had been to him that Torch had followed rather than preceded the Congressional elections for the United States.[93] More recently General Marshall has admitted: 'It would have been helpful, to put it mildly, for that operation to have been launched before the election then impending . . . A man of lesser stature than Mr. Roosevelt, with the authority of Commander-in-Chief, might have insisted that the election be timed for a week after the action. But not Mr. Roosevelt. I consider that it was a rare exhibition of courage and unselfishness.' [94]

General Marshall has done honor to himself with this postwar courtesy to his former Commander-in-Chief. But it must be said, to the credit of Mr. Roosevelt, that he did not permit his political interests to interfere with tactics; with both sides, of course, political factors frequently did determine grand strategy. In addition, there may have been some military basis for

Mr. Churchill's stress on speed since to at least one critic, General Frederick Fuller, the invasion of North Africa should have preceded General Montgomery's offensive at the Battle of El Alamein in order to force Rommel to look in two directions.[95] Certainly the effort was made, although principally for other reasons.

As a postscript to this controversy, because of the great Republican gains in the United States elections Roosevelt almost faced the dilemma of Woodrow Wilson in 1918 in losing control of Congress before he could attend the peace conference.[96] From the unconditional surrender formula down, Franklin Roosevelt would spend much of his wartime career plunging into new difficulties in his efforts to avoid repeating the mistakes of the Wilson administration.

Like the President, the American Army was still in the dark concerning the detailed plans which Winston Churchill was brewing for them in his opaque and teeming cauldron; the U. S. Army had not yet fully learned to take the initiative as a method of breaking down the indirect approach of the Prime Minister. For example, before leaving Britain for his new command post at Gibraltar in late October, Eisenhower told his colleague of the U.S.A.A.F., General Spaatz, that after Torch 'in all probability' he would return for the Roundup operation, a prospect to which he looked forward with satisfaction. In an attempted explanation, the U. S. Air Force historians surmise that Eisenhower may have been reflecting War Department hopes in 'the strategic fogs of late 1942,'[97] fogs in which Eisenhower was endeavoring to establish a fixed course without any directions from his more opportunist political superiors. Indeed, no formal directive was possible, for no Allied conference had determined operations beyond Torch.

In early November the strategic fogs seemed to part for Bedell Smith. To this keen participant it at last appeared that Mr. Churchill was losing enthusiasm for Roundup except as a *coup de grâce* after a more serious blow delivered against the Axis in the Mediterranean. To General Smith it also appeared that Churchill was substituting a British-sponsored Turkish military invasion of the Balkans in place of his old plan to invade

Norway. With Allied equipment, what the Prime Minister liked to consider as forty-five Turkish divisions of superior manpower should have a certain potential for distracting minor German forces from other regions of more immediate moment to Mr. Churchill.[98] Throughout 1943 he would not forget Turkey and her unemployed manpower.

Possibly Mr. Churchill's current accession of interest in Turkey had resulted, unbeknown to General Smith, from a suggestion of President Roosevelt for operations directed toward involving this easily overrated neutral power as a new ally. Without doubt this suggestion was most welcome to the Prime Minister. In mid-November Mr. Churchill explained more specifically to the President than before that an attack against Sicily or Sardinia was an essential step after the completion of Torch.[99]

At the same time, in a more private communication to his own Chiefs of Staff the Prime Minister complained: 'Torch is only thirteen divisions, whereas we had been prepared to move forty-eight divisions agianst the enemy in 1943. . . . No doubt we were planning too much for 1943 in the summer, but we are certainly planning too little now. . . . We have, in fact, pulled in our horns to an almost extraordinary extent, and I cannot imagine what the Russians will say or do when they realise it.' [100] Torch was beginning to appear to Winston Churchill himself an inadequate substitute for Roundup, the attack upon the Reich through France in 1943. To be sure, Lord Louis Mountbatten had also assured the British Chiefs of Staff that Torch ruled out Roundup, but this had only pleased these cautious and less politically aware officers.[101]

Although determined to employ North Africa as 'a springboard and not a sofa,' a view already anathema to the United States War Department, according to his own account the Prime Minister still felt that a cross-Channel invasion in July or August of 1943 was not impossible. To his Chiefs of Staff Churchill emphasized that inaction in both the Mediterranean and cross-Channel theaters of war, a thankless policy for which the American Army was, in effect, now forced to argue, would be intolerable to their Russian Ally. On November 9 the Prime Minister wrote: 'If French North Africa is going to be made an excuse for locking up great forces on the defensive and calling it a "commitment" it would be better not to have gone there at all.' [102] The United States War Department would gladly have echoed this last assertion before the actual execution of Torch, but now it was too late. The Allies had landed the day previously in northwest Africa, an action which President Roosevelt in agreement with his British colleague had publicly proclaimed an 'effective second front.' [103]

Somewhat less publicly, in July 1942 Mr. Churchill had also called Torch the Allies 'true second front of 1942.' On the other hand, by 1943 the Prime Minister had come to consider this true second front of the previous year a 'Third Front.' He stated in the later year that 'the Second Front . . . has not yet been engaged.' [104] Whatever may be said of the Prime Minister's strategy, his employment of the term 'second front' was flexible in the extreme.

On November 24, in a cable to President Roosevelt with which after the war he attempted to dispel the many American 'legends' that he was 'inveterately hostile' to Roundup, the Prime Minister declared that it seemed to him a 'most grievous decision to abandon Roundup. Torch is no substitute for Roundup . . . All my talks with Stalin . . . were on the basis of a postponed Roundup. But it was never suggested that we should attempt no second front in Europe in 1943, or even 1944.' [105]

Primary among the issues raised by this remarkable cable was that Mr. Churchill did not want the American Bolero build-up in Great Britain diverted to the Pacific in spite of the *de facto* abandonment of its *raison d'être* — Roundup. But the fact re-remained, as Churchill now admitted, that what the Western Allies were going to do about Roundup would constitute 'almost the sole thing' the Russians would want to know in the forthcoming months.[106]

In December Stalin would make clear that Torch was no substitute for Roundup and that it was also in no sense part of any Soviet conception of a second front. The Soviet ruler went on to express his confidence that 'the promises about the opening of a Second Front in Europe given by you, Mr. President, and by Mr. Churchill in regard to 1942, and in any case in regard to the spring of 1943, will be fulfilled, and that a Second Front in Europe will be actually opened by the joint forces of Great Britain and the United States of America in the spring of the next year.' Only a few weeks earlier the Soviet press had suggested more bluntly that the so-called Astor clique in the British Conservative party was inducing Mr. Churchill to postpone a second front in order to weaken Russia.

In the light of the evidence available today, it may be concluded that Mr. Churchill's post-war assertion to the effect that his conscience is 'clear,' since he did 'not deceive or mislead Stalin' [107] on this basic issue, is founded upon the hypothesis that notwithstanding repeated American warnings and his own immense experience in war, the Prime Minister had succeeded in deceiving himself so successfully that not until after November 1942 can he be said to have deliberately deceived his Russian ally.

In his cable of November 24 to the President, the Prime Minister went on to suggest that it might not now be possible to mass the necessary strength for an invasion of France in 1943, but 'if so, it becomes all the more important to make sure that we do not miss 1944.' Notwithstanding this broad hint regarding the real prospects for a 1943 cross-Channel invasion, on November 26 President Roosevelt replied to his British colleague as follows: 'Of course we have no intention of abandoning the plans for Roundup. It is impossible for anyone to say now whether or not we will be given the opportunity to strike across the Channel in 1943 . . . The mounting of Torch, according to the conclusions reached . . . last summer . . . by the Combined Chiefs of Staff, postponed necessarily the assembling of the required forces in the British Isles.' [108]

Although the intentions of President Roosevelt were both excellent and inspiring, one of his major weaknesses was his frequent lapses into opportunism. Domestically, this trait had enervated the hard bases of New Deal legislation; in military affairs it had a more immediate if similar effect in the realm of grand strategy. To Mr. Roosevelt in November 1942, when Winston Churchill himself was at last reluctantly facing reality, nobody could say yet whether or not Roundup was possible in 1943. In

July 1942 Henry Stimson had pushed his disagreement with the President 'to the limits prescribed by loyalty' and had again and again emphasized the fact that Torch destroyed Roundup in 1943.[109] Contradictions are rarely so flagrant for the easy convenience of the historian.

Probably some of the President's misunderstanding was based upon his belief, in common with those of many far better versed in tactics, that the African campaign would be concluded within a month or six weeks. Although Eisenhower had tried to make clear in August that the acceptance of the Casablanca landings instead of those nearer to Tunis had interdicted any such quick African campaign, his protests did not seem to have percolated through to the consciousness of the President, or more significantly, to that of General Marshall. Consequently, President Roosevelt was still set for a six-week Torch, followed by asaults against both the south and west of Europe in a politically most appealing fashion. Unhappily all of this could not be done, and those aware of the actual military resources of the Western Allies knew that a formal recognition of the Allied choice would soon have to be made. Otherwise even further Mediterranean operations would be crippled.

Exactly why General Marshall had informed Roosevelt in November that he estimated that the occupation of Tunisia could be accomplished in two or three weeks or a little longer, despite the opinions in August of both Eisenhower and the British that it would take much more time than that, remains obscure, particularly since Marshall had opposed Torch in the first place.[110] Possibly the unenthusiastic United States Chief of Staff had favored the Casablanca landings without completely grasping the delaying qualities inherent in these Moroccan operations; possibly, as Mr. Churchill may have implied, he had favored the Casablanca landings precisely because of their hampering effects. Unquestionably Marshall always wished to avoid 'dabbling' [111] any more in the Mediterranean than he could help in order to protect what would always remain to him the 'main plot,' [112] an invasion across the Channel. Nevertheless, the logistic ground was crumbling away under the feet of General Marshall and he knew it.[113]

Ironically, in Britain the appearance of Torch had evoked an extraordinary upsurge of desire to revive Roundup now that it was at last out of the question — an upsurge fostered both by a new confidence toward the suddenly less formidable enemy and by what may have been a rather tardy sense of guilt toward his Allies on the part of Mr. Churchill. What could have been almost as bad from the point of view of Sir Alan Brooke was that Churchill's characteristic last-minute switch in favor of Roundup was supported by the recent hero of the British victory at El Alemain, General Sir Bernard Montgomery. But Sir Alan was able to a large extent to conceal from the Americans this most unlikely change of front by Mr. Churchill and allow the actual realization of Torch henceforth to argue for itself.[114]

The Prime Minister's new position is worthy of scrutiny in order to perceive more closely the nature of his difficulties in strategy. If according to Mr. Churchill the Allies had lacked adequate resources for a cross-Channel invasion in 1943 before Torch had diverted most of their resources to the Mediterranean, they certainly would lack them afterwards. No wonder his Mediterranean-minded gray eminence, Sir Alan Brooke, found the Prime Minister 'quite the most difficult man to work with' that he had ever met. In Brooke's final conclusion: 'Perhaps the most remarkable failing of his is that he can never see a whole strategical problem at once. His gaze always settles on some definite part of the canvas and the rest of the picture is lost. It is difficult to make him realize the influence of one theatre against another . . . This failing is accentuated by the fact that often he does not want to see the whole picture, especially if the wider vision should in any way interfere with the operation he may have temporarily set his heart on.' [115]

In nonbelligerent circles, still beyond the immediate orbit of London and Washington, domestic politics were similarly influencing the uneven course of strategy. Primarily, in the opinion of the new American Ambassador, Carlton Hayes, as a means of readjusting the delicate internal political equilibrium in Spain, on September 3 Francisco Franco had replaced Serrano Suñer as Foreign Minister with the Count Jordana, an Allied sympathizer.[116] Despite this most opportune good fortune for the West, the position of Spain continued to remain extremely critical vis-à-vis Torch, since, as Eisenhower told Marshall, any sign of failure or hesitancy in Torch might enable the Axis to occupy Spain with unfortunate consequences for the Allies.[117]

Even before Torch, the increasingly obvious stalemate on the military fronts had been hardening the profound disagreements between the chief Axis partners. At the height of German successes in the early summer of 1942 Hitler declared that Japan should attack Russia only if Tokyo considered such a move profitable, although Ribbentrop had added that the time for Japan to attack Russia was probably at hand. Such unwonted Nazi restraint, perhaps based upon embarrassment as much as upon overconfidence, elicited markedly less Japanese sympathy in 1942 than in the previous year. In June the Japanese General Staff had reiterated earlier offers to mediate in the Russo-German war; by August Tokyo suggested sending Premier Tojo and other high officials to Europe to help negotiate a peace so essential to the parochial Japanese concept of the war. At first Ribbentrop favored such a mission but in September, evidently on orders from Hitler, he dropped the idea on the grounds that a German victory was certain.[118]

So far as Torch was concerned, since August the Italian Naval Command had suggested that an Allied invasion of northwest Africa was in the making and, in turn, it had attempted to plan a countermove to any such Allied action in the region of the greatest anxiety to Italy, Tunisia. But in September both the Germans and Italians were taken in for a time by the Allied cover plan and they accepted Dakar as the most probable point of danger. German submarines were, then, shifted to that region.[119]

That congenital pessimist, Count Ciano, was now about to see the realization of his darker forebodings, although like so many on the Allied side he could not anticipate the terrible consequences of the Italian inability to surrender effectively. On October 9 he claimed that he had been informed by Italian Military Intelligence that the British and Americans were preparing to land in French North Africa, and thereafter intended to attack Italy since 'geographically and logically' she would be their next objective.[120] If Ciano was correct, the Italians were crediting their American enemy with intentions of which the latter would for another few weeks still be officially unaware.

In mid-October, when it was much too late, Hitler decided to accept the conclusions of his Grand Admiral regarding the Mediterranean. Reasoning from his customarily limited naval point of view, Raeder had pointed out that after Malta the most important strategic position in the Mediterranean was Tunisia. Ignoring the fate of Bonaparte's Egyptian Army, Hitler now agreed to the seizure of Tunisia from the Vichy French only three weeks before the Allied invasion of North Africa.[121] The Allies can scarcely be blamed for their ignorance of this tardy conversion of the Fuehrer to what previously might have been a profitable German policy; however, the Allied debarkations in Morocco instead of in Eastern Algeria would, of course, reinforce the effect of Hitler's decision and emphasize the eventual tactical victory of the Allies in the African operation.

Hitler's change of front on the African issue may have been a reflection of his recently announced new strategy for the war, one of aggressive defense. Significantly in this period the Chief of Staff of the German Army, General Franz Halder, resigned, thus completing the process begun in 1938 with the removal of Blomberg and Fritsch from the Supreme Command of the Army. Hereafter, if not after Brauchitsch's resignation in December 1941, the German Army lacked any strategic leadership capable of functioning independently of Hitler. The consequences of this situation would become more and more obvious as time went on.[122]

By November 4, on the eve of the Allied invasion, Ciano learned of a great convoy being formed at Gibraltar and, in his own account, guessed that a landing was being prepared for Morocco.[123] If Ciano is to be trusted, by the seventh of the month both Il Duce and the Italian General Staff expected American landings in French North Africa against very slight resistance on the part of the adherents of Vichy. Upon receipt of definite news of Torch the next day, like General Marshall, Italian Military Intelligence foresaw the occupation of Tunisia within two weeks.[124] Although the Germans had not manifested the same foresight as the Italians, the Allies naturally regarded their reaction more seriously, especially if it appeared in Spain.

Indeed, on November 3 United States Ambassador Carlton Hayes cabled Cordell Hull that a week earlier Germany had asked Spain to allow her to send troops through the peninsula if the Allies attacked Morocco or the Canaries. Count Jordana had informed Hayes that Spain might not be able to refuse such German assistance in the event of an Allied landing in French North Africa. The Allied representatives in Madrid thereupon passed an anxious few days and elaborate arrangements were made in their embassies against the possibility of an immediate German occupation.[125]

At the opening of the North African invasion a warm letter from President Roosevelt to Generalissimo Franco promising friendship and the inviolability of Spanish territory was delivered by Ambassador Hayes. This letter, when coupled with the hard-won struggle of the new Spanish Foreign Minister to postpone the second meeting of the Spanish Council of Ministers for forty-eight hours, finally turned the scales in the Allies' favor. In the opinion of the British Ambasador, the Spanish interventionists had lost their case because of the swift and obvious success of the Torch landings.[126] But the crucial issue of intervention had hung upon a hair, and the conclusions of General Eisenhower in August regarding the extreme necessity for a rapid occupation had been amply justified.

Eisenhower, it would seem, had had even higher expectations of the benefits accruing from Torch than the speedy occupation of all of North Africa or even of the escape to Africa of the French Toulon fleet. Astonishingly, he had hoped that, intimidated by the Allied show of strength, the Germans would not seize the unoccupied zone in southern France.[127] The former General Staff planner must have been suffering from a peculiarly severe attack of theater commander 'localitis' when he propounded the thesis so close to the hopes of certain French generals, such as Giraud or de Lattre de Tassigny, for an immediate invasion of the French Riviera.[128] But the long-planned Nazi operation — Attila — brought about the immediate, if misleadingly weak, occupation of the unoccupied zone of France in mid-November. Hereafter the Latin sisters were not to offer the Fuehrer the problem of deciding whom most to favor.

Like Marshal von Rundstedt, Hitler logically expected an Allied invasion of the totally unfortified coast of southern France (via the Sardinian-Corsican route) to follow Torch as soon as possible in the next year. Subsequently Rundstedt admitted that had the Allies landed in southern France in 1943 they would have met with practically no resistance.[129] The German Marshal was closer to the perceptions of certain lesser Allied planners at the ensuing conference at Casablanca than to those of their superiors, both military and political.

Notwithstanding the long-prepared Attila plan, the shock to Hitler of what to him was the unexpected attack in North Africa was extreme. Furiously the Nazi leader put all the blame upon Francisco Franco and the 'nonsense' of which the latter had been guilty regarding Gibraltar in 1940.[130] In Franco's capital itself the American Ambassador saw that the Germans there had been taken unawares and were quite astounded. In Rome Ciano observed that Torch was an absolutely unexpected blow for the Germans in that city. This was true for Ribbentrop's Foreign Office as well; on the Wilhelmstrasse the landings had evoked complete surprise. The Germans had been thoroughly taken in by the Allied deceptions and had expected no more than another Allied convoy for the relief of Malta in the Mediterranean.[131]

Pursuant to the advice of his Grand Admiral, Hitler acted at once and, as he said, built up a bridgehead in Tunisia in a race for time against the Allied land assault from Algeria. Forgetting Malta for a moment, Raeder now declared: 'Tunisia always was and still is the decisive key position in the Mediterranean. The presence of Axis forces in Tunisia compels the enemy to employ considerable forces which must be supplied by long and vulnerable routes. It is, however, a simple task to supply our Armored Army since our lines are short.' [132]

The German Army was to pay for what seemed like such a simple business to the Mediterranean-minded German Navy. The latter service had, as usual, put its own interests and sense of values first, interests and values fundamentally opposed to those of the Army General Staff. By now even the German commander in Africa, Erwin Rommel, had recognized that henceforth any German forces sent across the Mediterranean would simply be destroyed.[133]

Too late, on December 22 Raeder advocated the occupation of the Iberian peninsula as 'of the utmost strategic importance' as a further counter to Torch.[134] The moment for this revival of Felix had passed; not merely would the Spanish Government no longer co-operate, but also the German Army and Air Forces having already undertaken the defense of Tunisia could not in the face of the first flush of the immense Soviet counterattack north of Stalingrad undertake this larger-scale, if safer and more effective, operation.

To sustain the new trans-Mediterranean German commitment in Tunisia the already overburdened Luftwaffe was called upon to send some five hundred aircraft to the Mediterranean of which the great majority came from the Russian front. On the other hand, instead of helping the Soviet Union by diversion of the German forces from the Soviet German front, by February 1943 the disclosure of the Allied hand with Torch had enabled the Germans to send twenty-seven fresh divisions from western Europe to the Russian front — or so Stalin estimated, although he misunderstood the causes of this movement. Subsequently Churchill lowered this estimate and Stalin raised his still higher, but neither disagreed that heavy German forces had been moved from west to east in the months after Torch.[135]

Moreover, for most of the next year the shipping required for the African operation helped limit the dispatch of Allied matériel to Murmansk to less than one-third of the levels of 1942, besides precipitating a world-wide crisis for the overstrained Allied merchant marine.[136] But the most serious effect of Mr. Churchill's successful campaign for a Mediterranean strategy remained the destruction of Roundup, although the unhappy Prime Minister would not admit as much to his Soviet Ally for many months to come.

When, following the Trident Conference in May 1943, it was no longer possible to deny to Moscow that Torch was a substitute for rather than a preliminary phase of a second front in

1943, not unnaturally Stalin charged Churchill with bad faith. Soon after, he withdrew his ambassadors from Great Britain and the United States. At the same time he postponed a meeting with President Roosevelt, eagerly desired by the latter.[137] Probably no more than as a threat of a more fundamental independence in action, Stalin then may have opened a series of none-too-covert negotiations pointing toward a truce with the Third Reich.[138]

Torch could not really help the Russians and Stalin now knew it, if President Roosevelt, as yet, did not. But in the months to come it would become apparent to the President that the crisis in Allied grand strategy was at hand.

10

ARCHITECT OF STALEMATE

THE CONSEQUENCES OF WINSTON CHURCHILL'S WAR DOCTRINE

1943–1945

'To say the truth, I do not believe we had in the last war, and, according to all appearance, we shall not have in the present one either, plans of a sufficiently large scale to force France to keep within her proper limits. Small measures produce only small results.' [1] — Horatio Nelson

'Has there ever been such a thing as absolute war since nations ceased to exterminate or enslave the defeated? Nineteenth Century Europe has passed beyond the Mongol stage.' [2] — Captain Liddell Hart

'The uncontrollable momentum of war, the inadequacy of unity and leadership among Allies, the tides of natural passion, nearly always force improvident action upon Governments or Commanders. Allowance must be made for the limits of their knowledge and power . . . But do not let us obscure the truth. Do not found conclusions upon error. Do not proclaim its melancholy consequences as the perfect model of the art of war or as the triumphant consummation of a great design.' [3] — Winston Churchill

'There is no greater fatuity than a political judgment dressed in a military uniform.' [4] — David Lloyd George

BY the time of the Casablanca Conference in January 1943, the form of war advocated so indirectly, yet so effectively, by the British Prime Minister had reached its apogee. The production priority of landing craft on the U. S. Navy's Shipbuilding Precedence List was dropped from second to twelfth place, or lower than in the dark days of March 1942, and in Great Britain field artillery shell production was drastically cut back.[5] Neither of these essential prerequisites of large-scale land warfare would be restored to their 1942 levels until early 1944.

The U. S. Army was to send only seven divisions abroad in the ten months following the North African landings, compared with double that number in 1942. The General Staff of the Army was forced to suspend, if not to abandon completely, its long-held concept of an immense force designed to operate as a single unit and solely against the army of the principal enemy. Consequently, as had also occurred to the British Army, the total United States troop list was again reduced, on this occasion from one hundred and fourteen to one hundred divisions.[6] Recognizing the implications for land warfare of the British narrowing-ring approach to the European Axis, General Marshall had found it necessary to insist upon this reduction in divisional strength against the unanimous advice of his staff.[7]

The results of the failure of the U. S. Army to achieve a durable agreement on a dominant theater in western Europe were now becoming more apparent. On January 14, at the first meeting at Casablanca of the Chiefs of Staff, in opposing 'interminable operations' in the Mediterranean, General Marshall joined Admiral King in the advocacy of further reinforcements for the South and Southwest Pacific as well as new assaults against Burma and the Marshall Islands.[8] Marshall was again reviving the old issue of the American Pacific threat despite his full awareness that only a few weeks before the President had complained that the United States was much more heavily engaged in the Southwest Pacific than he had expected. The U. S. Army Chief of Staff was also conscious of the current desire of the President to give the operations in North Africa precedence over all other projects until adequate preparations had been made against any Axis assault in Spanish Morocco or in Tunisia.[9]

The British Chiefs of Staff opposed their American colleagues on this Pacific proposal; instead at last they frankly urged an all-out effort in the Mediterranean. To thwart the emphasis of Marshall and King upon the Pacific, the British now discovered the necessity for a plan that would bring victory 'quickly and decisively' in the European theater.[10] As the Prime Minister would put it, the danger which faced his Grand Alliance was no longer defeat, but stalemate.[11]

Unfortunately, notwithstanding that, in Mr. Churchill's phrase, Admiral King had been 'paid off' once already in 1942, by May 1943 the American preoccupation with the war against Japan had risen to such a crescendo that it required a careful answer by Mr. Churchill before a Joint Session of the United States Congress.[12] Moreover, the United States Chiefs of Staff were not willing to sacrifice a full-fledged effort in their own popular Pacific theater for the sake of a limited campaign of expediency in the Mediterranean. War might be all hell and no glory, according to the prophetic General William Sherman, but by Calvinist definition there could be no mere purgatory of limited war in General Marshall's still absolute war doctrine.

Thus, with both United States military doctrine and popular opinion against him, there can be little doubt as to why the Americans had so unfavorable a reaction to Mr. Churchill's now triumphant conception of war. The Combined Chiefs were unable to answer General Eisenhower's request for his next objective, an impasse which Eisenhower terminated by remarking: 'Oh you just want to go on fighting, do you, well we can find plenty of places to do that.' [13]

Only a month previously the Prime Minister himself had conceded in a communication to President Roosevelt that 'at present we have no plan for 1943 which is on the scale or up to the level of events.' [14] More privately, Mr. Churchill would grumble to his own Chiefs concerning the inadequacy of the Western Allies 'playing about' with six German divisions while the Russians were facing one hundred and eighty-five.[15] For himself the Prime Minister favored an ample program which included not merely the conquest of Tunisia and Sicily and the recapture of Burma; he also still desired a preliminary invasion of France,[16] a weakening phrase which presumably reflected his exposure to the overwhelming fact of Torch.

So long as they had the decisive support of the President the British would win in the essentials, and this they did at Casablanca. It was decided to push ahead, officially at least, only to

Sicily in the Mediterranean. This new commitment was facilitated by the now obvious impossibility of conquering Tunisia in time to permit even a theoretical revival of Roundup in 1943.[17] Nevertheless, the United States Chiefs of Staff had extracted their price and would continue to do so. Of the sixteen American Army and Marine divisions arriving at United States Ports of Embarkation in 1942, two-thirds had been sent to the Pacific by the beginning of 1943. So late as January 1944 there were 40 per cent more of what Mr. Churchill has considered American divisions 'in fighting contact' with the enemy in the Pacific than in the Mediterranean.[18]

What, indeed, one might ask, had become of the concept of Germany first? By Casablanca the Allies were perilously close to the most deadly error of the Axis, that of fighting private and separate wars against their preferred and widely separated enemies. Between the late spring of 1940 and the surrender of Italy in September 1943, the bulk of Great Britain's fighting strength on land was engaged chiefly against Italians. Until the summer of 1944 the majority of American divisions actually in combat were waging war against Japan. The Soviets, of course, had been given no choice regarding the area of their basic conflict. The Western Allies alone could shift their weight in order to work with the U.S.S.R. against the strongest Axis partner; the United States alone, as would become ever more apparent throughout 1943, had the will to do so.[19]

From early 1941, when advance elements of Hitler's Afrika Korps began landing in Libya, until the final overture of the cross-Channel invasion in June 1944, the entire strength of the British Empire and Commonwealth intermittently fought between two and eight divisions of the principal Axis power, Germany. On the other hand, during all but the first six months of this same period the Russians contained an average of about one hundred and eighty German divisions in more or less continuous action. Moreover, in the policy advocated by the British, the United States was also compelled to limit its effort against Germany during 1943 and the first five months of 1944 to an average of four or five divisions in actual combat most of the time. As Mr. Churchill himself had explained, this contrasts most impressively with the original intention of the U. S. Army General Staff to wage a continuous and continental warfare against the Reich, a war designed to begin in the spring of 1943 with a commensurate force of some forty-eight British and American divisions.[20]

Under the inspiration of this essentially British colonial type of war, it took an average of twelve divisions of the Western Allies some two and one-half years to push about the same number of Axis divisions back from northwest Egypt to northeast Italy, a distance of some two thousand miles over terrain chiefly distinguished by its poverty of good communications and its frequency of highly defensible positions. At the end of several bitterly contested campaigns the greatest natural barrier in Europe, the Alps, still lay between the Anglo-American armies and the Reich.

Under the leadership of the U. S. Army, following the Anglo-American landings in France on June 6, 1944, an Allied land force averaging fifty to sixty divisions attacked German armies of nominally the same number of divisional units, but in fact a great deal weaker in all respects. Within eleven months the Allied troops had advanced a distance of some five hundred and fifty miles over a terrain notable chiefly for its comparative flatness, for a superb transportation network, and for the heart of Axis war industry.[21] At the termination of this type of campaign, undertaken in conjunction with the Red Army, there existed neither a German Army nor a German war economy.

As the German General Staff had warned Hitler in 1938, in no year between 1941 and 1944 did the German Army have the resources either in manpower or equipment to fight continental warfare on two fronts for any length of time. The long-planned German Army attempt upon Hitler's life in July 1944 merely recognized as much in an overdue, but finally concrete form. Conducting war according to Mr. Churchill's mode any longer than absolutely necessary played right into the hands of German policy; the Reich always could spare small forces to dally with the Allies in the Mediterranean. Mr. Broderick's charge so early as 1901 that Churchill suffered from a 'hereditary desire to run Imperialism on the cheap' may well be recalled.[22] In addition, the terrible dependence of the Western Allies upon Soviet military successes implicit in this form of war in the long run involved the grave danger of as great a political dependence.

From the evidence available today, it seems likely that the most important motive in policy for a Mediterranean denouement in 1942 lay in Mr. Churchill's desire to retain for at least another year the low British casualty rate established at the opening of the Second World War. So late as the period September 1943 through May 1944, land conflict in Europe resulted in only 14,300 deaths to soldiers from the British Empire during these nine ineffectual months.[23] To be sure, this conflict was at last necessarily fought against the German Army, but only within the narrow confines of the Italian peninsula. On the other hand, the decisive eleven-month campaign across the Channel so much dreaded by the Prime Minister and his whole generation of Britons, in fact, cost the British Isles no more than about 30,000 dead. Unlike the Italian campaign, the cross-Channel thrust would not drag on thereafter with further casualties and negligible rewards.

Above all, Mr. Churchill significantly has not pointed out that even with the American version of war policy superimposed upon his own, by the end of the Second World War the United Kingdom would suffer a total of no more than 264,000 military deaths, of which approximately one-quarter were in the Royal Air Force. By contrast, in the First World War the United Kingdom had sustained 744,000 deaths in the shorter period of four and one-quarter years.[24] Furthermore, in the First War almost all of these deaths were incurred in land warfare in France, while at that time the Salonika front afforded the safest, if also the most futile theater of war for the British Army.[25]

This immense drop in war losses was more than simply desirable in Great Britain for, as Wing Commander J. C. Slessor had put it in 1937 in his influential Gold Medal Essay: 'In war we could not afford again to be the mainstay of an alliance at sea, in the air, and in the economic sphere, while at the same time maintaining huge armies in the field. Moreover — and the sooner we face the fact the better — *the country will not stand it again*. It will take a very just cause, cleverly stated, to get the

British people to go to war again at all; for that just cause they will fight with air forces, they will spend their money and energies; but they will not again tolerate casualties in the scale of those suffered by the National Armies in the Great War.' [26]

Hitler was no further off in this basic postulate of his, that Britain did not have the determination to fight an all-out land war against Germany,[27] than he had been in his belief that the Soviets would collapse in 1941 or that the Americans would have to fight a war principally directed against Japan. But in each case these relatively narrow misses proved decisive.

A closely related aspect of the current triumph of the war of attrition advocated by Winston Churchill may be found in the frank dependence of the Casablanca Conference upon air power as the principal weapon of the West for the defeat of Germany. Certainly the increasingly discrete impersonality of life in the more civilized Western states, in a military and, perhaps, moral sense, led directly to the theories of Douhet in the air and of Liddell Hart on land. Facing the practical consequences of personal and infantry combat was now too distasteful to societies which in other realms had already successfully evaded so many of the traditional agonies of the human condition. In the famous air directive issued at the Conference which accurately foreshadowed the war of the future, breaking of the German will-to-fight was openly admitted to be a major objective of the bombing offensive, although it was subordinated somewhat by references to military, industrial, and economic targets.[28]

Perhaps the chief rational, if not necessarily the principal intended, object of this renewed stress upon area bombing would be for the sake of appeasing the popular clamor for action while at the same time diverting attention from the all-too-visible possibility of conducting major land warfare across the Channel. To be sure, the Air Force Chiefs, if not Mr. Churchill, believed that they could win the war by their action alone.[29] At the very least, however, should the Allied public, if not the Axis populations, become fully enough convinced of the value of strategic bombing, an invasion of France even in 1944 might be deflected.

It is only fair to emphasize that the faith in the effectiveness of bombing so frequently manifested by the Allied leaders at this time stemmed in part from mistaken intelligence analyses. Far from recognizing that German munitions production was increasing more than three times between 1942 and 1944, Allied Intelligence circles held as a fixed article of belief that Germany had passed her production maximum in the previous year. It was only too easy to jump to the conclusion that the totalitarian German state must have achieved her full production by the start of the war she had initiated in 1939.[30] Nevertheless, as Max Werner could still write so late as 1943, 'the algebraic sum total of a land defensive and an air offensive will not be offensive, but defensive action.' [31]

By March 1944, when Britain was at last irrevocably committed to the cross-Channel invasion, Sir James Grigg, the British Secretary of State for War estimated that there were as many workers employed on the R.A.F. heavy bomber program alone as upon the whole British Army program for the large-scale land campaign then imminent. At this late date the United Kingdom was still devoting 40 to 50 per cent of her war production to her air forces. Under these circumstances it can be understood why authorities such as General Fuller, Allen Dulles, and Admiral Gallery believe that because of its cost in raw materials and manpower this air policy up to the spring of 1944 did not shorten the war but instead prolonged it.[32] There is certainly no mystery why Mr. Churchill's Britain, of her own accord, would never have been able and ready to cross the Channel and wage major land battles in France.

While, in effect, postulating the defeat of Germany without large-scale land warfare on the part of the Western Allies at Casablanca in January 1943, at the same time, quite inconsistently, Mr. Churchill also accepted President Roosevelt's policy of unconditional surrender. The policy of the President was, of course, a political reflection of the American Army's philosophy of absolute war rather than of the Prime Minister's own more limited form of warfare. As that apostle of Winston Churchill's strategy, Captain Liddell Hart, has pointed out in an uncharacteristic exposition of Clausewitz, a strategy of a limited aim is usually a result of a war policy of a limited aim.[33] Subsequently the Prime Minister was uncomfortable over the consequences of unconditional surrender; decidedly less than the President was Mr. Churchill a pacifist in war-paint, inclined 'to overact the unfamiliar part' [34] he was at last able to play.

Not merely was Mr. Churchill incorrect with regard to his *de facto* reliance before 1944 upon area bombing as the West's principal contribution to defeating Germany, he was also fundamentally mistaken in treating Africa as one of Hitler's major objectives before the defeat of the U.S.S.R. After the survival of Russia in the battle of Moscow, and notwithstanding the simultaneous American entry into the war, it may be concluded that Churchill quite consciously used the continuing fear of a German threat to Africa — a threat which he had done so much to evoke — as the method by which he was able to initiate an Anglo-American offensive against Italy instead of Germany. Unlike those of the Nazi Fuehrer, the intentions of Winston Churchill were never essentially defensive on the periphery and, in particular, not in the Mediterranean.

On the other hand, like Adolph Hitler in the summer of 1940, the British Prime Minister staved off the continuing possibility of a campaign across the Channel from 1941 until 1944, choosing instead to suffer comparable losses elsewhere in campaigns which could never lead to the defeat of the Reich. As the Duke of Marlborough had emphasized to his cautious, overburdened, and weary Dutch ally, in the long run the pursuit of victory without slaughter is likely to eventuate in slaughter without victory.[35] But, Mr. Churchill has written, Marlborough was not attracted 'by small warfare or limited objects.' His purpose was to annihilate the French Army in a great battle.[36]

Like Hitler with respect to Great Britain,[37] Winston Churchill's significant if subconscious fear of an absolute decision in a general war made him prefer no more than a *guerre d'usure* against his German enemy. Each man displayed an excessive anxiety concerning operations within the chosen realm of the other, e.g. on land and sea respectively. But only through the admittedly difficult and unattractive Channel route could either obtain a final decision as opposed to simply another triumph.

The parallels between the attitudes of Hitler and Churchill toward war and strategy go deeper than the problem of a cross-

Channel invasion and beyond the tedious ambivalence of Anglo-German relations in the last century. If, for example, as romantics each man tended to overestimate the newer technological factors in war, more suprisingly they also seemed to have underemphasized such traditional military influnces as the terrain of the supposed soft underbelly of the Axis or the climate and immensity of Russia. Yet neither ignored geography; indeed both generally pursued geographical objectives to the exclusion of any real concentration upon the destruction of the chief forces of their enemies.

Actually their successes resulted from their keen insight in politics rather than from their military proclivities — fortunately for Mr. Churchill's reputation his opportunity for political judgment came late in a victorious war won, as in 1918, by others; a war which, however, had gradually excluded Hitler from any further chance to exercise his remarkable talents for political blackmail.

It is hardly surprising that with personalities so opposed to the authority of others, and imbued with such similar conclusions concerning the fatuity and parochialism of the military in the First World War, the Prime Minister and the Fuehrer should have desired to make their respective General Staffs vehicles for the expression of their own strategic views. To be sure, unlike Hitler, Mr. Churchill would hardly reproach his generals for their 'obsolete concepts of the chivalrous conduct of war.' [38] It is also questionable whether anyone but a parvenu with his back to the wall would express himself so bluntly as did Hitler in 1945 when he told Guderian: 'It is intolerable to me that a group of intellectuals should presume to press their views upon their superiors. But such is the General Staff system and that system I intend to smash.' [39] Unquestionably there could be no easy reconciliation between the improvisation and opportunism inherent in the strategy of these forceful advocates and the emphasis upon long-range and determinist planning embodied in such a revolutionary development as the General Staff system.

The similarities between the great British nationalist and the rulers of Japan are equally illuminating. Like the Japanese government, Winston Churchill saw in the opening of the decisive struggle of the Second World War between Germany and Russia a better opportunity to seize territory from a still weak opponent in the south than to open a second front against his more powerful enemy in the north. Like the Japanese on their Manchurian frontier in 1938–39, Winston Churchill made a pretense at a correct coalition strategy at Dieppe in 1942; in each instance the timing was premature and in the case of Dieppe any real punch was lacking as well. In August 1942, in Mr. Churchill's concept of land warfare, Dieppe was not planned to lead anywhere, as the great air raid on Cologne in May 1942 was planned to accomplish so much — with Allied public opinion.[40] As a wit had said of the elder Pitt's raid on Rochefort in 1757:

> We went, we saw, were seen, like Valiant Men
> Sailed up the Bay and then — sailed back again.[41]

It is interesting to recall why Britain's Prime Minister at the beginning of the First World War, Herbert Asquith, had begun to lose faith in Winston Churchill's judgment even before the Dardanelles. According to Lord Beaverbrook, Asquith's disillusionment had resulted from a series of hit-and-run raids launched by Churchill along the Flemish coast with the intention of encouraging the Belgians and alarming the Germans 'by making a great parade of force without fighting any general action.'[42] In September 1943 a still purer theatrical enterprise — a part of which was appropriately named 'Harlequin' — was staged by British forces in the Channel in an unsuccessful simulation of a second front assault.[43] Wisely, with the high cost of Dieppe in mind, on this occasion the British Army did not disembark in France at all.

Certainly in the art of staging martial drama the nautical impresario of the Dunkirk Circus, as the actions of 1914 were known, had few peers. But it can be seen why that realistic organizer of mass British Armies, Lord Kitchener, had then become so weary of what he called Churchill's 'wild-cat schemes' that he threatened to resign the War Office to his irrepressible rival, although the latter already held the Admiralty.[44] Churchill had long grated on the feelings of so rigid a planner as Kitchener,[45] and the latter may be forgiven for doubting whether what Churchill advocated was magnificent, let alone whether or not it constituted war. After all, few Puritans had approved of theater, even in times of peace.

In the Second World War the policy of Mr. Churchill in many fundamentals also resembled that of the more conservative elements among the military masters of Japan, who according to Herbert Rosinski did not realize that they had 'no *choice;* that their cautious, "independent" and "limited" strategy was radically unsound in a world-wide conflict and that the only slender chance of salvation depended precisely on such a seemingly reckless, "unlimited" global strategy. The fatal effect of their plan for a "limited war" also prevented them from acting with full concentrated energy in any direction.' [46] Unlike the Japanese military conservatives, however, Mr. Churchill was saved from the full force of a war of attrition on the part of Hitler's Reich by the unexpected recovery of the Soviet Union. Of course the Prime Minister had already received his share of bad luck in the First World War.

Lastly, this British statesman so often considered a soldier of fortune [47] was admittedly an opportunist, quite willing to engage in a great conflict without any clear-cut and responsible plans or methods for obtaining a final military decision; essentially the military doctrines of Winston Churchill, like those of the Axis, made sense only in terms of a mediated peace. Although in 1918 Mr. Churchill may have favored such a peace or, as was his aristocratic custom, a magnanimous victory,[48] in the Second World War he would engage in no negotiations of any sort with the Third Reich.

On the other hand, Hitler at least did seek such a peace in 1940 with Great Britain and possibly in 1943 with the U.S.S.R.; this latter an effort eagerly fostered by his Japanese ally. Likewise, Tokyo's whole policy in undertaking war with America was dependent upon the theory that eventually the Americans would weary of fighting and accept a Japanese *fait accompli* in the Far East.[49] The Axis rulers did not direct societies which, after fighting no more than limited wars, still demanded the absolute victories of Puritanism.

The question may be posed as to what extent any British belief that Hitler would win in Russia would enhance their desire to advance in the Mediterranean while this theater was not dominated by Germany. Of course, it is perfectly possible that, like the Japanese, the British Government formulated its policy after June 22, 1941, on the hypothesis that, sooner or later, the Soviet Union would be defeated by Germany. If so, like Tokyo, Mr. Churchill held to the strategic consequences of his probable beliefs regarding the course of the Barbarossa campaign in 1941 with remarkable tenacity thereafter. In 1942 the Japanese would not even help their German ally through India, let alone in the Russian Far-Eastern provinces, although with the wrong timing, as usual, and for their own purposes, they attempted to invade India from Burma in 1944. Similarly in 1942, Mr. Churchill refused to stick to a more or less settled engagement to attack Germany rather than Italy; even at the end of 1943 he was willing to reaccept a major attack upon Germany perhaps only because of *force majeure* applied by his more powerful Allies.[50]

Most surprisingly, in the course of an eloquent tribute to Mr. Churchill, Sir James Grigg has illuminated one of the Prime Minister's most salient characteristics, his seeming inability to grow with the war.[51] Although starting from a lower level of military experience than the Prime Minister, neither of the leaders of the other two chief Allied states reflected this particular weakness to the same degree; as deliberate social innovators, their development in military affairs was both obvious and profound.[52] As statesmen, using nationalism rather than being used by it, Roosevelt and Stalin would in time come to dominate the course of the Second World War perhaps as much through their aggressive military attitudes as through the immense potentials of their respective nations. On the other hand the Axis leaders, men of the extreme Right, far from growing with their war, shrank almost to nothingness as it developed. With the dubious exception of Mussolini, they had little of that extraordinary understanding of the world outside their national states which so enlightened a moderate Conservative such as Otto von Bismarck.

If, unlike the Axis leaders, Mr. Churchill's peculiar qualities of magnanimity, imagination, courage, and humor led him to the utmost magnificence in defeat, as a man of the moderate Right he would also diminish in size as victory approached without reference to his policies. To be sure, his great design of imposing a war strategy based on the stringent British necessities of 1940–41 upon the Grand Alliance of 1942–43 can be explained on the grounds that his countrymen had not sufficiently abandoned the pacifism of the earlier 1930's to be able to conduct an effective coalition war on the land against the German Army. At the same time an important explanation for the desire for a limited war manifest in the dominant circles of the British Government after Pearl Harbor must be sought in its predominantly conservative cast.

In contrast to the First World War, the Second World War was essentially a struggle favored by the political Left among the Allied coalition; it seems improbable that a British Government of the Left would have sought to resist the early creation of a second front to relieve Russia with either the persistence or the passion manifested by Mr. Churchill for three full years. Moreover a British Labour Government, in spite of occasional yearnings toward its traditional pacifism, would hardly have opposed the desire of the United States General Staff for a war conducted according to a long-range plan with the ideological enthusiasm of this great Conservative advocate of strategic opportunism.

Indeed, in discussing an era more to his taste, Mr. Churchill has written of the early eighteenth century that, like his own mentor in strategy, Admiral Fisher, the British Tories had 'obstinately championed the policy that if we were drawn into a war we should go as little to the Continent, send as few troops, fight as near to the coast as possible, and endeavor to secure territory and traffic across the oceans.' As Mr. Churchill's Liberal Imperialist colleagues had done in the First World War, so the eighteenth-century Whigs dwelt upon 'the theory familiar to us as the doctrine of "the decisive theatre" and sought, with the largest army that could be maintained, to bring the war to an end by a thrust at the heart of France, the supreme military antagonist, arguing that thereafter all the rest would be added unto them. It should be noticed that the Tories favored the popular idea that the Navy should be stronger and the Army stinted . . . Marlborough's march to Blenheim was therefore . . . the greatest violation of Tory principles which could be conceived.' [53]

Winston Churchill, then, as a Conservative, looked to the past in preference to the future, although it has been pointed out that it was his knowledge of history which helped distinguish him from the more common run of Conservatives.[54] As occurred with the U. S. Army in the Second World War, Churchill had won the distrust of many Britons of an earlier generation for his notably plangent and impulsive romanticism — a romanticism obliquely recognized in the once popular appellation of poor judgment.[55]

As a romantic Winston Churchill could see the cinema *Lady Hamilton* for the fifth time with deep emotion.[56] As a romantic Winston Churchill was the man who in 1914 wished to abandon the Admiralty for the 'glittering commands' of the Army, then in his opinion in the hands of 'dug-out trash' or of 'mediocrities who have led a sheltered life, mouldering in military routine.' Churchill had gone on to tell Herbert Asquith that a political career was nothing to him in comparison with military glory. He also was the man who told Henry Stimson in the Second World War that any blow to President Roosevelt's basic war policy, such as that which would result from the abandonment of a cross-Channel attack in 1944, could be cured by victories elsewhere.[57] As a romantic he was the man who would consider the alternatives between attacking southern Italy or the island of Sardinia as the difference between a 'glorious campaign and a mere convenience.' [58] As a romantic he always felt it would be 'very foolish to discard the reasons of the heart for those of the head.' [59] Like Admiral Fisher he wanted to enjoy both.

In fact, Mr. Churchill's dislike of the drab impersonality of contemporary warfare went hand in hand with his distaste for democratic or mass warfare as a whole. Certainly the grimly predetermined warfare of the political Left, so explicitly proletarian and Puritan, as in the Bolshevik Reformation, or even the bourgeois New Models inspired by Gustavus Adolphus and

his successors, would distress Mr. Churchill regardless of what
the ablest practitioners of such warfare — Cromwell, Marlborough, and Napoleon — actually achieved in the field.[60]

Unfortunately for Mr. Churchill, as the great connoisseur of
chivalric postures, Edmund Burke, had long ago conceded: 'It
is a dreadful truth, but is a truth that cannot be concealed: in
ability, in dexterity, in the distinctness of their views, the Jaco-
bins are our superiors. They saw the thing right from the beginning. . . . The British and the Austrians, [on the other hand]
refused to take any steps which might strike at the heart of
affairs. . . . They always kept on the circumference; and the
wider and remoter the circle was, the more eagerly they chose it
as their sphere of action in this centrifugal war. The plan they
pursued, in its nature, demanded great length of time.'[61] Or as
Mr. Churchill's *bête noire* in Calvinist warfare, Oliver Cromwell,
put it, 'without a more speedy, vigorous and effectual prosecution
of the War — casting off all lingering proceedings like [those of]
soldiers of fortune . . . we shall make the kingdom weary of
us, and hate the name of a Parliament.'[62] Probably, as his earlier
career had demonstrated, Mr. Churchill did not recognize that
overdisciplining the means of war is a necessary compensation
for the disorder inherent in its ends.

The rather complex nature of Winston Churchill's deliberate
rejection of Clausewitz and his disciples in World War II did not
grow out of the traumatic experiences of the First World War
alone, although of that war Mr. Churchill has readily admitted
that his general principles ran counter to the dominant military
views.[63]

Between 1919 and 1939 the bitter legacy of Passchendaele and
the Somme had enthroned Captain Liddell Hart as the prophet
of a more traditional form of warfare for Britain, a form of warfare which the modern military theorist, Delbrück, has termed
the 'Ermattungsstrategie,' or strategy of exhaustion. Recognized
by Clausewitz only shortly before his death, this strategy is in
many fundamentals diametrically opposed to that strategy of annihilation at any cost more generally associated with this famous
theorist.

Embodying, as Winston Churchill did, a rather Anglican repudiation of any Calvinist tendency toward clear-cut or absolute solutions, the strategy of exhaustion would encounter a most sympathetic pupil in this conserver of so many of the older and finer values of Occidental society. Such a form of warfare was condoned in Clausewitz either when the political ends or conflicts of the war were small or when the military means were inadequate to bring about an absolute victory.[64] The political tensions between the Anglo-Americans and the Third Reich were unquestionably beyond compromise in the Second World War; more germane, after Pearl Harbor the military means of the Western Allies were not inadequate to accomplish a war of annihilation should they really set out to do so.

Nevertheless, from the start of the conflict in 1939, the future Prime Minister had thrown all his influence on behalf of that type of warfare so persuasively presented by Hart, Fuller, and others in post-1918 Britain; a defensive warfare of limited liability on land, of blockade, of economic conflict, and of a small but elite army concentrated in Britain and the Middle East instead of in France. He was naturally supported by the Royal Air Force and Navy; more important, the C.I.G.S. after 1941, Sir Alan Brooke, and many Army generals of Churchill's generation agreed with their Prime Minister wholeheartedly. One long-standing critic of Mr. Churchill, Victor Germains, summed up the demoralizing influence of the period before 1939 when he wrote: 'For more than a decade the British public was trained to put faith in every conceivable means of winning wars save by fighting battles and beating the enemy.'[65]

Mr. Churchill believed at the beginning of his career that wars of the people might be more terrible than those of the kings, but as Captain H. M. Curteis felt compelled to point out after Munich: 'It may not be entirely coincidence that the last two major wars — the Napoleonic and the German — in which Great Britain has fought, have not been decided by "traditional" or "amphibious" strategy . . . The chances that our strategical problems in any future European war would more nearly resemble 1914–1918 than those of the XVIIIth Century appear too

strong to ignore; and traditional strategy applied in circumstances
no longer traditional is likely to prove inadequate and perhaps
disastrous.' [66]

In order to preserve and, if possible, to exalt such a traditional
type of war, Mr. Churchill had only to resort to his conclusion
from 1915 that the least-guarded strategic points should be
selected for attack, rather than the more guarded.[67] Unfortunately, the least-guarded points, in the Second World War at
any rate, were almost invariably the least important points. Combat undertaken for its own sake rather than for a decision violated
another principle of Clausewitz, that of not losing time. In the
Prussian theorist's well-known interpretation, everything that
does not happen is to the credit of the defense. The defender
'reaps where he had not sowed.' [68]

Another closely related example of Mr. Churchill's strategic
principles for land warfare derived from the First World War
merits a more extended analysis, for it lies even closer to the
heart of his strategic thesis in the Second World War. 'In any
hostile combination,' wrote the future Prime Minister, 'once it
is certain that the strongest cannot be directly defeated itself,
but cannot stand without the weakest, it is the weakest that
should be attacked.' Leaving aside the infinitely debatable issue
of whether or not Germany could have been attacked directly
through France in 1943, it would in any event seem clear that
the defeat of the weakest hostile power does not necessarily
bring about either the certain or probable defeat of the strongest.
Furthermore, the dissipation of military resources against such
a secondary enemy as Italy militated against the decisive conflict with the major hostile power. Nevertheless, to Mr. Churchill,
his Eastern policy in the First World War was vindicated in
the end since 'the collapse of Bulgaria . . . was the signal for
the general catastrophe of the Central Powers.'

The belief that the surrender of Bulgaria in 1918 had enforced
that of Germany is indeed remarkable, and certainly a belief at
variance with many of Churchill's civilian colleagues, not to mention the military, in the First War.[69] For example, Lord Grey,
who had played such a decisive role at the Foreign Office, de-

cided that the principal mistakes in British strategy between 1914 and 1918 could be summed up in the phrase 'side-shows.' Grey concluded that Britain had not sufficiently concentrated on the one cardinal point: 'It was the German Army which had to be beaten and this could be done only on the Western Front. For to attempt it anywhere else was to give the Germans the advantage of interior and safe lines of communication as compared with our own.' [70] In fact, on occasion Mr. Churchill himself appears to have recognized full well both the necessity for raising large British armies in 1914 and their absolute essentiality as a means of achieving victory in 1918.[71]

Whatever may be said of the merits of the Dardanelles, without the immense potential of the American Expeditionary Force in the First World War, without that terrible main *and* decisive theater sustained by ravaged armies of Sir Douglas Haig in France, there would have been no 'black day' for Erich Ludendorff and no capitulation of the Second Reich. Hitler's propaganda notwithstanding, in 1918 Germany faced an overwhelming and inescapable land assault in the next year aimed directly at her fatherland, an assault which she had no reasonable assurance of resisting. Unlike Hitler, the rulers of the Kaiserreich were men as relatively reasonable as the peace terms of their enemies.

An additional basis in strategic theory on which Winston Churchill disagreed with Clausewitz and, for that matter, with his own General Frederick Morgan, is in his apparent opinion that an attack on exterior lines is preferable to one on interior lines. In *The World Crisis* Mr. Churchill asserted: 'If the fronts of centres of armies cannot be broken their flanks should be turned. If these flanks rest on seas the manoeuvers to turn them must be amphibious and dependent on sea power.' [72] Clausewitz, however, has written that in strategy, he who finds himself 'in the midst of his enemies is better off than his opponent who tries to envelop him, particularly if the forces on each side are equal, and, of course, still more so if there is an inferiority on the enveloping side. . . . The strategic enveloping movement is therefore never advisable unless we are (physically and morally) so superior, that we shall be strong at the decisive point, and yet can, at the same time, dispense with the detached corps.' No better commentary upon Mr. Churchill's North African operation and its consequences can be found.

One authority has interpreted Clausewitz as being particularly interested in the problems arising from coalition warfare. To him the basic problem confronting the strategist is 'one of discerning the "center of gravity" against which the military push must be directed. . . . In wars of coalition, the "center" lies in the army of the strongest of the allies or in the community of interest between the allies.' [73] Here lies Winston Churchill's best military base in Clausewitz; nonetheless, we notice a choice is posed by Clausewitz even in this instance.

From 1939 the destruction of the community of interest between Germany and Italy was continuously planned by the future Prime Minister, but far from seriously damaging the Reich by the destruction of this uneasy Axis rapport, the Anglo-Americans found themselves entangled in a situation in which the possibility of returning to their original coalition plan of attacking the army of their strongest enemy tended more and more to put a strain upon their own alliance. Yet, as the United States War Department had anticipated, having bet wrongly on the alliance between the Axis powers as the enemy's true center of gravity, the British and Americans would still have to face that inescapable German Army again. Fundamentally, the bet was misplaced because the power of Germany so enormously outweighed that of Italy that it made little difference one way or another what happened to the Latin partner.[74] With Allies of more equal strength such as Britain and France in 1940, the destruction of the alliance might well have yielded decisive fruit.

The efforts of Mr. Churchill and his supporters after the Second World War to refute the impressive evidence of his own earlier attitude in order to maintain that he always favored the Allied assault-in-force of 1944 across the Channel has taken two principal forms. The first, in general adduced for the public, can be termed the timing or *coup de grâce* argument. The second, more frequently employed by and against the professional military critic, has been dressed up into a philosophy of expediency or of opportunism.

The first argument has been well presented by Mr. Churchill's wartime personal chief of staff, General Sir Hastings Ismay. In 1948, accurately anticipating the Prime Minister's own dialectic in a review of Eisenhower's *Crusade in Europe*, he wrote: 'Mr. Churchill and his military advisors always recognized that ultimately the death blow to Germany must be delivered across the Channel; but they were determined that it should not be delivered prematurely. There was no difference as to the principle, but only as to the timing.' [75]

With respect to the thesis that the wartime Prime Minister always favored the principle of a major cross-Channel invasion, wishing to delay it only until it was a reasonably safe bet, the true character of this cross-Channel operation emerges in Ismay's expressions, 'ultimately' and 'death blow.' Not for small reason had his old friend Jacky Fisher terminated his historic controversy with Mr. Churchill in 1915 on the following note: 'You are bent on forcing the Dardanelles and nothing will turn you from it — *nothing*. I know you so well!' [76]

So late as 1943, in no fundamental had Winston Churchill abandoned his belief of 1941 in a cross-Channel assault undertaken solely in the event that German morale showed signs of a serious weakening. As before, his concept of a safe and sound cross-Channel venture constituted a technique to exploit a German collapse rather than a method of evoking it.

For example, in early May 1943, Admiral Leahy heard that the British Chiefs of Staff would not agree to an invasion, such as was envisaged in the American Roundup plan, until Germany had collapsed under pressure from Russia and from the Allied air attack. In the same month General Eisenhower, who had been told by Mr. Churchill himself in January of this year that the British did not plan 'to scuttle Roundup,' understood Sir Alan Brooke to say that he would be glad to reconsider the cross-Channel project to the point of eliminating it entirely. [77]

Returning to the inverted logic which served them so well in 1942, and with the cordial approval of Mr. Churchill, in late 1943 the British Chiefs of Staff officially declared that without continued major operations in the Mediterranean, Overlord would be impossible in 1944. Justifying the profound doubts of both their Russian and American Allies concerning their sincerity on this fundamental issue, the British Chiefs then suggested that Overlord might involve no more than a limited number of divisions against weak opposition (that is, actually, their own Rankin plans) and that no cross-Channel operation on 'a fixed date' should be regarded 'as the pivot of our whole strategy on which all else turns.' [78] In short, regardless of the hegemony implicit in its name, Overlord would merely remain no more than one peer among many.

In this period the Prime Minister left Eisenhower uncertain regarding his own views, but, as the American general has indicated suspiciously, in the spring of 1943 Churchill did want to pour into Italy the maximum number of Allied forces available in the Mediterranean instead of saving at least a part of these forces for the cross-Channel invasion in 1944.[79] Rather less guardedly, Mr. Churchill told Eisenhower that he would prefer to wait until after the war and then write 'impressions, so that, if necessary, he could correct or bury his mistakes.' [80] Perhaps, like d'Alembert, Mr. Churchill believed a man of letters should be very careful of what he writes, fairly careful of what he does, and relatively careless of what he says — in private.

Again in October 1943, in protesting the movement of landing craft from the Mediterranean for Overlord, Mr. Churchill had told President Roosevelt that the latter operation was possible 'only if certain hypothetical conditions are fulfilled which may very likely not be fulfilled.' When the Prime Minister made his customary affirmation to the principle of Overlord, he emphasized to the President that he did not wish his agreement with the United States on this score to be interpreted 'rigidly and without review in the swiftly-changing situations of war.' [81] Mr. Churchill had a hearty dislike of the 'lawyer's' covenants with which his distrustful Allies attempted to bind him irrevocably to Overlord.

Another strong advocate of an all-out cross-Channel attack, Henry Stimson, has likewise expressed grave doubts concerning the real determination of the Prime Minister for such an operation. In preparing the President for the Quadrant Conference in August 1943, Mr. Stimson wrote:

First: We cannot now rationally hope to be able to cross the Channel and come to grips with our German enemy under a British commander. His Prime Minister and his Chief of the Imperial [General] Staff are frankly at variance with such a proposal. . . . Though they have rendered lip service to the operation their hearts are not in it. . . .

Second: The difference between us is a vital difference of faith. . . . The British theory (which cropped out again and again in unguarded sentences of the British leaders . . .) is that Germany can be beaten by a series of attritions in northern Italy, in the eastern Mediterranean, in Greece, in the Balkans, in Rumania and the other satellite countries. . . .

To me in the light of the postwar problems we shall face, that attitude . . . seems terribly dangerous. We are pledged quite as clearly as Great Britain to the opening of a real second front. None of these methods of pinprick warfare can be counted on by us to fool Stalin into the belief that we have kept that pledge.[82]

Over the years the British have had plenty of experience in opportunist raids such as those dispatched by both Pitts to warm the coasts of France and the Netherlands in preference to a serious and effective war in Germany. So fine a British soldier as Sir John Moore had then, perforce, employed that 'disastrous term "a littoral warfare"' [83] and Charles James Fox had aptly compared these operations to 'breaking windows with guineas.' [84] A British general who certainly should know has written of the Second World War that if the Allies had continued such 'non-profit making' raids — as Mr. Churchill advocated against Norway and the Dodecanese in 1943 — the chances for the success of their invasion of France in 1944 would have been 'gravely jeopardized.' [85]

If President Roosevelt was also an opportunist in military affairs, as his reaction to Stimson's pressure had made clear,[86] Winston Churchill alone was prepared by training and temperament to elevate opportunism into a philosophy of war. To the Prime Minister, 'the American mind runs naturally to broad, sweeping logical conclusions on the largest scale,' but the British mind does not work quite this way. 'We do not think,' Mr. Churchill maintains, 'that logic and clear-cut principles are necessarily the sole keys to what ought to be done in swiftly changing and indefinable situations. In war particularly we assign a larger importance to opportunism and improvisation, seeking rather to live and conquer in accordance with the unfolding event than to aspire to dominate it often by fundamental decisions. There is room for much argument about both views. The difference is one of emphasis, but is deep-seated.' [87] Or in the phrase of another slightly chastened romantic:

When precept and the pedantry
of dull mechanic battle do enslave.[88]

One Briton who fortunately did not think in such Arminian terms as Winston Churchill was General Frederick Morgan, in 1943 the chief of the tremendous and long-range planning project for the Overlord invasion of France in 1944. In his disarmingly restrained and modest reminiscences General Morgan has written that in the beginning of 1943 there was much talk in Britain of the need for flexibility in her strategy, and it seemed to him at this time that the British authorities had 'no real plan for the day when they would have to stop being flexible.' Of course, Morgan had been one of that something more than a minority of Englishmen in the First World War, a 'confirmed' Westerner. In World War II he again reflected a marked preference for a Puritan straight line from London to Berlin, namely that across the Channel. Whether or not these opinions represented the true Briton's outlook, as General Morgan avers, or whether the typical inhabitant of the British Isles thought so flexibly as Mr. Churchill has judged, would seem to be a matter of individual interpretation.[89]

The Calvinist crusader who was to carry out General Morgan's predetermined cross-Channel plan in the field, Dwight Eisenhower, has recorded that in 1943 he also had to cope with the theory that 'opportunity should be exploited as it arises, and . . . if things went well in the "soft underbelly" we should not pause merely because we had made up our minds to conduct the cross-Channel operation.' Like Morgan, Eisenhower concluded sharply: 'The doctrine of opportunism, so often applicable in tactics, is a dangerous one to pursue in strategy. Significant changes in the field of strategy have repercussions all the way back to the factory and the training center.' [90]

In reluctantly facing the formal demise of Roundup at the Casablanca Conference General Marshall had likewise considered Mr. Churchill's strategy as one of opportunity or expediency. Yet in so reacting to the Prime Minister's concept of war Marshall had gone further and had questioned the sincerity of the term so freely accepted by Winston Churchill himself. He had asked pointedly whether the British Chiefs of Staff considered that an attack now against Sicily was a means to an end or an end in itself.[91]

In short, by this date General Marshall was coming to recognize the purpose behind the British strategy, a strategy so opportunely called opportunist. Actually, as the U. S. Army Chief may have now perceived, Mr. Churchill almost certainly knew perfectly well where he was going and had known it years in advance — his old Influx and Whipcord war plans of 1941–42 for the invasion of Sicily are cases in point.[92] At Casablanca Mr. Churchill and his military chiefs must have been aware that they could get the U. S. Army to accept a further Mediterranean push chiefly because the American Army would hope that this also would be the last such effort. In other words, Marshall had accepted Sicily as the next Allied objective, partly because the island's geographic position made it a fine place to close down all subsequent operations in the Mediterranean [93] in order to give priority to a revivified cross-Channel assault.

When the logical denouement of the Sicilian campaign necessarily unfolded in the southern or wrong end of the Italian peninsula, General Marshall — like Kitchener with the Dardanelles — did not wish 'a vacuum' created in Italy into which the resources of the cross-Channel operation would be again dissipated [94] in 1943 as they had been the previous year.

Had the British suggested at Casablanca that in their conception the seizure of Sicily was designed to lead on to Italy the American Army would instead have preferred Sardinia as the logical Mediterranean objective to follow the conquest of Tunisia. From Sardinia, and its natural corollary, Corsica, it would have been infinitely simpler to have cut off the bulk of Italy by landings in Liguria or Tuscany without fighting all the way up the crenelated boot of the peninsula.[95] Alternatively, and of far greater potential importance, as actually took place in 1944, the still unfortified and under-garrisoned coast of southern France might have been assaulted in 1943 from this Sardinian-Corsican *point d'appui.*

But although such British amphibious planners as Morgan and Mountbatten had preferred Sardinia to Sicily as the militarily sensible way of approaching even Italy, they had been over-ruled by the Prime Minister and his Chiefs of Staff on the grounds that the political effect of Sicily's surrender was a more important consideration.[96] In fact, Mountbatten, who finally seemed to string along with the American desire for Sicily, appeared embarrassed when the Americans learned of his switch from a Sardinian approach to the nominal dead-end in Sicily and cautioned them to say nothing to his superiors concerning his own advocacy of the Sardinian route.[97] The trouble with Sardinia may have been that too obviously it did lead somewhere, and Mr. Churchill's careful and patient policy of winning American acquiescence in what is too often represented as a strategy of opportunism or expediency could not tolerate such an honest and logical anticipation of the future. One may decide that although the Prime Minister's strategy might be termed opportunist in the larger sense that he followed the easier rather than the harder path in waging war, it can scarcely be considered completely improvised, as it was disclosed to his Allies, step by step.[98]

The parallel between the pattern of the unduly cautious or self-defeating approach set at Casablanca and that of Torch is striking, and it was a pattern which would continue onto the Italian mainland in a manner which General Fuller eventually described as 'daft.'[99] In each case, in order to evade a direct American refusal to countenance the prospect of an indefinite advance in the Mediterranean in the direction of southeastern Europe, the British sacrificed their initially logical plans for the execution of their strategy, e.g. the landings at Bône and Philippeville or in Sardinia. For the policy of concealment of Mr. Churchill and the obstinacy of the U. S. Army with respect to this so-called eccentric [100] approach many Allied soldiers would die unnecessarily and much time and matériel would be expended in the mountains of southern and central Italy. While two of Mr. Churchill's true objectives in his war policy, namely a political as well as a military victory and one at a low cost in casualties to Great Britain, were in no sense morally reprehensible objectives from the point of view of the United Kingdom alone, the necessity of concealing these objectives from his more powerful Allies would have most unhappy consequences for Britain in the long run as in the short.

It may well be felt that the role and responsibility of Winston Churchill for British war policy and strategy after he became Prime Minister in 1940 has been overstressed. There are, however, very substantial grounds for emphasizing it. A variety of Americans have taken note of the unquestioned dominance of Mr. Churchill in the Second World War over a tremendous variety of British military issues, great and small.

General Arnold, for one, observed at the first general Allied Conference following Pearl Harbor, the Arcadia Conference, that the British Chiefs of Staff seemed to be reluctant to commit themselves to any new war plans until they could check them over with their Prime Minister.[101] General Eisenhower, who was in a better position to know, expressed himself more forcefully. He considered the Prime Minister a 'virtual member' of the British Chiefs of Staff. He could not remember any major discussion with the British Chiefs in which Churchill did not participate. According to Eisenhower, Mr. Churchill even joined his Chiefs of Staff in tactical instructions.[102] Indeed, in 1915 the resignations of Fisher and Churchill had been precipitated, at least nominally, over this very issue.[103] Harry Hopkins might well write the President in his first report on Winston Churchill: 'Your "former Naval person" is not only the Prime Minister, he is the directing force behind the strategy and the conduct of the war in all of its essentials.'[104]

Churchill himself has made no bones about the Erastian nature of his conception of the duties of the British Chiefs of Staff. As he wrote of the First World War: 'A series of absurd conventions became established in the public mind. First and most monstrous was that generals and admirals were more competent to deal with the broad issues of war than abler men in other spheres of life.' [105] In 1943 Mr. Churchill reiterated this theme: 'Modern war is total, and it is necessary for its conduct that the technical and professional authorities should be sustained and if necessary directed by the Heads of Government, who have the knowledge which enables them to comprehend not only the military but the political and economic forces at work, and who have the power to focus them all upon the goal.' [106] Of the Second World War Winston Churchill could wind up contentedly that, for his Britain, at least, there had been 'no division, as in the previous war, between politicians and soldiers, between the "Frocks" and the "Brass Hats" — odious terms which darkened counsel.' [107]

It is, of course, difficult to say how much such unwonted felicity had resulted from Mr. Churchill's having learned from previous unhappy experience not to overrule his Chiefs on strictly military issues when they stood firm and united against him [108] and how much this agreement was evoked by his selection of military chiefs in fundamental accord with himself. In any event it is clear that Winston Churchill had not the slightest intention of finding himself, like his political colleague and rival in the First World War, David Lloyd George, in the position of being unable to impose his will on the military. Like Churchill, and most of their generation, including Adolf Hitler, Lloyd George had come to believe that British statesmen had shown undue caution in exerting their authority over their subordinates in uniform. Another dedicated man of crisis, the witty and cynical Georges Clemenceau, had already immortalized this overwhelming lesson of 1914–18 in the aphorism that war was too important a matter to leave to the generals.[109]

Far more than Lloyd George with his hard-won conception of the proper relationship between the Prime Minister and his Chiefs of Staff, Winston Churchill was prepared in World War II to resume his continuous conflict with the expert — in this war with the American expert.[110] Such more or less independent Britons as Beaverbrook, Morgan, and occasionally, Mountbatten, the Prime Minister could ignore without especial difficulty. Furthermore, by 1942, Mr. Churchill could cut a very fine figure as a military expert himself. His fervent supporter, Air Marshal Sir Arthur Harris, had never known Churchill without an answer for any question of pure strategy.[111]

As his biographers have often recognized, Winston Churchill had been trained primarily for war, at the Admiralty, at the Ministry of Munitions, and at the War Office, and almost all his writings involved military issues.[112] The Prime Minister was an acknowledged expert on espionage and had played a significant role in founding the Royal Air Force. Moreover, in some measure he was responsible for the conversion of the Royal Navy from coal to oil before the First World War. In addition to his pioneer work with tanks in the First World War and with landing craft in the Second, Mr. Churchill had worked closely with the Air Defence Research Committee in connection with the development of radar for the R.A.F. and for the Admiralty.[113]

In his exaltation of the civilian head of government over the military chiefs, Mr. Churchill was in close accord with orthodox military doctrine. Clausewitz — normally so repugnant to the Prime Minister as the formulator of the revolutionary military practices of Napoleon — has written: 'The subordination of the political point of view to the military would be contrary to common sense, for policy has declared the war; it is the intelligent faculty, War only the instrument, and not the reverse. The subordination of the military point of view to the political is, therefore, the only thing which is possible.' [114]

It may be contended that it was precisely because in this instance the British Prime Minister was in such essential accord with the classic theory that he proved ultimately correct in his continuing dispute with the United States War Department in 1944–45. In the desperate argument over the Anvil plan for a French and American landing in southern France in August 1944, a landing proposed in part to drain Allied divisions out of Mr. Churchill's beloved Mediterranean, the now probably dominant anxiety of the Prime Minister over the post-war position of the West in Eastern Europe may well have deserved priority over the logistic needs of the American Army for the port of Marseille.[115] Certainly, having been sucked into Italy in 1943 by her surrender, the U. S. Army was more determined than ever not to allow the eager Hungarians to have a similar effect, and in 1944 President Roosevelt backed up his Army leaders.[116]

Mr. Churchill was on still stronger ground in the spring of 1945 when he urged the Anglo-American seizure of Berlin and his Chiefs urged that of Prague. Fortunately for the Soviet Union, even at this point amid the collapsing ruins of the Third Reich, and notwithstanding lip service to the contrary theory, General Eisenhower continued to operate on the assumption that military plans should be devised with 'the single aim of speeding victory.' Ignoring the point of any war, General Marshall backed up Eisenhower's crusade in Europe. He cabled: 'I would be loath to hazard American lives for purely political purposes.' [117] It may be that to Puritans, facing the evil of war is only to be condoned by fighting for purely moral purposes, although the U. S. Army's Prussian model had reflected a similar military egocentricity after the intoxicating victories of the elder Moltke.[118] But however much he might wish to limit Great Britain's casualties, Winston Churchill was an old hand at accepting the struggle for political power endemic in war.

To a very considerable extent this gross U. S. Army violation of the doctrines of Clausewitz must have resulted from its now confirmed and fundamental distrust of the sincerity of the military policies of Mr. Churchill, a distrust which at the Trident and Quadrant conferences Stimson and Marshall had finally succeeded in conveying to President Roosevelt. After the middle of 1943 the President could no longer be induced to believe that his British colleague was driving deeper and deeper into the Mediterranean for the sake of a cross-Channel invasion. When this American disillusionment was accentuated by the apparent alienation of the Russians at this time, it is not surprising that in Mr. Churchill's careful language: 'There was emerging a strong current of opinion in American governmental circles, which seemed to wish to win Russian confidence even at the expense of co-ordinating the Anglo-American war effort.' [119]

The ultimate effect of this distrust appeared at the Teheran Conference in November-December 1943, when after the United States joined up with the Russians to push through the cross-

Channel invasion, this policy of Russo-American military collaboration tended to continue in the even more delicate realm of politics, a realm in which Mr. Churchill was a true master, a master solidly based on Clausewitz. But by 1944–45 the British Prime Minister had misled the Americans too often on the military end to expect to be respected and heeded on the political. Conversely, General Marshall, who had made no public speeches concerning his many 'difficult scenes' with President Roosevelt in 1942, had so won the latter's confidence by 1944–45 that there was no debate 'whatsoever' between them in this era in which political considerations should have dominated the scene.[120]

Stalin, who followed Clausewitz in the military sphere properly enough until the realization of a true second front in the West had sealed the fate of Germany, abruptly suspended his own drive upon Berlin in August 1944, and concentrated upon conquering the Balkans himself, notwithstanding the fact that he had discouraged Mr. Churchill from doing the same thing the year before.[121] Although subsequent to the war he formally repudiated some of the military theses of the great military theorist, Stalin understood and followed Clausewitz in both his political and military senses; the Soviet ruler first and necessarily had concentrated everything upon defeating the strongest force of the chief Axis power, the German Army, and only afterward started to cash in his political chips.[122] Mr. Churchill made the serious mistake of attempting to reverse this logical order of action under the cloak of a policy of supposed opportunism.

It is a striking fact that the two states which emerged from the Second World War with the most power, the United States and the U.S.S.R., were also the two states with the most effective coalition strategies in this war. Of course, this was no accident. Only these two states had the resources to support the self-confidence and courage which led to a long-range strategy of concentration. After 1943, when the full effects of the growing mobilization of their enormous resources began to be felt,[123] both of these states could look primarily outward to the problem of defeating the enemy rather than essentially inward to the questions of domestic opinion, tradition, or morale.

By the autumn of 1943 the U.S.S.R. had largely overcome her

grave problem of internal dissidence and was prepared to commit herself to aid the United States against Japan following the defeat of Germany; [124] by the autumn of 1943 the United States had the strength to impose long-planned and truly offensive strategies of concentration directly against the seats of Axis power in both the Central Pacific and in the Western European theaters on top of those opportunist and defensive strategies, based on conditions of comparative impotence, which for political reasons had been accepted in 1942 in the South Pacific and in the Mediterranean.

As a result, regardless of their motives, both states would eventually face and successfully encompass their fundamental problems in two-front strategies, first with Germany and then with Japan. In subordinating a war not yet won to personal inclinations or to considerations of domestic policy, Great Britain under Winston Churchill's otherwise inspiring leadership never could achieve this. That in 1944–45 the Americans either forgot that war is no more than an instrument of foreign policy, or followed a foreign policy based upon false assumptions, illustrates again what Mr. Churchill himself once wrote with such prophetic irony: 'those who can win a war well can rarely make a good peace and those who could make a good peace would never have won the war.' [125]

Notes

PREFACE

1. Winston Churchill, *The Story of My Early Life, A Roving Commission* (New York, 1945), 65.
2. Field Marshal Sir William Robertson, *Soldiers and Statesmen* (London, 1926), vol. I, 92.
3. *Burke — Select Works*, edited by E. J. Payne (Oxford, 1892), vol. II, 89.
4. *Arms and the Man*.
5. Gertrude Himmelfarb, *Lord Acton — A Study in Conscience and Politics* (Chicago, 1952), 198.
6. Admiral of the Fleet Lord Fisher, *Memories* (London, 1919), vol. I, 57.
7. George Kennan, *American Diplomacy 1900–1950* (Chicago, 1951).
8. See below, chap. x, n. 48.
9. Isaac Deutscher, *The Prophet Armed — Trotsky: 1891–1929* (New York, 1954), 482; cf. D. F. White, *The Growth of the Red Army* (Princeton, 1944), chap. VI, or his 'Soviet Philosophy of War,' *Political Science Quarterly*, vol. LI, no. 3 (New York, September 1936), 537ff.

Chapter 1. FELIX AND IL DUCE UNDONE

1. Adolf Hitler, *Mein Kampf* (New York, 1939), 183, 950.
2. Herman Rauschning, *The Voice of Destruction* (New York, 1940), 623.
3. Capt. A. T. Mahan, *The Influence of Sea Power upon the French Revolution and Europe 1793–1812* (Boston, 1898), vol. I, 327.
4. Winston Churchill, *Step by Step 1936–1939* (London, 1949), 333.
5. Jacob Burckhardt, *Force and Freedom, Reflections on History*, edited by James Nichols (New York, 1943), 43.
6. *Mein Kampf*, 892–3.
7. *Nazi Conspiracy and Aggression*, Office of U. S. Chief of Counsel for Prosecution of Axis Criminality (Washington, 1946), vol. II, 754 (cited hereafter as N.C.A.); MS. Gen. Franz Halder's *War Diary*, Office of the Chief of Counsel for Prosecution of War Crimes (Nuremberg, 1946), vol. IV, 35 (May 24–25, 1940); F. H. Hinsley, *Hitler's Strategy* (Cambridge, 1951), 6.
8. Adolf Hitler, *My New Order, Speeches 1922–1941*, edited by Raoul de Roussy de Sales (New York, 1941), 901–24.
9. *Nazi-Soviet Relations, 1939–1941, Documents from the Archives of the German Foreign Office* (cited hereafter as N.-S. R.), edited by R. J. Sontag and J. S. Beddie, Dept. of State (Washington, 1948), 147.

10. N.-S. R., 154.
11. Halder's *Diary*, vol. IV, 193 (September 14, 1940).
12. J. Davenport and C. Murphy, *The Lives of Winston Churchill, A Close Up* (New York, 1945), 40.
13. Isaac Deutscher, *Stalin, A Political Biography* (New York, 1949), 457; Gerhard Weinberg, *Germany and the Soviet Union 1939–1941* (Leiden, 1954), 101ff.
14. *Trial of the Major War Criminals before the International Military Tribunal* (Nuremberg, 1947–48), vol. XXVI, 330 (translation, cited hereafter as *War Trials*); cf. Peter de Mendelssohn, *Design for Aggression, The Inside Story of Hitler's War Plans* (New York, 1946), 221, and *The United States Strategic Bombing Survey, The Effects of Strategic Bombing on the German War Economy*, Over-all Economic Effects Division (Washington, 1945), 15ff. (cited hereafter as *Strategic Bombing Survey*).
15. General Franz Halder, *Hitler als Feldherr* (Munich, 1949), 36; Gen. Guenther Blumentritt, *Von Rundstedt, The Soldier and The Man* (London, 1952), 37.
16. *Documents on International Affairs 1939–1946*, vol. I, March–September, 1939, edited by the Royal Institute of International Affairs, under Arnold J. Toynbee (New York, 1951), 188–9; Gaetano Salvemini, 'Pietro Badoglio's Role in the Second World War,' *The Journal of Modern History*, vol. XXI, no. 4 (Chicago, December 1949), 326.
17. *Documents on German Foreign Policy 1918–1945, From the Archives of the German Foreign Ministry*, U. S. Dept. of State (Washington, 1949–55), series D, vol. VIII; *The War Years, September 4, 1939–March 18, 1940*, 907.
18. Marshal Pietro Badoglio, *Italy in the Second World War, Memoirs and Documents* (New York, 1948), 14–15.
19. Halder's *Diary*, vol. IV, 27 (May 22, 1940); a twice translated version of a letter whose original is impossible to obtain.
20. Paul Schmidt, *Hitler's Interpreter* (New York, 1951), 146; Gen. George C. Marshall, *The War Reports, 1939–1945* (New York, 1947), 144; and N.C.A., vol. X, 931.
21. Halder's *Diary*, vol. I, 28–33 (August 26–28, 1939); *Documents on German Foreign Policy 1918–1945*, series D, vol. VIII, 263.
22. *Documents on International Affairs*, vol. I, 176–7. Felix Gilbert, 'Ciano and His Ambassadors,' *The Diplomats 1919–1939*, edited jointly with Gordon Craig (Princeton, 1953), 532ff.
23. *Documents on German Foreign Policy 1918–1945*, series D, vol. VIII, 1–24, 605–13, 902–7; cf. Count Galeazzo Ciano, *The Ciano Diaries 1939–1943*, edited by Hugh Gibson (New York, 1946), 120–31; Badoglio, op. cit. 14–15; Major General I. S. O. Playfair with Commander Stitt, Brigadier Molony, Air Vice-Marshal Toomer, *The Mediterranean and Middle East*, vol. I, *The Early Successes against Italy (to May 1941)* (London, 1954), 39–89; Bernadotte Schmitt, 'Italian Diplomacy 1939–1941,' *The Journal of Modern History* (Chicago, June 1955), 160ff.
24. *War Trials*, vol. XXVI, 339. Translation.
25. *The Memoirs of Ernst von Weizsäcker* (London, 1951), 235; Ciano's *Diaries*, 135.

26. Halder's *Diary,* vol. v, 29 (November 18, 1940); cf. Alan Bullock, *Hitler, A Study in Tyranny* (London, 1952), 541.
27. Count Galeazzo Ciano, *Diplomatic Papers,* edited by Malcolm Muggeridge (London, 1948), 372–6.
28. Sir Samuel Hoare, *Complacent Dictator* (New York, 1947), 19–31; Ciano's *Diplomatic Papers,* 376n.1; Halder's *Diary,* vol. iv, 116 (July 13, 1940); Gen. Alfred Jodl, *War Diary,* July 13, 1940, German MS., Princeton University Library.
29. *Documents on International Affairs,* vol. i, 443–6; cf. Marshall, op. cit. 145.
30. *My New Order,* 837.
31. Halder's *Diary,* vol. iv, 117 (July 13, 1940).
32. N.C.A., vol. i, 795; cf. John Wheeler-Bennett, *The Nemesis of Power: The German Army in Politics, 1918–1945* (New York, 1954), 509n.4; and Jodl, ms. cit. June 30, 1940.
33. Halder's *Diary,* vol. iv, 100–128 (July 2–22, 1940); N.C.A., vol. x, 942–4; cf. Weinberg, op. cit. 110ff.
34. DeWitt C. Poole, 'Light on Nazi Foreign Policy,' *Foreign Affairs,* October 1946, vol. xxv, no. 1, 145–7; cf. N.C.A., vol. v, C–170, 741, and Supplement B, 1635–7.
35. Capt. B. H. Liddell Hart, *Reputations* (London, 1928), 58.
36. Halder's *Diary,* vol. iv, 144–5 (July 13, 1940), Jodl, ms. cit. July 31, 1948; N.C.A., vol. x, 944–56.
37. N.C.A., vol. i, 796; Field Marshal Gustav Mannerheim, *The Memoirs of Marshal Mannerheim* (New York, 1954), 398ff.
38. *Mein Kampf,* 180–83.
39. *The Memoirs of Field Marshal Kesselring* (London, 1953), 109; 'Goering's Unpublished Interview,' edited by Brig. Gen. W. W. Quinn, *U. S. News and World Report* (Washington, May 14, 1954), 56ff.
40. Gen. Heinz Guderian, *Panzer Leader* (London, 1952), 136–7; Hinsley, op. cit. 96; cf. Milton Shulman, *Defeat in the West* (New York, 1948), 49–56, and Anthony Martienssen, *Hitler and His Admirals* (New York, 1949), 76–87.
41. Halder's *Diary,* vol. iv, 135–41 (July 29–30, 1940).
42. Poole, loc. cit. 131.
43. Rear Adm. Robert de Belot, *La Guerre aéronavale en Méditerranée 1939–1945* (Geneva, 1947), 22. Translation.
44. General Frederick Fuller, *The Second World War, 1939–1945, A Strategical and Tactical History* (New York, 1949), 90.
45. U. S. Dept. of State *Bulletin* (Washington, March 17, 1946), vol. iv, no. 350, 413–14; Halder's *Diary,* vol. iv, 17–175 (May 18–Aug. 27, 1940); Ciano's *Diplomatic Papers,* 388.
46. Elizabeth Wiskemann, *The Rome-Berlin Axis, A History of the Relations between Hitler and Mussolini* (New York, 1949), 224–6; Playfair, op. cit. 225; Ciano's *Diary,* 285.
47. *Fuehrer Conferences on Matters Dealing with the German Navy,* Office of Naval Intelligence, Navy Dept. (Washington, 1947), 1940, vol. ii, 20–24 (Cited hereafter as *Fuehrer Conferences: German Navy*).
48. Sir Julian Corbett, *England in the Mediterranean — A Study of the Rise and Influence of British Power in the Mediterranean 1603–1713*

(London, 1917), vol. I, vi. In the First World War Adm. Tirpitz had likewise been inclined to overestimate the importance of the Mediterranean for the Reich. See Brig. Gen. C. F. Aspinwall-Oglander, *History of the Great War, Military Operations, Gallipoli* (London, 1929), 303.

49. U. S. Dept. of State *Bulletin*, March 17, 1946, vol. IV, no. 350, 415–16; Ciano's *Diplomatic Papers*, 389–97.
50. *War Trials*, vol. XXVIII, 577; Herbert Feis, *The Spanish Story, Franco and the Nations at War* (New York, 1948), chap. XIII.
51. Serrano Suñer, *Entre les Pyrénées et Gibraltar, notes et réflexions sur la politique espagnole depuis 1936* (Geneva, 1948), 161–2. Translation. Cf. Ciano's *Diplomatic Papers*, 389.
52. Weizsäcker, op. cit. 239.
53. *Fuehrer Conferences: German Navy*, 1940, vol. II, 25; Halder's *Diary*, vol. IV, 233 (October 15, 1940).
54. Suñer, op. cit. 169; cf. U. S. Dept. of State *Bulletin*, March 17, 1946, vol. IV, no. 350, 414.
55. Ciano's *Diplomatic Papers*, 392–6.
56. Suñer, op. cit. 181.
57. Winston Churchill, *The Second World War*, vol. II, *Their Finest Hour* (Boston, 1949), 26; Wiskemann, op. cit. 229–30.
58. Hermann Rauschning, *The Revolution of Nihilism, Warning to the West* (New York, 1939), 219; Gordon Craig, *The Politics of the Prussian Army 1640–1945* (Oxford, 1955), 285.
59. Halder's *Diary*, vol. IV, 225 (October 8, 1940). The German Army was already giving North Africa first priority in its war production program. Hinsley, op. cit. 99.
60. Shulman, op. cit. 56; Martienssen, op. cit. 100; Vice Adm. Kurt Assmann, 'The Battle for Moscow, Turning Point of the War,' *Foreign Affairs*, vol. XXVIII, no. 2 (January 1950), 311.
61. Halder's *Diary*, vol. IV, 246 (October 24, 1940); Capt. B. H. Liddell Hart, *The German Generals Talk* (New York, 1948), 155.
62. Adm. Franco Maugeri, *From the Ashes of Disgrace* (New York, 1948), 14–21; cf. Playfair, op. cit. 146, and Aldo Fraccaroli, 'The Italian Navy in the Late War,' *Journal Royal United Service Institution*, vol. XCIII, no. 571 (London, August 1948), 436ff.
63. N.C.A., vol. VII, 925.
64. Playfair, op. cit. 255.
65. *Documents on German Foreign Policy, 1918–1945*, series D, vol. II, *Germany and Czechoslovakia, 1937–1938* (Washington, 1949), 999; and Ciano's *Diaries*, 183ff.
66. Ciano's *Diaries*, 300; cf. Howard Smyth, 'The Command of the Italian Armed Forces in World War II,' *Military Affairs*, vol. XV, no. 1 (Spring 1951), 41–3.
67. Weizsäcker, op. cit. 130–84; Ciano's *Diaries*, 42–54.
68. John Lukacs, *The Great Powers and Eastern Europe* (Philadelphia, 1953), 344; N.C.A., vol. X, 930–31; Weizsäcker, op. cit. 244; Wiskemann, op. cit. 229–37; Playfair, op. cit. 225–6.
69. Schmidt, op. cit. 200.
70. *Les Lettres secrètes éxchangées par Hitler et Mussolini* (Paris, 1946), 82ff., translation (cited hereafter as *Les Lettres secrètes*); cf. A. Rossi,

The Russo-German Alliance, August 1939–June 1941 (Boston, 1951), 155; *The German Campaigns in the Balkans (Spring 1941)*, Dept. of the Army (Washington, November 1953), 5.

71. Suñer, op. cit. 206; cf. *Fuehrer Conferences: German Navy*, 1940, vol. II, 32–50; N.C.A., vol. VII, 926, and Lukacs, op. cit. 346–7, 768.

72. Halder's *Diary*, vol. V, 5–29 (November 4–18, 1940).

73. Ibid.

74. Ulrich von Hassell, *The Von Hassell Diaries, 1938–1944, The Story of the Forces against Hitler inside Germany* (New York, 1947), 159; cf. Halder's *Diary*, vol. IV, 233 (October 15, 1940).

75. Ciano's *Diplomatic Papers*, 295, and his *Die Stellung Italiens zum internationales Konflikt* (Basel, 1939), 84–94; Schmitt, loc. cit. 164ff.

76. *Documents on German Foreign Policy 1918–1945*, series D, vol. III, *Germany and the Spanish Civil War 1936–1939* (Washington, 1950), 932ff.; Halder's *Diary*, vol. V, 4 (November 2, 1940).

77. Ciano's *Diplomatic Papers*, 401–4.

78. Schmidt, op. cit. 197; cf. Ciano's *Diaries*, 297, and Bullock, op. cit. chap. X.

79. *Fuehrer Conferences: German Navy*, 1940, vol. II, 33; N.C.A., vol. X, 898–900; cf. Mendelssohn, op. cit. 162, and Feis, op. cit. chaps. XVII–XVIII.

80. Suñer, op. cit. 207; cf. Belot, op. cit. 23ff.

81. *Les Lettres secrètes*, 86.

82. Halder's *Diary*, vol. V, 34 (November 24, 1940).

83. Shulman, op. cit. 56–8.

84. *Fuehrer Conferences: German Navy*, 1940, vol. II, 41.

85. Weinberg, op. cit. 137–8.

86. Deutscher, op. cit. 450; and Gustav Hilger and Alfred Meyer, *The Incompatible Allies, A Memoir History of German-Soviet Relations, 1918–1941* (New York, 1953), 317ff.

87. N.-S.R., 218–21.

88. N.-S.R., 330–31.

89. N.C.A., *Opinion and Judgment*, 43.

90. *Fuehrer Conferences: German Navy*, 1940, vol. II, 65; Poole, loc. cit. 145; Halder's *Diary*, vol. V, 98 (January 28, 1941); Martienssen, op. cit. 91.

91. See below, chapter III; Mannerheim, op. cit. 407; Telford Taylor, *Sword and Swastika, Generals and Nazis in the Third Reich* (New York, 1952), 227–309; William Langer and S. F. Gleason, *The Challenge to Isolation, 1937–1940* (New York, 1952), 378–9.

92. *Fuehrer Conferences: German Navy*, 1941, vol. I, 4.

93. Robert E. Sherwood, *Roosevelt and Hopkins, An Intimate History* (New York, 1948), 782.

94. Suñer, op. cit. 220.

95. *Les Lettres secrètes*, 99–100.

96. Ian Colvin, *Master Spy, The Incredible Story of Admiral Wilhelm Canaris, Who While Hitler's Chief of Intelligence Was a Secret Ally of the British* (New York, 1951), 152–5; Walter Goerlitz, *History of the German General Staff, 1657–1945* (New York, 1953), 384.

97. Suñer, op. cit. 224–5; cf. U. S. Dept. of State *Bulletin*, March 17, 1946, vol. IV, no. 350, 422, and Ciano's *Diplomatic Papers*, 421–30.

98. Belot, op. cit. 24–5; cf. Halder's *Diary*, vol. v, 60–2 (December 8–9, 1940).
99. *Fuehrer Conferences: German Navy*, 1941, vol. i, 5–7; Halder's *Diary*, vol. v, 61–2 (December 9, 1940); *The German Campaign in the Balkans*, 6.
100. Burckhardt, op. cit. 41.
101. Halder's *Diary*, vol. v, 83 (December 24, 1940).
102. Ciano's *Diaries*, 325–36; cf. Smyth, loc. cit. 43.
103. Halder's *Diary*, vol. v, 85 (January 16, 1941).
104. *Fuehrer Conferences: German Navy*, 1941, vol. i, 1–4.
105. *My New Order*, 914.
106. Wing Commander Asher Lee, *The German Air Force* (New York, 1946), 87; N.C.A., vol. x, 903–4; Mendelssohn, op. cit. 165; Playfair, op. cit. 315.
107. W. F. Craven and J. L. Cate, *The Army Air Forces in World War II*, vol. i, *Plans and Early Operations, January 1939 to August 1942* (Chicago, 1948), 97.
108. Mendelssohn, op. cit. 170.
109. Halder's *Diary*, vol. v, 98 (January 28, 1941).
110. *Fuehrer Conferences: German Navy*, 1941, vol. i, 3; Mendelssohn, op. cit. 212–48.
111. *War Trials*, vol. xxvi, 396. Translation.
112. Martienssen, op. cit. 128; cf. Mendelssohn, op. cit. 173; *The German Campaign in the Balkans*, 120.
113. Ciano's *Diplomatic Papers*, 421–30; U. S. Dept. of State *Bulletin*, March 17, 1946, vol. iv, no. 350, 422–6.
114. Geoffrey Bruun, *Europe and the French Imperium, 1799–1814, The Rise of Modern Europe*, edited by William Langer (New York, 1938), 184.
115. Hinsley, op. cit. 226–7; cf. Weizsäcker, op. cit. 239–40.
116. N.-S.R., 351–3.

Chapter 2. 'MARLBROUCK S'EN VA T'EN GUERRE'

1. Jonathan Swift, *The Conduct of the Allies and of the Late Ministry in the Beginning and Carrying on the Present War* (Edinburgh, 1711), 19.
2. Frank Owen, *Tempestuous Journey, Lloyd George, His Life and Times* (London, 1954), 166.
3. *The Parliamentary Register, House of Commons Debates* (London, 1801), vol. xiv, 577.
4. *Fear God and Dread Nought, The Correspondence of Admiral of the Fleet Lord Fisher of Kilverstone*, edited by Arthur Marder, vol. ii, *Years of Power 1904–1914* (London, 1956), 437; cf. ibid. 143, 218.
5. Lord Beaverbrook, *Men and Power 1917–1918* (London, 1956), 361.
6. Winston Churchill, *The Second World War*, vol. i, *The Gathering Storm* (Boston, 1948), 251–4. This was also a passion of another Edwardian convert to a link with America, at a time when he was becoming close to Churchill. See Adm. Fisher, *Correspondence*, vol. ii, 298ff., 361–7.
7. *The Gathering Storm*, 440–41.

8. *The Gathering Storm*, 415–16; cf. Dennis Richards, *Royal Air Force 1939–1945*, vol. i, *The Fight at Odds* (London, 1953), 33ff.; *The Secret Diary of Harold L. Ickes*, vol. iii, *The Lowering Clouds 1939–1941* (New York, 1954), 176; *House of Commons Debates*, fifth series, vol. 345, 682–4.

9. Langer and Gleason, *The Challenge to Isolation*, 385, and *The Undeclared War* (New York, 1953), 393; J. R. M. Butler, *History of the Second World War, United Kingdom Military Series*, edited by J. R. M. Butler, *Grand Strategy*, vol. ii, *September 1939–June 1941* (London, 1957), 10–11.

10. Sherwood, op. cit. 141.

11. Maj. L. F. Ellis, *History of the Second World War, United Kingdom Military Series*, edited by J. R. M. Butler, *The War in France and Flanders, 1939–1940* (London, 1953), 57; and Richards, op. cit. 112–22.

12. Winston Churchill, *The Second World War*, vol. ii, *Their Finest Hour* (Boston, 1949), 26; *House of Commons Debates*, fifth series, vol. 360, 1502.

13. Fuller, op cit. 22, 221–2; Winston Churchill, *While England Slept, A Survey of World Affairs 1932–1938* (New York, 1938), 12, 41; Harry Truman, *Memoirs* (New York, 1955), vol. i, 419.

14. *Strategic Bombing Survey*, 1; Richards, op. cit. 234ff., 378ff.

15. Dr. E. B. Straus, 'The Psychological Effects of Bombing,' *Journal Royal United Service Institution* (London, May 1939), vol. xxxiv, 534; cf. ibid. 270ff.; cf. Butler, op. cit. 17; John Kennedy, *Why England Slept* (New York, 1940), 190–206; Air Marshal E. J. Kingston-McCloughry, *The Direction of War — A Critique of Political Direction and High Command in War* (New York, 1955), 128ff. Captain Liddell Hart persisted in advocating the psychological road to air victory as late as 1941, perhaps because by then he had run out of any other: *The Current of War* (London, 1941), 405. By 1946, however, he had decided that strategic bombing was a form of 'slow suicide' for Britain, hurting her more than it did Germany in 1940–41: 'War, Limited,' *Harper's Magazine* (New York, March 1946), vol. 192, no. 1150, 199.

16. Air Chief Marshal Sir Philip Joubert de la Ferté, 'Churchill the Airman,' *Churchill by His Contemporaries*, edited by Charles Eade (London, 1953), 167; Winston Churchill, 'Let the Tyrant Criminals Bomb,' *Collier's* (New York, January 14, 1939), 36; Herbert Dinerstein, 'The Impact of Air Power on International Security 1933–1940,' *Military Affairs*, vol. xix, no. 2 (Washington, Summer 1955), 65ff.

17. Mark Watson, *The United States Army in World War II*, edited by K. R. Greenfield, *The War Department. Chief of Staff: Prewar Plans and Preparations*, Office of the Chief of Military History, Dept. of the Army (Washington, 1950), 108–11.

18. *Their Finest Hour*, 126–7; cf. Frank Friedel, *Franklin D. Roosevelt, The Apprenticeship* (Boston, 1952), 362ff.

19. Winston Churchill, *Blood, Sweat and Tears, War Speeches*, compiled by Charles Eade (New York, 1941), 455.

20. Adm. of the Fleet Viscount Cunningham of Hyndhope, *A Sailor's Odyssey* (London, 1951), 231; cf. Maj. Gen. J. F. C. Fuller, *A Military History of the Western World* (New York, 1955), vol. ii, *From the Defeat*

of the Armada, 1588, to the Battle of Waterloo, 1815, 379; Winston Churchill, *Marlborough, His Life and Times* (New York, 1950), vol. III, 100ff.

21. *Their Finest Hour,* 164.
22. John J. McCloy, 'The Great Military Decisions,' *Foreign Affairs,* vol. XXVI, no. 1 (October 1947), 54.
23. *Their Finest Hour,* 147.
24. Cunningham, op. cit. 244–5. For his useful summary of the material available on this old desire of Adm. Fisher, see Sidney Fay, *The Origins of the World War,* vol. I, *Before Sarajevo: Underlying Causes of the War* (New York, 1927), 198; and Adm. Fisher, *Correspondence,* vol. II, 2.
25. *Their Finest Hour,* 642.
26. Charles de Gaulle, *War Memoirs,* vol. I, *The Call to Honour* (New York, 1955), 93; Adm. Sir Herbert Richmond, *Statesmen and Sea Power* (Oxford, 1946), 356ff.; Playfair, op. cit. chap. VII; Lord Hankey, *Politics, Trials and Errors* (Chicago, 1950), 70–79; Butler, op. cit. 97ff., 226.
27. *Their Finest Hour,* 222–3. For the opinions of two men on the spot in disagreement with the Prime Minister on this score, see Desmond Young's *Rommel* (London, 1950), 78, and General Maxime Weygand, *Recalled to Service* (New York, 1952), 257ff.; cf. Butler, op. cit. 432.
28. *Their Finest Hour,* 440–43, 408; see also Playfair, op. cit. chap. v.
29. Lord Riddell's *War Diary 1914–1918* (London, 1933), 199; cf. Lord Sydenham of Combe, 'Mr. Churchill as Historian,' *The World Crisis by Winston Churchill — A Criticism* (London, undated), 24–32; and Flag-Officer, 'Lest We Forget — The Tragedy of the Dardanelles,' *National Review* (London, October 1925), vol. LXXXVI, 280.
30. The Earl of Oxford and Asquith, *Memoirs and Reflections, 1852–1927* (Boston, 1928), vol. II, 108 (cited hereafter as Asquith).
31. For the former First Lord's complaints along this line see *The Diary of Lord Bertie of Thane 1914–1918,* edited by Lady Algernon Lennox (New York, n.d.), vol. II, 185.
32. W. S. Blunt, *My Diaries — Being a Personal Narrative of Events 1888–1914* (New York, 1929), part II, 271.
33. *Their Finest Hour,* 458–60; Richards, op. cit. 229. For similar views as early as 1916, see *House of Commons Debates,* fifth series, vol. LXXXII, 1590.
34. Cunningham, op. cit. 268–9, and Sir James Grigg, *Prejudice and Judgment* (London, 1948), 342; Winston Churchill, *The War Speeches* compiled by Charles Eade (Cambridge, 1953), vol. I, 50, and *Mr. Broderick's Army* (London, 1903), 23ff.; Adm. Fisher, *Correspondence,* vol. II, 232–3, 330–59.
35. *History of the Second World War, United Kingdom Civil Series,* edited by Sir Keith Hancock; W. K. Hancock, and M. M. Gowing, *British War Economy* (London, 1949), 67–96; M. M. Postan, *British War Production* (London, 1952), 27–136; Butler, op. cit. 255ff., 344ff.
36. Richard Challener, *The French Theory of the Nation in Arms, 1866–1939* (New York, 1955), 248ff.; General Charles de Gaulle, *The Army of the Future* (New York, 1941), 105ff.
37. *House of Commons Debates,* fifth series, vol. 364, 1159–71; *Blood, Sweat and Tears,* 341–2.

38. *Their Finest Hour*, 115.
39. L. S. Amery, 'The Great War Leaders,' *Servants of Crown and Commonwealth* (London, 1954), 64–5; cf. *House of Commons Debates*, fifth series, vol. 380, 63–262; Kingston-McCloughry, op. cit. 238–9; and Churchill's own argument, *The Second World War*, vol. IV, *The Hinge of Fate* (Boston, 1950), 89ff. and *Their Finest Hour*, 15.
40. Thomas Jones, *Lloyd George* (Cambridge, 1951), 285; *A Diary with Letters 1931–1950* (London, 1954), 465.
41. Samuel Eliot Morison, *History of United States Naval Operations in World War II*, vol. II, *Operations in North African Waters, October 1942 — June 1943* (Boston, 1947), 4 (cited hereafter as Morison Africa); Langer and Gleason, *The Undeclared War*, 64.
42. *Their Finest Hour*, 474–87; Butler, op. cit. 313–19.
43. Weygand, op. cit. 257; Playfair, op. cit. 215.
44. Halder's *Diary*, vol. IV, 212 (September 27, 1940).
45. Watson, op. cit. 117.
46. *Their Finest Hour*, 513–26; cf. Langer and Gleason, *The Undeclared War*, 65–86; Cordell Hull, *The Memoirs of Cordell Hull* (New York, 1948), vol. I, 849ff.
47. William L. Langer, *Our Vichy Gamble* (New York, 1947), 78–90; Louis Rougier, *Mission secrète à Londres, Les Accords Pétain-Churchill* (Paris, 1947), 72–8; *Their Finest Hour*, 513ff.
48. *Their Finest Hour*, 503–30; cf. Weygand, op. cit. 357–60; and *F. D. R., His Personal Letters, 1928–1945*, edited by Elliott Roosevelt (New York, 1950), vol. II, 1080–81 (cited hereafter as *Roosevelt Letters*).
49. Langer, op. cit. 120ff.

Chapter 3. RAINBOWS ACROSS THE ATLANTIC

1. Mahan, op. cit. vol. I, 119.
2. Frederick Oliver, *Ordeal by Battle* (London, 1915), 422–3; cf. Philip Guedalla, *The Duke* (London, 1946), 41ff.
3. Harold Begbie, *The Mirrors of Downing Street, Some Political Reflections* (New York, 1921), 100ff.
4. C. R. Attlee, *As It Happened* (London, 1954), 140; cf. Frances Perkins, *The Roosevelt I Knew* (New York, 1946), 383.
5. Watson, op. cit. 113–14.
6. Maurice Matloff and Edwin Snell, *United States Army in World War II*, edited by K. R. Greenfield, *The War Department, Strategic Planning for Coalition Warfare 1941–1942*, Office of the Chief of Military History, Dept. of the Army (Washington, 1953), 23–4; Butler, op. cit. 342–4.
7. A naval bias more obvious in Churchill's cicerone in war strategy. See Adm. Fisher, *Correspondence*, vol. II, 454–69 and 168n.2.
8. Watson, op. cit. 122; cf. Samuel Eliot Morison, *History of United States Naval Operations in World War II*, vol. I, *The Battle of the Atlantic September 1939–May 1943* (Boston, 1947), 37–42 (cited hereafter as Morison Atlantic).
9. Richard Leighton and Robert Coakley, *United States Army in World War II*, edited by K. R. Greenfield, *The War Department, Global*

Logistics and Strategy 1940–1943, Office of the Chief of Military History, Dept. of the Army (Washington, 1955), 43–56.

10. *Their Finest Hour,* 690–91.
11. Craven and Cate, op. cit. vol. i, 136.
12. Ray Cline, *United States Army in World War II,* edited by K. R. Greenfield, *The War Department, Washington Command Post: The Operations Division,* Office of the Chief of Military History, Dept. of the Army (Washington, 1951), 59.
13. British troops were, of course, landing in Greece during the enunciation of these basic war plans. *Pearl Harbor Attack, Hearings before the Joint Committee on Investigation of the Pearl Harbor Attack,* First Session, 79th Congress (Washington, 1946), Part 1, 998, Part 15, 1490–92; Watson, op. cit. 376–7; Morison Atlantic, 48.
14. A theory which Mr. Churchill has reiterated in the title of his fifth volume on the Second World War, *Closing the Ring* (Boston, 1951), a volume which, however, actually records the triumph of the ring theory's antithesis, a concentrated Allied thrust in France.
15. *Pearl Harbor Attack,* Part 15, 1491.
16. *Roosevelt Letters,* vol. ii, 1148; Winston Churchill, *The Second World War,* vol. iii, *The Grand Alliance* (Boston, 1950), 424–5.
17. Craven and Cate, op. cit. vol. i, 130, 476–592; Morison Atlantic, 48.
18. *Their Finest Hour,* 565; Sherwood, op. cit. 261ff.; a denial not in agreement with some of his own generals, *House of Commons Debates,* fifth series, vol. 374, 90–91.
19. *House of Commons Debates,* fifth series, vol. xiv, 1494ff., vol. lxxxii, 2023; cf. fourth series, vol. xciii, 1574, vol. civ, 3; Winston Churchill, *The Story of My Early Life, A Roving Commission,* and *Mr. Broderick's Army;* Colonel John Dunlop, *The Development of the British Army 1899–1914* (London, 1938), 157; Adm. Fisher, *Correspondence,* vol. ii, 359.
20. Lord Haldane, *An Autobiography* (Garden City, 1929), 198; cf. Viscount Esher, *Journals and Letters* (London, 1934–38), vol. iv, 120–22; Sir George Forrest, *The Life of Lord Roberts* (New York, n.d.), 339–40; L. S. Amery, *My Political Life,* vol. i, *England before the Storm 1896–1914* (London, 1953), 10. However, one particularly bitter naval critic of Churchill, closely associated with him during 1914–15, has written of the former that, as First Lord of the Admiralty, he was no more than an 'absurd amateur historian' whose thought in naval matters was 'crooked' and dangerous. *Portrait of an Admiral, The Life and Papers of Sir Herbert Richmond,* edited by Arthur Marder (Cambridge, Mass., 1952), 94–113, 203.
21. Sir Arthur Bryant, *The Turn of the Tide 1939–1943, A Study Based on the Diaries and Autobiographical Notes of Field Marshal the Viscount Alan Brooke* (London, 1957), 330, 386.
22. Sherwood, op. cit. 272.
23. *Blood, Sweat and Tears,* 440–41.
24. In this connection see, especially, Sir John Dill's remarkable warning to Sir Claude Auchinleck in June 1941 concerning the 'great and often undue pressure by the government on most British Commanders from Wellington to Haig and Wavell.' Butler, op. cit. 531.

25. *Their Finest Hour,* 623; Weygand, op. cit. 364–5.
26. Cunningham, op. cit. 291; cf. *The Grand Alliance,* 7–58; Playfair, op. cit. 307–25; Capt. S. W. Roskill, *History of The Second World War, United Kingdom Military Series,* edited by J. R. M. Butler, *The War at Sea,* vol. I, *The Defensive* (London, 1954), 304; Butler, op. cit. 370–71.
27. Winston Churchill, *The World Crisis* (New York, 1923), *1915,* 6; cf. Lt. Gen. Sir Gerald Ellison, *The Perils of Amateur Strategy as Exemplified by the Attacks on the Dardanelles Fortress in 1915* (London, 1926), 99.
28. *Mr. Broderick's Army,* 34; *House of Commons Debates,* fifth series, vol. LXXXII, 2023.
29. *The Grand Alliance,* 34, 64, 169; Richards, op. cit. 278ff.; Playfair, op. cit. 345ff.
30. Gen. Alexander Papagos, *The German Attack on Greece* (London, 1946), 10ff.; Butler, op. cit. 376ff., 441ff.; Maj. Gen. Sir Francis de Guingand, *Operation Victory* (New York, 1947), 47; *The Rommel Papers,* edited by Capt. B. H. Liddell Hart (London, 1953), 95.
31. *The United States and World Sea Power,* edited by E. B. Potter (Englewood Cliffs, N.J., 1955), 498ff.; Maj. Gen. Sir C. E. Callwell, *The Dardanelles* (Boston, 1924), 337; Richmond, *Papers,* 111–13, 148. Although Churchill's own early experiences in what is quaintly known as the last of the chivalric wars had afforded him a considerable insight into military logistics. Winston Churchill, *The River War — An Account of the Reconquest of the Sudan* (London, 1951), 162ff.
32. A. L. Rowse, *The Early Churchills, An English Family* (New York, 1956), 205–6; cf. Butler, op. cit. 562.
33. With consequences more apparent in 1942 in the Far East than immediately. *The Hinge of Fate,* 58, 155; cf. Butler, op. cit. 446–8.
34. *The Grand Alliance,* 96ff.; Bryant, op. cit. 248; B. H. Liddell Hart, *Defense of the West* (New York, 1950), 17–27; Richards, op. cit. 281ff.; Cunningham, op. cit. 310ff.; Butler, op. cit. 411ff.
35. *House of Commons Debates,* fifth series, vol. 359, 346ff.
36. *The Grand Alliance,* 365; Assmann, loc. cit. 309; Blumentritt, op. cit. 101; Playfair, op. cit. 349 and vol. II, *The Germans Come to the Help of Their Ally 1941* (London, 1956), 149ff.; de Guingand, op. cit. 77ff.; *The German Campaign in the Balkans,* 150ff.
37. David Lloyd George, *War Memoirs* (London, 1933–37), vol. III, 1072; cf. Butler, op. cit. 562.
38. *House of Commons Debates,* fifth series, vol. 371, 733.
39. Playfair, op. cit. vol. I, 371ff.; vol. II, 150; cf. Cunningham, op. cit. 310ff.; *The Grand Alliance,* 106–7; Butler, op. cit. 442–6.
40. de Guingand, op. cit. 58–9; cf. Capt. Russell Grenfell, *Main Fleet to Singapore* (London, 1951), 86.
41. Field Marshal Lord Wilson of Libya, *Eight Years Overseas, 1939–1947* (London, 1950), 73ff.; *The German Campaign in the Balkans,* 74, 116–18; John Wrench, *Geoffrey Dawson and Our Times* (London, 1955), 432. *House of Commons Debates,* fifth series, vol. 128, 371, 770–74; vol. 372, 63–155; Butler, op. cit. chap. XIX.
42. For Mr. Churchill's similar exuberance of ambitions in this region in the First World War, see J. C. Spender and Cyril Asquith, *Life of Herbert*

Henry Asquith, Lord of Oxford and Asquith (London, 1932), vol. II, 197.

43. Playfair, op. cit. vol. I, 371–96; cf. Gavin Long, *Greece, Crete and Syria* (Canberra, 1954), chaps. I, IX; Lukacs, op. cit. 356ff., 770–71; Playfair, op. cit. vol. II, 236; Bryant, op. cit. 340, 626.
44. Bryant, op. cit. 247–8.
45. Hoare, op. cit. 95–106; Langer and Gleason, *The Undeclared War*, 400.
46. Gen. H. H. Arnold, *Global Mission* (New York, 1949), 237–8.
47. Butler, op. cit. 436; Langer, op. cit. 142–5.
48. *The Grand Alliance*, 236.
49. U. S. Dept. of State *Bulletin*, May 17, 1941, 584.
50. Langer, op. cit. 153; cf. Fleet Admiral William D. Leahy, *I Was There, The Personal Story of the Chief of Staff of Presidents Roosevelt and Truman Based on His Notes and Diaries Made at the Time* (New York, 1950), 33.
51. Leahy, op. cit. 29; *Roosevelt Letters*, vol. II, 1149.
52. Leighton and Coakley, 68–70; *Pearl Harbor Attack*, part 5, 2309, part 15, 1523.
53. Morison Atlantic, 66–7; *The Grand Alliance*, 143–5.
54. Gen. Joseph Stilwell, *The Stilwell Papers*, edited by T. H. White (New York, 1948), 16.
55. Cline, op. cit. 44.
56. *The Public Papers and Addresses of Franklin D. Roosevelt*, 1941 volume, *The Call to Battle Stations* (New York, 1950), 185.
57. Halder's *Diary*, vol. VI, 117; Langer, op. cit. 402–11, Appendix II.
58. Morison Atlantic, 67; Langer, op. cit. 160.
59. *Pearl Harbor Attack*, part 16, 2161.
60. Henry L. Stimson and McGeorge Bundy, *On Active Service in Peace and War* (New York, 1947), 386–7 (cited hereafter as Stimson).
61. Morison Pacific, 57.

Chapter 4. THE GRAND ALLIANCE

1. Keith Feiling, *The Life of Neville Chamberlain* (London, 1947), 314; cf. ibid. 426.
2. Capt. B. H. Liddell Hart, 'The Defence of the Empire,' *Fortnightly Review*, No. 853 (London, January 1938), 28.
3. *House of Commons Debates*, fifth series, vol. 346, 1358–9.
4. *Hitler's Table Talk 1941–1944* (London, 1953), 166.
5. Winston Churchill, *The Unrelenting Struggle. War Speeches* (Boston, 1942), 171; cf. R. W. Seton-Watson, *Britain in Europe 1789–1914, A Survey of Foreign Policy* (Cambridge, 1937), 25.
6. *The Grand Alliance*, 372; *Secret Session Speeches* (New York, 1946), 40.
7. Goerlitz, op. cit. 394; Mendelssohn; op. cit. 251–2; Rossi, op. cit. 189; Hinsley, op. cit. 137–8; Bryant, op. cit. 241–2.
8. *The Grand Alliance*, 370–425; D. Richards and H. Saunders, *Royal Air Force 1939–1945*, vol. II, *The Fight Avails* (London, 1954), 159; Richards, op. cit. 347; Butler, op. cit. 509, 549.

9. Sherwood, op. cit. 303–14; Leahy, op. cit. 54–5; Langer and Gleason, *The Undeclared War,* 563–91; Pearl Harbor Attack, part 44, 1344.
10. *The Unrelenting Struggle,* 343.
11. Hans Rothfels, 'Clausewitz,' *Makers of Modern Strategy, Military Thought from Machiavelli to Hitler,* edited by E. M. Earle in collaboration with G. Craig and F. Gilbert (Princeton, 1943), 111; cf. *The Rommel Papers,* 191–2.
12. According to Nikita Khrushchev, if not Harry Hopkins. 'Stalin Depicted as Savage Despot,' *The New York Times* (New York, June 5, 1956), 12ff.; and see below.
13. *The Grand Alliance,* 383–5.
14. Col. C. P. Stacey, *Official History of the Canadian Army in the Second World War,* vol. I, *Six Years of War — The Army in Canada, Britain and the Pacific* (Ottawa, 1955), 326.
15. *Their Finest Hour,* 253.
16. *Their Finest Hour,* 249; Commander Kenneth Edwards, R.N., *Operation Neptune* (London, 1946), 23.
17. Sherwood, op. cit. 343.
18. In December 1941 the President, Mr. Churchill, and several other civilian dignitaries would agree that Hitler might stage Felix because of the failure of Barbarossa rather than because of its success! *The Grand Alliance,* 664.
19. Elliott Roosevelt, *As He Saw It* (New York, 1946), 22–30.
20. Matloff and Snell, op. cit. 161; Leighton and Coakley, op. cit. 133.
21. William McNeill, *Survey of International Affairs 1939–1946 — America, Britain and Russia, Their Cooperation and Conflict 1941–1946* (New York, 1953), 52ff.; Grenfell, op. cit. 87; *House of Commons Debates,* fifth series, vol. 374, 78. This was, of course, another policy advocated by David Lloyd George in the First World War. Lloyd George, op. cit. vol. I, chaps. XIII–XV; vol. IV, chap. IV, 477–8.
22. Bryant, op. cit. 276, 376–7.
23. Sherwood, op. cit. 355.
24. *Pearl Harbor Attack,* part 4, 1785; *The Grand Alliance,* 437.
25. *The Grand Alliance,* 593; cf. Butler, op. cit. 548.
26. Watson, op. cit. 402; Leighton and Coakley, op. cit. 119.
27. W. F. Craven and J. L. Cate, *The Army Air Force in World War II,* vol. II, *Europe: Torch to Pointblank, August 1942 to December 1943* (Chicago, 1949), 42.
28. *Pearl Harbor Attack,* part 4, 1786.
29. Sherwood, op. cit. 358.
30. Watson, op. cit. 402–3; *The Grand Alliance,* 508. For an early warning against the elite armor escape from large-scale infantry war, see Victor Germains, *The Mechanization of War* (London, 1927), 217. See also Col. J. F. C. Fuller, *The Reformation of War* (New York, 1923), 142–3, and *On Future Warfare* (London, 1928); Capt. B. H. Liddell Hart, 'Our Military Correspondent,' *The Times* (London, October 25–27, 1937), 15–16, for the then more influential proponents of such views. Mr. Churchill's own faith in tanks to some extent came from the days of his pioneer work in overcoming the infantry deadlock of the First World War in France. See Winston Churchill, *The World Crisis,* rev.

ed. in one vol. (New York, 1949), 310ff.; Maj. Gen. Sir. C. E. Callwell, *Field Marshal Sir Henry Wilson, His Life and Diaries* (New York, 1923), vol. ii, 68.

31. Gordon Harrison, *The United States Army in World War II*, edited by K. R. Greenfield, *The European Theater of Operations, The Cross-Channel Attack*, Office of the Chief of Military History, Dept. of the Army (Washington, 1951), 6.

32. Immediately after Pearl Harbor, Churchill contemplated the employment of approximately forty British and American armored divisions which he suggested would attack Europe in 1943 from several points across the Mediterranean as well as from Britain herself. *The Grand Alliance*, 655–9; see below, chap. iv.

33. Watson, op. cit. 408; cf. Capt. Norman MacMillan, 'The Influence of Air Forces on the Course of the War,' *Journal Royal United Service Institution*, vol. lxxxvi, no. 541 (London, February 1941); Hancock and Gowing, op. cit. 98–100.

34. *The Unrelenting Struggle*, 187.

35. Harris, op. cit. 78; cf. Winston Churchill, *The Second World War*, vol. vi, *Triumph and Tragedy* (Boston, 1953), 541; and Butler, op. cit. 411ff., 485.

36. Butler, op cit. 484; Thomas Greer, 'Air Arm Doctrinal Roots, 1917–1918,' *Military Affairs*, vol. xx, no. 4 (Washington, Winter 1956), 213.

37. Sherwood, op. cit. 410–15; cf. Craven and Cate, op. cit. vol. i, 145.

38. Matloff and Snell, op. cit. 59–61; McCloy, loc. cit. 57.

39. H. A. De Weerd, 'Marshall, Organizer of Victory,' part 1, *Infantry Journal* (Washington, December 1946), vol. liv, no. 6, 13.

40. Craven and Cate, op. cit. vol. i, 143–9; Sherwood, op. cit. 413–17.

41. Matloff and Snell, op. cit. 55–6.

42. Leighton and Coakley, op. cit. 139.

43. Craven and Cate, op. cit. vol. i, 143–4.

44. Raymond Garthoff, *Soviet Military Doctrine* (Glencoe, Ill., 1953), 67, 373ff.; D. F. White, *The Growth of the Red Army* (Princeton, 1944), chap. vi; Khrushchev, loc. cit. 15.

45. *The Grand Alliance*, 379ff., 460ff.; cf. Jan Ciechanowski, *Defeat in Victory* (New York, 1947), 91ff.

46. Blumentritt, op. cit. 161–97; cf. Lt. Gen. Hans Speidel, *Invasion 1944, Rommel and the Normandy Campaign* (Chicago, 1950), 43–8; Shulman, op. cit. 90–92; Gen. Dwight D. Eisenhower, *Crusade in Europe* (New York, 1948), 322.

47. *The Grand Alliance*, 461ff.

48. Bryant, op. cit. 256–62.

49. *The Grand Alliance*, 466.

50. Maj. Gen. Sir Edward Spears, *Assignment to Catastrophe*, vol. ii, *The Fall of France* (New York, 1955), 151. For French anxieties as a consequence of the British preference in the 1930's for a limited liability army, cf. Victor Germains, 'Some Problems of Imperial Strategy,' *National Review*, vol. cx, no. 663 (London, May 1938); Gen. Baratier, 'A French View of the *Times* Article: "Defence or Attack"' *Army Quarterly*, xxxvi, no. 1 (London, April 1938).

51. *The Private Papers of Douglas Haig 1914–1919*, edited by Robert Blake

(London, 1952), 346–469; cf. Lloyd George, op. cit. vol. vi, 3350; *House of Commons Debates*, fifth series, vol. 125, 1448.

52. *The Grand Alliance*, 509–10, 851; Postan, op. cit. 345. The official British War History's estimate of fifty divisions for the Empire in 1942 is far more realistic. Butler, op. cit. 480.

53. Bryant, op. cit. 323–4.

54. Fuller, *The Second World War*, 265; cf. John Maynard Keynes, *Essays in Biography* (New York, 1933), 73; and *The Grand Alliance*, 852.

55. In June 1941 Beaverbrook was ordered to transfer his impressive attentions from fighters to tanks, since Erwin Rommel, first in British production priorities. But by autumn the Prime Minister was chiefly concerned with spurring the lagging heavy bomber program. Postan, op. cit. 118–25.

56. *Strategic Bombing Survey*, 6–9.

57. Duff Cooper, *Old Men Forget* (London, 1954), 98ff.

58. McNeill, op. cit. 503; Tom Driberg, *Beaverbrook, A Study in Power and Frustration* (London, 1956), 248, 285; Emrys Hughes, *Winston Churchill, British Bulldog* (New York, 1955), 210ff.

59. Sherwood, op. cit. 393–4.

60. William H. Standley and Arthur Ageton, *Admiral Ambassador to Russia* (Chicago, 1955), 74; Driberg, op. cit. 268ff. Political ambitions evidently lay behind Beaverbrook's discovery of the Second Front issue. *President Roosevelt Secretary File*, Box 9, *Hyde Park Papers* (Hyde Park, N.Y.); Driberg, op. cit. 280ff.

61. Henry Morgenthau, *Ambassador Morganthau's Story* (Garden City, 1919), 205.

62. *House of Commons Debates*, fifth series, vol. 377, 600; cf. vol. 376, 119ff., 226ff., 689ff.

63. Forrest Pogue, *The United States Army in World War II, The European Theater of Operations, The Supreme Command*, edited by K. R. Greenfield, Office of the Chief of Military History, Dept. of the Army (Washington, 1954), 98–9.

64. Lt. Gen. Sir Frederick Morgan, *Overture to Overlord* (Garden City, N.Y., 1950), 39; cf. Bryant, op. cit. 237–8, 386.

65. Arnold, op. cit. 376.

66. Edwards, op. cit. 28.

67. Morgan, op. cit. 69.

68. *The Grand Alliance*, 544–6.

69. Langer, op. cit. 193; cf. Leahy, op. cit. 60.

70. *The Grand Alliance*, 540–52; cf. Matloff and Snell, op. cit. 101ff.; *Roosevelt Letters*, vol. ii, 1223.

71. Ralph Ingersoll, *Top Secret* (New York, 1946), 58.

72. *The Grand Alliance*, 549–53; cf. Roskill, op. cit. 520–21.

73. *Pearl Harbor Attack*, part 14, exhibit 16, 1016–62.

74. Morison Atlantic, 47; Trumbull Higgins, 'East Wind Rain,' *United States Naval Institute Proceedings*, vol. 81, no. 11 (Annapolis, November 1955).

75. Winston Churchill, *The End of the Beginning, War Speeches* (Boston, 1943), 66.

76. *The Grand Alliance*, 606–8.

Chapter 5. ARCADIAN IDYLL

1. *The Dispatches of Field Marshal The Duke of Wellington During His Various Campaigns 1799–1839* compiled by Lt. Col. Gurwood (London, 1837–39), vol. xi, 35.
2. Duff Cooper, *Haig* (Garden City, 1936), p. 72.
3. Gen. Sir Ian Hamilton, *The Soul and Body of an Army* (London, 1921), 185.
4. *House of Commons Debates*, fifth series, vol. 378, 48; *The End of the Beginning*, 92.
5. Sherwood, op. cit. 441.
6. *Fuehrer Conferences: German Navy 1941*, vol. ii, 79–80; *The German Campaign in Russia, Planning and Operations 1940–1942*, Dept. of the Army (Washington, March 1955), 92–4.
7. *Fuehrer Conferences: German Navy 1942;* cf. *The Gathering Storm*, 544–8. Sir John Slessor, *The Central Blue, Recollections and Reflections* (London, 1956), 260ff.
8. With somewhat improbable naïveté, the much-tried C.I.G.S., Sir Alan Brooke, has wondered why Churchill 'wanted to go back, and what he would have done there [in Norway] . . . we never found out.' Bryant, op. cit. 340ff.
9. Captain T. B. Kittredge, 'A Military Danger — The Revelation of Secret Strategic Plans,' *United States Naval Institute Proceedings* (Annapolis, July 1955).
10. Blumentritt, op. cit. 129; cf. Martienssen, op. cit. 199; and Pogue, op. cit. 177; Stacey, op. cit. 349ff.
11. *The Grand Alliance*, 643.
12. *Secret Session Speeches*, 87.
13. *Roosevelt Papers, 1942 Volume, Humanity on the Defensive*, 34.
14. Eisenhower, op. cit. 27.
15. Craven and Cate, op. cit. vol. i, 238.
16. Sherwood, op. cit. 445.
17. Playfair, op. cit. vol. i, 23.
18. Bryant, op. cit. 278–80.
19. *The Grand Alliance*, 645–59; cf. Challener, op. cit. 250ff.; and Hoffman Nickerson, *The Armed Horde 1793–1939 — A Study of the Rise, Survival and Decline of the Mass Army* (New York, 1940), 337ff.
20. Butler, op. cit. 549.
21. See Adm. Fisher, *Memories*, vol. i, 77, for the use of this Admiralty term in the First World War.
22. Lloyd George, op. cit. vol. iv, 2347–8; cf. Jere King, *Generals and Politicians, Conflict between France's Higher Command, Parliament and Government, 1914–1918* (Berkeley, 1951), chaps. ix–x; and Owen, op. cit. 439.
23. Stimson, op. cit. 414; cf. Lloyd George, op. cit. vol. iii, 1067; Cline, op. cit. 100; Eisenhower, op. cit. 191; Bryant, op. cit. 316.
24. Sherwood, op. cit. 469ff.
25. De Weerd, 'Marshall, Organizer of Victory,' loc. cit. part ii, 13.

26. 'Marshall Joins Truman in Urging Free-World Unity,' *The New York Times* (New York, June 6, 1949), 1.
27. Langer, op. cit. 204–9; cf. Hull, op. cit. vol. ii, 1044–5.
28. Arnold, op. cit. 279.
29. Ciano's *Diaries*, 426–37.
30. Arnold, op. cit. 275.
31. *The Grand Alliance*, 663–4.
32. Craven and Cate, op. cit. vol. i, 240–41.
33. Stilwell, op. cit. 11–14.
34. Arnold, op. cit. 285; and Ernest J. King and W. M. Whitehill, *Fleet Admiral King, A Naval Record*, cited hereafter as King (New York, 1952), 363.
35. Craven and Cate, op. cit. vol. i, 560. Delayed news on heavy British naval losses would tend to perpetuate this situation hereafter.
36. Bryant, op. cit. 296.
37. Sherwood, op. cit. 459.
38. Stilwell, op. cit. 14–36.
39. Arnold, op. cit. 303.
40. Stilwell, op. cit. 20–21; Eisenhower, op. cit. 22; Craven and Cate, op. cit. vol. i, 561–2.
41. Eisenhower, op. cit. 77–8.
42. Matloff and Snell, op. cit. 104–5.
43. *The Grand Alliance*, 665–85; Craven and Cate, op. cit. vol. i, 239–40.
44. Sherwood, op. cit. 460.
45. That is that the British be able to invade Tunisia from Libya at the same time as an American invasion of French Morocco. Stilwell, op. cit. 25; Young, op. cit. 105.
46. *The Grand Alliance*, 700–705; cf. Craven and Cate, op. cit. vol. i, 239–40.
47. Sherwood, op. cit. 465–6.
48. Arnold, op. cit. 302; cf. Stilwell, op. cit. 23; and Harrison, op. cit. 11.
49. Craven and Cate, op. cit. vol. ii, 42.

Chapter 6. ROUNDUP—AMERICAN STYLE

1. *The Writings and Speeches of Oliver Cromwell*, edited by W. C. Abbott, vol. ii, *The Commonwealth 1649–1653* (Cambridge, 1939), 444.
2. R. S. Baker, *Woodrow Wilson, Life and Letters* (New York, 1927–39), vol. viii, 76.
3. Carl von Clausewitz, *On War* (London, 1911), vol. iii, 154.
4. Winston Churchill, *Amid These Storms — Thoughts and Adventures* (New York, 1932), 155–6.
5. Cline, op. cit. 145.
6. Morison Africa, 12.
7. Sherwood, op. cit. 495–6.
8. Harris, op. cit. 74.
9. Adolf Galland, *The First and the Last, The Rise and the Fall of the German Fighter Forces, 1938–1945* (New York, 1954), 226; *Strategic Bombing Survey 2;* Richards and Saunders, op. cit. 118ff.; Capt. Harry Butcher, *My Three Years with Eisenhower, The Personal Diary of Cap-*

tain Harry C. Butcher, U.S.N.R., Naval Aide to General Eisenhower 1942–1945 (New York, 1946), 498ff.
10. Craven and Cate, op. cit. vol. I, 593.
11. Stimson, op. cit. 415–16.
12. Cline, op. cit. 148–9.
13. Harrison, op. cit. 11; cf. Sherwood, op. cit. 495.
14. Deutscher, op. cit. 470.
15. Cline, op. cit. 148–50; Craven and Cate, op. cit. vol. I, 563.
16. Harrison, op. cit. 12.
17. Craven and Cate, op. cit. vol. II, 45.
18. *The Grand Alliance*, 706; Matloff and Snell, op. cit. 176.
19. Leahy, op. cit. 76. Cf. Langer, op. cit. 286; and Craven and Cate, op. cit. vol. II, 43.
20. Craven and Cate, op. cit. vol. I, 561–2.
21. Stimson, op. cit. 416.
22. Craven and Cate, op. cit. vol. I, 588; Cline, op. cit. chap. VI.
23. H. A. De Weerd, 'Organizer of Victory,' loc. cit. part II, 15–17.
24. Craven and Cate, op. cit. vol. I, 562; Sherwood, op. cit. 519.
25. Matloff and Snell, op. cit. 166–80; cf. Cline, op. cit. 153, 364–5; and Pogue, op. cit. 100.
26. Lloyd George, op. cit. III, 1391.
27. Stimson, op. cit. 416–17.
28. Stimson, op. cit. 417–18.
29. Craven and Cate, op. cit. vol. I, 563; Harrison, op. cit. 15.
30. Sherwood, op. cit. 520; Cline, op. cit. 157.
31. *The Grand Alliance*, 657–9.
32. Harrison, op. cit. 16.
33. Cline, op. cit. 154–7; cf. Craven and Cate, op. cit. vol. I, 563.
34. Sherwood, op. cit. 520.
35. Eisenhower, op. cit. 43–5.
36. Arnold, op. cit. 304; Marshall, op. cit. 158.
37. Sherwood, op. cit. 519–20.
38. *The Grand Alliance*, 852.
39. Sherwood, op. cit. 520; cf. Eisenhower, op. cit. 45.
40. Cline, op. cit. 156.
41. Eisenhower, op. cit. 45–6.
42. Martin Sommers, 'Why Russia Got the Drop on Us,' *The Saturday Evening Post* (Philadelphia, Feb. 8, 1947), 25.
43. Sherwood, op. cit. 521; Matloff and Snell, op. cit. 183–4.
44. *Roosevelt Letters*, vol. II, 1305.
45. Arnold, op. cit. 305; cf. Ingersoll, op. cit. 74.
46. *The Hinge of Fate*, 314.
47. Sherwood, op. cit. 554; Donald Nelson, *Arsenal of Democracy* (New York, 1946), 252–3; Leighton and Coakley, op. cit. 377–80.
48. Bryant, op. cit. 358–60; cf. ibid. 255; and Sherwood, op. cit. 523.
49. Sherwood, op. cit. 523–6; *The Grand Alliance*, 423, 688.
50. Matloff and Snell, op. cit. 187; cf. Craven and Cate, op. cit., vol. I, 563; and Cline, op. cit. 158.
51. Harrison, op. cit. 17–18; cf. Bryant, op. cit. 354.
52. *The Hinge of Fate*, 317; cf. Richards and Saunders, op. cit. 66; Harri-

son, op. cit. 18; Charles Romanus and Riley Sunderland, *The United States Army in World War II*, edited by K. R. Greenfield, *China-Burma-India Theater, Stilwell's Mission to China*, Office of the Chief of Military History, Dept. of the Army (Washington, 1953), 100–140; Bryant, op. cit. 357.

53. *The Hinge of Fate*, 317–25; cf. Craven and Cate, op. cit. vol. I, 564.
54. Harrison, op. cit. 18; cf. Sherwood, op. cit. 535.
55. Sir Frederick has written that since by 1943 Norfolk House had acquired such a reputation 'as a home of lost causes' he had suggested, half seriously, renaming the famous old building Suffolk House, 'or something of the sort,' as a method of protecting the morale of his own Anglo-American planning staff. Morgan, op. cit. 45.
56. Sherwood, op. cit. 534–42.
57. *The Hinge of Fate*, 319; Cline, op. cit. 159.
58. Cline, op. cit. 160; cf. De Weerd, loc. cit. 14; Stimson, op. cit. 419; Matloff and Snell, op. cit. 189.
59. *On War*, vol. III, 222.

Chapter 7. 'STRATEGIC NATURAL SELECTION'

1. *The Hinge of Fate*, chap. xx; cf. *The Story of My Early Life — A Roving Commission*, 28; in a phrase of Mr. Churchill's characteristically more Darwinian than Calvinist in its attitude toward what Cromwell has said is 'falsely called the chance of war.' Robert Paul, *The Lord Protector, Religion and Politics in the Life of Oliver Cromwell* (London, 1955), 217.
2. Winston Churchill, *Onwards to Victory, War Speeches* (Boston, 1944), 147; *House of Commons Debates*, fifth series, vol. 390, 561.
3. *House of Commons Debates*, third series, vol. CLXXII, 1130; cf. Esher, op. cit. vol. III, 210; Lloyd George, op. cit. vol. IV, 2419.
4. Lloyd Lewis, *Sherman: Fighting Prophet* (New York, 1932), 424.
5. *On War*, vol. III, 210.
6. *Fuehrer Conferences, German Navy, 1942*, 10–18; and Martienssen, op. cit. 123–5; F. C. Jones, *Japan's New Order in East Asia, Its Rise and Fall* (London, 1954), 403.
7. Mitsuo Fuchida and Masatake Okuniya, *Midway, The Battle that Doomed Japan. The Japanese Navy's Own Story* (Annapolis, 1955), 51ff.; Herbert Rosinski, 'Strategy of Fear,' *The Infantry Journal*, vol. LVIII, no. 6 (Washington, June 1946), 30.
8. But Hitler had fewer illusions on this score than his Mediterranean-minded navy. *Table Talk*, 202.
9. Halder's *Diary*, vol. VIII (June 12, 1942), 325.
10. In Admiral Cunningham's phrase, Roskill, op. cit. 438.
11. Cunningham, op. cit. 420–21; *Fuehrer Conferences, German Navy, 1942*, 18, 95–6; Kesselring, op. cit. 109.
12. Marshall, op. cit. 155; *The Grand Alliance*, 553.
13. Romanus and Sunderland, op. cit. 100–140.
14. Kesselring, op. cit. chaps. XIII and XIV; cf. Maugeri, op. cit. chap. VII; *The Rommel Papers*, 203–88; General Ugo Cavallero, *Commando Su-*

premo, diaro 1940–1943 del Capo di Stato Maggiore Generale (Bologna, 1948), December 29, 1941, June 24, 1942.

15. *Fuehrer Conferences, German Navy, 1942*, 102; cf. Hinsley, op. cit. 211.
16. Langer, op. cit. 241–3; cf. Sherwood, op. cit. 539.
17. Langer, op. cit. 279–81.
18. Sherwood, op. cit. 556; *The Hinge of Fate*, 340.
19. Harrison, op. cit. 23–4.
20. Hull, op. cit. vol. II, 1249; Sherwood, op. cit. 528.
21. Although to the dismay of Sir Alan Brooke Molotov's visit made the Prime Minister restless and eager for some sort of action on the Continent. Bryant, op. cit. 372ff., 487. Mr. Churchill's restlessness probably was decisive in pushing through the ill-fated raid on Dieppe in August 1942. See below.
22. Sherwood, op. cit. 556–77; cf. Morgan, op. cit. 155–7.
23. *Roosevelt Papers*, 1942, 269; cf. McNeill, op. cit. 184.
24. Sherwood, op. cit. 577; Matloff and Snell, op. cit. 231–2.
25. *Falsifactors of History*, Soviet Information Bureau, Soviet Embassy (Washington, February 1948), 57–8.
26. Standley, op. cit. 204–13; chap. XVII and see below, chap. IX.
27. This statement, so damaging to Mr. Churchill's argument, has been removed from the bound version of *The Hinge of Fate*, published in the United States, 335–42. For the original see 'The Hinge of Fate,' *New York Times* (October 21, 1950). Cf. Matloff and Snell, op. cit. 233–4.
28. Craven and Cate, op. cit. 573.
29. Arnold, op. cit. 316–17; *Closing the Ring*, 518–19; cf. Harris, op. cit. 110, and Richards and Saunders, op. cit. 133ff.
30. Maj. Alexander de Seversky, *Victory through Air Power* (New York, 1942). William Ziff, *The Coming Battle of Germany* (New York, 1942).
31. Max Werner, *Attack Can Win in 1943* (Boston, 1943); Col. W. F. Kernan, *Defense Will Not Win the War* (Boston, 1942).
32. Hanson Baldwin, *Strategy for Victory* (New York, 1942), 149–50.
33. Kernan, op. cit. 152.
34. Sherwood, op. cit. 588.
35 Eisenhower, op. cit. 66
36. Cline, op. cit. 163.
37. Edwards, op. cit. 2, 29; Matloff and Snell, op. cit. 234–5.
38. Stacey, op. cit. 315.
39. Sommers, loc. cit. 25; Lt. Gen. L. K. Truscott, Jr., *Command Missions — A Personal Story* (New York, 1954), 46–7.
40. *The Hinge of Fate*, 353.
41. Harrison, op. cit. 23.
42. Sherwood, op. cit. 582–4; cf. *The Hinge of Fate*, 353.
43. Stimson, op. cit. 419–23.
44. Craven and Cate, op. cit. vol. I, 571.
45. Craven and Cate, op. cit. vol. II, 46.
46. Harrison, op. cit. 32n., 113.
47. Alexander Werth, *The Year of Stalingrad* (London, 1946), 91–139.
48. Sherwood, op. cit. 590; Bryant, op. cit. 395, 405.
49. See, for example, Fitzroy MacClean's account, *Eastern Approaches* (London, 1949), 281, for the Prime Minister's still apolitical views

toward Marshal Tito and the Balkans so late as 1943–44 in contrast
with Chester Wilmot's strongly political interpretation of Churchill's
motives even in 1942, *The Struggle for Europe* (New York, 1952),
636ff. In his own volumes Churchill stresses no particularly anti-Communist sentiments vis-à-vis the Balkans before May 1944: *Closing the
Ring*, 708; *The Dawn of Liberation, War Speeches* (Boston, 1945),
21–2. Cf. John Ehrman, *History of the Second World War, United Kingdom Military Series, Grand Strategy*, vol. v, *August 1943–September 1944*
(London, 1956), 555; Louis Halle, 'Strategy versus Ideology,' *The Yale
Review*, vol. xlvi (New Haven, Autumn 1956), 4; Sherwood, op. cit.
590–91; Lukacs, op. cit. 678ff.

50. *The World Crisis, 1915*, 1–5.
51. *Marlborough, His Life and Times*, vol. iv, 31; cf. Sir John Fortescue,
    Following the Drum (London, 1931), 185.
52. *The Story of My Early Life, A Roving Commission*, 338; cf. ibid. 301.
53. This was, of course, a moot point in 1915 as in 1942.
54. *The World Crisis, 1915*, 14–32.
55. Grigg, op. cit. 359.
56. Capt. B. H. Liddell Hart, *The War in Outline* (New York, 1936), 83;
    C. R. Cruttwell, *The Role of British Strategy in the Great War* (Cam-
    bridge, Great Britain, 1936), 35; *The World Crisis*, rev. ed., 308–9.
57. King, *A Naval Record*, 425.
58. J. A. Spender, *Life, Journalism and Politics* (New York, 1927), vol.
    ii, 70; cf. *The Hinge of Fate*, 433; George Smalley, *Anglo-American
    Memories*, second series (New York, 1912); Butler, op. cit. 561.
59. Adm. Fisher, *Memories*, 50–52.
60. Craven and Cate, op. cit. vol. i, 570; David Woodward, *The Tirpitz and
    and the Battle for the North Atlantic* (New York, 1954), 98.
61. *The Hinge of Fate*, 382–3. For a softer view of Tobruk see de Guin-
    gand, op. cit. 122–3.
62. *The End of the Beginning*, 163–86 and see below.
63. Sherwood, op. cit. 592. With his customary political perception Hitler
    surmised the Allied difficulties at this juncture. *Hitler's Table Talk*, 538.
64. Marshall, op. cit. 154.
65. Robertson, op. cit. 273.
66. Stimson, op. cit. 423–5; cf. Sherwood, op. cit. 591.
67. Sommers, loc. cit. 90–94. As Field Marshal Wavell has pointed out, in
    the First World War Sir William Robertson's efforts to educate Lloyd
    George on those same logistic factors were quite unavailing. Field Mar-
    shal Earl Wavell, *Soldiers and Soldiering, or Epithets of War* (London,
    1953), 40–41; Lloyd George, op. cit. vol. i, 386.
68. King, op. cit. 395; Harrison, op. cit. 25–6; Bryant, op. cit. 405.
69. Craven and Cate, op. cit. vol. i, 571.
70. Harrison, op. cit. 26; cf. *The Hinge of Fate*, 384.
71. Stimson, op. cit. 424.
72. Craven and Cate, op. cit. vol. i, 571–2; Harrison, op. cit. 25–6.
73. *The Hinge of Fate*, 438–41.
74. *Roosevelt Papers, 1942*, 462; *Onwards to Victory*, 242. Even that pur-
    portedly all-out Africa man, Sir Alan Brooke, reflected doubt and in-
    consistency in this enigmatic period. Bryant, op. cit. 402–3.

Chapter 8. TORCH

1. Capt. B. H. Liddell Hart, *The Defence of Britain* (London, 1939), 125.
2. Esher, op. cit. vol. III, 263.
3. *Marlborough, His Life and Times,* vol. v, 243–4.
4. Callwell, op. cit. vol. I, 215–16.
5. Sherwood, op. cit. 595–600.
6. Edwards, op. cit. 18; and Capt. W. D. Puleston, *The Influence of Sea Power in World War II* (New Haven, 1947), 168.
7. Butler, op. cit. 381–2, 524.
8. Ingersoll, op. cit. 57–9.
9. Sherwood, op. cit. 603; Marshall, op. cit. 77.
10. Bryant, op. cit. 357–62; Matloff and Snell, op. cit. 378ff.
11. Capt. B. H. Liddell Hart, *The War in Outline,* 108; T. H. Thomas 'British War Policy and the Western Front,' *Foreign Affairs,* vol. I, no. 4 (June 1923), 160–61; Robertson, op. cit. 277, 324; Beaverbrook, *Men and Power,* 158.
12. *The World Crisis, 1915,* 36.
13. Hardly a practical or even desirable proposition with a strong Prime Minister. See Lt. Gen. Sir Ian Jacob, 'The High Level Conduct and Direction of World War II,' *Journal Royal United Service Institution* (London, August 1956), vol. CI, no. 603, 364.
14. *House of Commons Debates,* fifth series, vol. 380, 261, vol. 381, 237–576; cf. *The Hinge of Fate,* 89–91, 432.
15. *House of Commons Debates,* fifth series, vol. 381, 237–576; cf. John Wheeler-Bennett, *Munich, Prologue to Tragedy* (New York, 1948), 384; and Richmond *Papers,* 98.
16. For example, Bevan's characteristic belief of the doctrinaire Left that Churchill had 'intelligence but not intellect' and that he expressed 'the values of a boy of seventeen or eighteen.' Vincent Brome, *Aneurin Bevan* (London, 1953), 160; cf. H. G. Wells, *Men Like Gods* (New York, 1923).
17. Butcher, op. cit. 12.
18. Eisenhower, op. cit. 68–70.
19. Bryant, op. cit. 415–19.
20. Harrison, op. cit. 27.
21. *The Hinge of Fate,* 434; cf. Leighton and Coakley, op. cit. 385–7.
22. Matloff and Snell, op. cit. 328.
23. Stacey, op. cit. 349ff.
24. Butcher, op. cit. 11.
25. Stimson, op. cit. 424.
26. King, op. cit. 387–99.
27. Sherwood, op. cit. 594–600.
28. Harrison, op. cit. 28.
29. *The Hinge of Fate,* 440.
30. Matloff and Snell, op. cit. 215. Cf. *Triumph and Tragedy,* 57; and Maj. Gen. Courtney Whitney, *MacArthur, His Rendezvous with History* (New York, 1956), 68–74.
31. Sherwood, op. cit. 600–605.

32. Ibid. Cf. King, op. cit. 399–400; and Pogue, op. cit. 101.
33. Butcher, op. cit. 22. Cf. McNeill, op. cit. 187ff.
34. As Mr. Churchill has admitted. *The Hinge of Fate,* 433.
35. Butcher, op. cit. 24–6.
36. Bryant, op. cit. 627; cf. ibid. 415–24.
37. Lord Beaverbrook, *Politicians and the War 1914–1916* (London, 1932), vol. II, 82; cf. Lord Brabazon of Tara, *The Brabazon Story* (London, 1956), 206; Cooper, op. cit. 349; and Bryant, 298ff.
38. Rowse, op. cit. 195–6.
39. Butcher, op. cit. 24–6; cf. King, op. cit. 401ff.
40. Sherwood, op. cit. 607.
41. Eisenhower, op. cit. 71.
42. *The Hinge of Fate,* 441; Harrison, op. cit. 29.
43. *The Hinge of Fate,* 270–71; Bryant, op. cit. 425.
44. Craven and Cate, op. cit. vol. I, 572; Marshall, op. cit. 155; *The Hinge of Fate,* 447.
45. Butcher, op. cit. 29–30.
46. Sherwood, op. cit. 609–10; cf. Bryant, op. cit. 423–5.
47. Stacey, op. cit. 317.
48. King, op. cit. 402; Butcher, op. cit. 29.
49. Harrison, op. cit. 30.
50. Sherwood, op. cit. 615; Bryant, op. cit. 427.
51. Stimson, op. cit. 426.
52. King, op. cit. 404; cf. Harrison, op. cit. 30; Craven and Cate, op. cit. vol. I, 572–3; and Leighton and Coakley, op. cit. 387.
53. Sherwood, op. cit. 611. Sir Alan Brooke, for one, seems to have known about Hopkins' switch to Africa at least ten days before this. Bryant, op. cit. 422–5.
54. Harrison, op. cit. 31.
55. Sherwood, op. cit. 612.
56. Butcher, op. cit. 82.
57. Morison Africa, 15.
58. *The Hinge of Fate,* 448.

Chapter 9. A SECOND FRONT

1. Henry Adams, *The Education of Henry Adams* (New York, 1931), 417.
2. Garthoff, op. cit. 130.
3. Brig. Gen. E. L. Spears, *Prelude to Victory,* with preface by Winston Churchill (London, 1939), 12–13; cf. Lloyd George, op. cit. vol. III, chap. XLVIII, vol. IV, 2316–32.
4. Blanche Dugdale, *Arthur James Balfour, First Earl of Balfour* (London, 1936), 129.
5. Butcher, op. cit. 33; cf. Cline, op. cit. 164; *Roosevelt Letters,* vol. II, 1313.
6. Richard Leighton, 'Preparation for Invasion,' *Military Affairs,* vol. X, no. 1 (Washington, Spring 1948), 4.
7. Robertson, op. cit. 319ff.; Bryant, op. cit. 398, 574, 626, 712–13.
8. Harrison, op. cit. 88; Leighton and Coakley, op. cit. 610.

9. Arnold, op. cit. 323; cf. Craven and Cate, op. cit. vol. i, 574–5; Matloff and Snell, op. cit. 317–22.
10. Craven and Cate, op. cit. vol. ii, 61.
11. Stacey, op. cit. 325–41; cf. Bryant, op. cit. 487.
12. Stimson, op. cit. 425–6.
13. Marshall, op. cit. 155.
14. Ingersoll, op. cit. 75.
15. Sherwood, op. cit. 600–615; cf. Stimson, op. cit. 424.
16. Sherwood, op. cit. 943.
17. H. A. De Weerd, 'Marshall — Organizer of Victory,' loc. cit. part ii, 14.
18. 'Marshall Scores "Back Door" Forces,' *The New York Times* (New York, May 19, 1949), 21.
19. Eisenhower, op. cit. 72.
20. Butcher, op. cit. 84; cf. Bryant, op. cit. 495.
21. *The Forrestal Diaries,* edited by Walter Millis with E. S. Duffield (New York, 1951), 17; cf. Morison Africa, 16; Bryant, op. cit. 652n.1; Sherwood, op. cit. 648; Butcher, op. cit. 54–5.
22. Eisenhower, op. cit. 72.
23. Harrison, op. cit. 29–30.
24. Butcher, op. cit. 50–51; Omar N. Bradley, *A Soldier's Story* (New York, 1951), 189.
25. *The Hinge of Fate,* 495; author's conversation with Gen. Smith, August 1949; cf. the implications behind Adm. Sir. Ernle Erle-Drax's advocacy of bombing in lieu of the invasion of France, 'The British War Effort,' *Journal of the Royal United Service Institution,* vol. xxxvii, 548 (London, Nov. 1942), 320.
26. Bryant, op. cit. 422–3.
27. Harrison, op. cit. 30.
28. Sherwood, op. cit. 343.
29. Bryant, op. cit. 412.
30. Harrison, op. cit. 32n.113.
31. *House of Commons Debates,* fifth series, vol. 385, 29.
32. *The Grand Alliance,* 380. This was in spite of the fact that in 1942 he had assured Stalin that in 1943 he could hope to send eight or ten times as much across the Channel as in the previous year. *The Hinge of Fate,* 478.
33. Harrison, op. cit. 32.
34. Sherwood, op. cit. 615; and cf. below.
35. Craven and Cate, op. cit. vol. i, 573.
36. Sherwood, op. cit. 954; cf. King, op. cit. 409, and for similar reactions to Mr. Churchill's diverse projects in World War I, see Spender and Asquith, op. cit. vol. ii, 163.
37. Craven and Cate, op. cit. vol. ii, 47; cf. Leighton and Coakley, op. cit. 456.
38. Cunningham, op. cit. 468.
39. Harrison, op. cit. 31–3.
40. Butcher, op. cit. 49–50.
41. Butcher, op. cit. 37–73; cf. King, op. cit. 410–11; Grigg, op. cit. 369–70.
42. *The Hinge of Fate,* 530.
43. Butcher, op. cit. 74; cf. Bryant, op. cit., 533–4.

44. Eisenhower, op. cit. 80; cf. Leighton and Coakley, op. cit. 420ff.
45. For the development and application of Calvinist dualism in this connection see Paul, op. cit. 62; Maurice Ashley, *Oliver Cromwell — The Conservative Dictator* (London, 1937), 107–8.
46. Gen. Mark Clark, *Calculated Risk* (New York, 1950), 31–52.
47. In which a fleet forced a strait to 'quell' a rebellious capital. *The Story of My Early Life, A Roving Commission,* 154.
48. Sherwood, op. cit. 628–9; Butcher, op. cit. 83.
49. *The Hinge of Fate,* 540.
50. Grigg, op. cit. 369.
51. *Onwards to Victory,* 129.
52. Eisenhower, op. cit. 156.
53. George Trevelyan, *England under Queen Anne, Blenheim* (London, 1930), 260; *Marlborough, His Life and Times,* vol. III, 100ff., vol. IV, 131ff.; Corbett, *England in the Mediterranean,* vol. II, chaps. XXX–XXXI.
54. Clark, op. cit. 43–4; Eisenhower, op. cit. 78–95; Leighton and Coakley, op. cit. 670ff.; *The Dawn of Liberation,* 116; Truman, op. cit. vol. I, 358; Leahy, op. cit. 133; Morgan, op. cit. 4–5.
55. *The Hinge of Fate,* 473–8.
56. Sherwood, op. cit. 617.
57. Of the First World War Mr. Churchill had already expatiated on 'the naked belly' of Austria in the Balkans. *The World Crisis 1918–1928, The Aftermath,* 474.
58. *The Hinge of Fate,* 482–3; cf. Sherwood, op. cit. 617–18.
59. Sherwood, op. cit. 617–20; cf. H. A. De Weerd, 'On Overestimating the Enemy,' *The Reporter,* Aug. 15, 1950, 26–7.
60. Sherwood, op. cit. 620; cf. *The Hinge of Fate,* 490–91, and Col. R. H. Beardon, 'Reply to "Does Defence Mean Defeat," ' *Journal Royal United Service Institution,* vol. LXXXIII, no. 531 (London, August 1938).
61. Edward Stettinius, Jr., *Roosevelt and the Russians — The Yalta Conference* (Garden City, 1949), 219ff.
62. *The Grand Alliance,* 380.
63. Bryant, op. cit. 460–65.
64. *The Hinge of Fate,* 491–2.
65. Matloff and Snell, op. cit. 39.
66. *House of Commons Debates,* fifth series, vol. 383, 95.
67. Lord Riddell, *More Pages from My Diary, 1908–1914* (London, 1934), 78.
68. *Onwards to Victory,* 35; Matloff and Snell, op. cit. 325–6.
69. Butcher, op. cit. 75–7; cf. Clark, op. cit. 51; Bryant, op. cit. 373, 505; Leighton and Coakley, op. cit. 422ff. In the Australian War History it is stated: 'Rather than take the risk that this blow at Gallipoli might not be delivered at all, Churchill's impatient desire — the father of his judgment — committed his country to delivering it at once under wrong conditions,' C. E. W. Bean, *The Official History of Australia in the War of 1914–1918,* vol. II, *The Story of Anzac from May 1915 to the Evacuation* (Sydney, 1937), 764. Cf. Sir John Fortescue, *Following The Drum,* 234; E. T. Raymond, *Uncensored Personalities* (New York, 1919), 109; Aspinwall-Oglander, op. cit. vol. I, 108; *Dardanelles Commission — First Report* (London, 1917); Richmond *Papers,* 96–108.

70. *The Hinge of Fate*, 528–9.
71. Sherwood, op. cit. 628.
72. Butcher, op. cit. 68.
73. Clark, op. cit. 45–7.
74. Bryant, op. cit. 502.
75. Stimson, op. cit. 426–8.
76. Butcher, op. cit. 61.
77. Nelson, op. cit. 254–6; Leighton and Coakley, op. cit. 682–3; Matloff and Snell, op. cit. 192ff.; Sherwood, op. cit. 554ff.; *Official Munitions Production of United States, July 1, 1940 — August 31, 1945*, prepared by the War Production Board and Civilian Production Administration (Washington, May 1, 1947), 99.
78. Puleston, op. cit. 161; Wilmot, op. cit. 42–114.
79. Morison Atlantic, 410–12.
80. Ross Munro, *Gauntlet to Overlord, The Story of the Canadian Army* (Toronto, 1946), 11; Stacey, op. cit. 327ff., 399ff.; Harrison, op. cit. 54; *The United States and World Sea Power*, 73ff.
81. Eric McDermott, S.J., 'The Elder Pitt and His Admirals and Generals,' *Military Affairs*, vol. xx, no. 2 (Washington, Summer 1956), 70; cf. Sir Julian Corbett, *England in the Seven Years War — A Study in Combined Strategy* (London, 1907), vol. i, 190ff.; O. A. Sherrard, *Lord Chatham — A War Minister in the Making* (London, 1952), 162ff.
82. Adm. Fisher, *Memories*, 73; Jeter Iseley and Philip Crowl, *The U. S. Marines and Amphibious War — Its Theory and Its Practice in the Pacific* (Princeton, 1951), 21; Driberg, op. cit. 288ff.
83. Lt. Col. Frank Osmanski, 'The Logistical Planning of Operation Overlord,' part iii, *Military Review*, vol. xxix, no. 10, Command and General Staff School (Fort Leavenworth, Kansas, Jan. 1950), 57.
84. Harrison, op. cit. 137–40.
85. Shulman, op. cit. 96.
86. *The Hinge of Fate*, 479; cf. Ingersoll, op. cit. 71–3.
87. Harrison, op. cit. 141ff.
88. Butcher, op. cit. 90–91.
89. Leighton and Coakley, op. cit. 484; cf. Harrison, op. cit. 35; Matloff and Snell, op. cit. 325–6.
90. Bryant, op. cit. 501.
91. Ibid. 373.
92. Sherwood, op. cit. 630; *The Hinge of Fate*, 545.
93. Eisenhower, op. cit. 195; cf. Sherwood, op. cit. 630.
94. 'Marshall Scores "Back Door" Forces,' loc. cit. 21.
95. Fuller, *The Second World War*, 240.
96. Sherwood, op. cit. 634.
97. Craven and Cate, op. cit. vol. ii, 63–4.
98. Sherwood, op. cit. 657; Bryant, op. cit. 571ff. This was also another tenet of the Kingfisher's Fishpond. See Adm. Fisher, *Correspondence*, vol. ii, 19, 385.
99. Harrison, op. cit. 35.
100. *The Hinge of Fate*, 650–51.
101. Rear Adm. H. E. Horan, 'Combat Operations 1939–1945,' *Journal Royal United Service Institute*, vol. xcviii, no. 589 (London, Feb. 1953), 62; Wilmot, op. cit. 118–19.

102. *The Hinge of Fate*, 649–51; cf. Harrison, op. cit. 35.
103. *The New York Times* (New York, Nov. 8, 1942), 1; cf. *The Hinge of Fate*, 492.
104. *The Hinge of Fate*, 434; *House of Commons Debates*, fifth series, vol. 392, 97.
105. *The Hinge of Fate*, 651ff.
106. Matloff and Snell, op. cit. 349; cf. Leighton and Coakley, 483ff.
107. *The Hinge of Fate*, 659–67; cf. Bryant, op. cit. 530–31; Beaverbrook, *Politicians and the War*, vol. i, 133; and MacNeill, op. cit. 213.
108. Sherwood, op. cit. 657.
109. Stimson, op. cit. 426; Bryant, op. cit. 525.
110. Sherwood, op. cit. 657–8.
111. Matloff and Snell, op. cit. 364ff., and see above.
112. Harrison, op. cit. 40.
113. Craven and Cate, op. cit. vol. ii, 285; Harrison, 37–8.
114. Bryant, op. cit. 528–35; 574.
115. Bryant, op. cit. 722–3.
116. Carlton Hayes, *Wartime Mission in Spain 1942–1945* (New York, 1945), 57–8.
117. Butcher, op. cit. 59; Eisenhower, op. cit. 93.
118. N.C.A., vol. v, 580; David Dallin, *Soviet Russia and the Far East* (New Haven, 1948), 176.
119. Belot, op. cit. 160.
120. Admiral Maugeri, not one of Ciano's admirers, suspects the Foreign Minister of *ex post facto* revisions of his famous diary in this instance. See Maugeri, op. cit. 88, and Ciano's *Diaries*, 528–9.
121. Martienssen, op. cit. 145.
122. Werner, op. cit. 167; Speidel, op. cit. 7–30; Halder, *Hitler als Feldherr*, 15.
123. Actually the Moroccan convoys sailed directly from the United States; the Gibraltar forces landed in Algeria. Belot, op. cit. 154–5.
124. Ciano's *Diaries*, 538–41; Belot, op. cit. 160.
125. Hull, op. cit. vol. ii, 1191.
126. Hayes, op. cit. 91; Hoare, op. cit. 170.
127. Langer, op. cit. 354.
128. Ibid. 322–38.
129. Blumentritt, op. cit. 168–73; cf. Hart, *The German Generals Talk*, 229–30; and Kesselring, op. cit. 139.
130. Wiskemann, op. cit. 290.
131. Hayes, op. cit. 92; Ciano's *Diaries*, 540; Fuller, op. cit. 241.
132. *Fuehrer Conferences, German Navy, 1942*, 126; cf. Martienssen, op. cit. 145–7.
133. *The Rommel Papers*, 361–7.
134. *Fuehrer Conferences, German Navy, 1943*, 53–5; Hinsley, op. cit. 226–7.
135. Lee, op. cit. 134; *The Hinge of Fate*, 745–51.
136. Leighton and Coakley, op. cit. 462, 558–84; *Closing the Ring*, 261; Clark, op. cit. 56; Matloff and Snell, op. cit. 309ff.; C. B. A. Behrens, *History of the Second World War, United Kingdom Civil Series*, edited by Sir Keith Hancock, *Merchant Shipping and the Demands of War* (London, 1955), chap. xiv.

137. Sherwood, op. cit. 734.
138. Peter Kleist, *Zwischen Hitler und Stalin, 1939–1945* (Bonn, 1950); Maxim Mourin, *Les Tentatives de paix dans la seconde guerre mondiale* (Paris, 1949), chap. vii; Bryant, op. cit. 531–5.

Chapter 10. ARCHITECT OF STALEMATE

1. Capt. A. T. Mahan, *The Life of Nelson — The Embodiment of the Sea Power of Great Britain* (Boston, 1897), vol. ii, 183; cf. Esher, op. cit. vol. iii, 210.
2. Capt. B. H. Liddell Hart, *The British Way in Warfare* (New York, 1933), 18.
3. Winston Churchill, *The World Crisis 1916–1918*, vol. i, 50–51.
4. Lloyd George, op. cit. vol. ii, 751.
5. Leighton and Coakley, op. cit. 683–6; Sherwood, op. cit. 554; Nelson, op. cit. 256; *The Dawn of Liberation*, 347; H. D. Hall, *History of the Second World War, United Kingdom Civil Series*, edited by Sir Keith Hancock, *North American Supply* (London, 1955), 357–8.
6. Leighton, loc. cit. 20; cf. K. R. Greenfield, R. Palmer, B. Wiley, 'Reorganization of Ground Troops for Combat,' *United States Army in World War II*, edited by K. R. Greenfield, *The Army Ground Forces, The Organization of Ground Combat Troops*, Dept. of the Army, Office of the Chief of Military History (Washington, 1947), 286; Bryant, op. cit. 658–9; Postan, op. cit. 348; and see below.
7. De Weerd, 'Marshall — Organizer of Victory,' loc. cit. 15.
8. John Miller, Jr., 'The Casablanca Conference and Pacific Strategy,' *Military Affairs* (Washington, Winter 1949), vol. xiii, no. 4, 210–13.
9. Sherwood, op. cit. 657.
10. Leighton and Coakley, op. cit. 662ff.; cf. Miller, loc. cit. 210–13.
11. *Closing the Ring*, v.
12. *The Hinge of Fate*, 540; cf. Butcher, op. cit. 311–12; *Onwards to Victory*, 122–3; Bryant, op. cit. 540n.1, 545, 620; Harrison, op. cit. 42–3.
13. Samuel Eliot Morison, *History of United States Naval Operations in World War II*, vol. ix, *Sicily, Salerno, Anzio January 1943–June 1944* (Boston, 1954), 7. Cited hereafter as Morison Mediterranean.
14. *The Hinge of Fate*, 664; cf. Arnold, op. cit. 388; and Sherwood, op. cit. 671. According to German records there were seven German divisions in Africa at this time and 204 on the Russian front. Stacey, op. cit. 314.
15. *The Hinge of Fate*, 935; cf. Bryant, op. cit. 530.
16. Bryant, op. cit. 544.
17. Sherwood, op. cit. 668–75.
18. *Their Finest Hour*, 5; cf. Samuel Eliot Morison, *History of United States Naval Operations in World War II*, vol. v, *The Struggle for Guadalcanal August 1942–February 1943* (Boston, 1944), 12, 334; 'The Building and Training of Infantry Divisions,' in R. Palmer, B. Wiley, and W. Keast, *United States Army in World War II*, edited by K. R. Greenfield, *The Army Ground Forces — The Procurement and*

Training of Ground Combat Troops, Office of the Chief of Military
History, Dept. of the Army (Washington, 1948), 492; Bryant, op. cit.
651–6.

19. As was indicated in Stalin's significant tribute to President Roosevelt.
Sherwood, op. cit. 869.

20. Harrison, op. cit. chap. i; Fuller, *The Second World War,* chaps. iii–viii;
Sherwood, op. cit. 333; Eisenhower, op. cit. chaps. viii–xii; Field Marshal Sir Henry Maitland Wilson, *Report by the Supreme Allied Commander Mediterranean to the Combined Chiefs of Staff on the Italian
Campaign, 8 January to 10 May 1944* (London, 1946), and see above.

21. See Eisenhower, op. cit. chaps. xiii–xxi, in preference to Churchill's
rather misleading conception of an engaged division in *Their Finest
Hour,* 5; cf. Shulman, op. cit. chap. xiii.

22. *Mr. Broderick's Army,* 33.

23. It is obvious why between June 1941 and December 1943 some 94 per
cent of German army casualties were incurred on her front with Russia.
Harrison, op. cit. 142n.49.

24. *History of the Second World War — United Kingdom Civil Series,*
edited by Sir Keith Hancock, *Statistical Digest of the War* (London,
1951), 13; Frances Hirst, *The Consequences of the War to Great Britain*
(London, 1934), 297; Pogue, op. cit. 544; *The Dawn of Liberation,*
148.

25. Capt. Peter Wright, *At the Supreme War Council* (London, 1921),
35–6.

26. Wing Commander J. C. Slessor, 'Gold Medal Essay,' *Journal Royal
United Service Institution,* vol. lxxxii, no. 527 (London, August 1937),
465–6. For post-war reiterations of this view see Brig. C. N. Barclay,
'British Generalship,' *Army Quarterly,* vol. lix, 2 (London, January
1950), 244 and Kingston-McCloughery, op. cit. 257–8.

27. See Halder's *Diary,* vol. i, 6 (August 14, 1939); Ciano's *Diplomatic
Papers,* 297–310; *Hitler's Table Talk,* 166–87, 253.

28. *Strategic Bombing Survey,* 2.

29. See Morgan, op. cit. 73; Butcher, op. cit. 447; Harris, op. cit. 192;
Kingston-McCloughery, op. cit. 122ff.; Richards, op. cit. 378–9.

30. George Pettee, 'Strategic Intelligence Part I: Faults and Errors in World
War II,' *Infantry Journal,* October 1946, vol. liv, no. 4, 31–3; cf.
Strategic Bombing Survey, 6–7.

31. Werner, op. cit. 178.

32. Fuller, op. cit. 230–31; Adm. D. V. Gallery, 'An Admiral Talks Back
to the Airmen,' *The Saturday Evening Post* (Philadelphia, June 25,
1949); Allen Dulles, *Germany's Underground* (New York, 1947), 168–79.

33. *The British Way in Warfare,* 97–8.

34. Oliver, op. cit. 262; cf. Friedel, op. cit. 370ff.

35. *Marlborough, His Life and Times,* vol. ii, 259. For the application of
this dictum to Mr. Churchill's truer prototype in war policy, David
Lloyd George, see Maj. Gen. Sir Frederick Maurice, 'Intrigues of the
War, Important Military Secrets Now Disclosed,' *Westminster Gazette*
(London, June 1922), 16ff.

36. *Marlborough, His Life and Times,* vol. iii, 126.

37. Arnold, op. cit. 483; Butler, op. cit. 270.

38. Vice Adm. Kurt Assmann, 'Hitler and the German Officer Corps,' *United States Naval Institute Proceedings* (Annapolis, May 1956), vol. 82, no. 5, 519; *Hitler's Table Talk*, xiv–xxx, 14; Halder, *Hitler als Feldherr*, 15–18; Bryant, op. cit. 445.
39. Guderian, op. cit. 397; cf. Forrestal, op. cit. 145.
40. Arnold, op. cit. 317; Stacey, op. cit. 61; Richmond *Papers*, 136; Rosinski, loc. cit. 30.
41. F. J. Hudleston, *Gentleman Johnny Burgoyne, Misadventures of an English General in the Revolution* (Indianapolis, 1927), 8.
42. Beaverbrook, *Politicians and the War*, vol. II, 26ff.; cf. Asquith, op. cit. vol. II, 55–82.
43. Morgan, op. cit. 81–102; Hart, *The German Generals Talk*, 231.
44. Callwell, *Field Marshal Sir Henry Wilson, His Life and Diaries*, vol. I, 193; cf. Bryant, op. cit. 322. See Field Marshal Viscount French of Ypres, *1914* (Boston, 1919), 308ff., for a favorable military view of Churchill on this issue.
45. E. T. Raymond, *Portraits of the Nineties* (New York, n.d.), 79; *The Story of My Early Life, A Roving Commission*, 162ff. An attitude reciprocated for several years by Mr. Churchill. Blunt, op. cit. part II, 270–76.
46. Rosinski, loc. cit. 30; cf. Richard Storry, 'Fascism in Japan,' *History Today* (London, November 1956), vol. VI, no. 11, 717ff.
47. Philip Guedalla, *Mr. Churchill*, 152; G. M. Young, *Stanley Baldwin* (London, 1952), 157; Viscount Templewood, *Nine Troubled Years* (London, 1954), 33; Richard Harding Davis, *Real Soldiers of Fortune* (New York, 1906); Philip Gibbs, *More That Must Be Told* (New York, 1921), 32–55; Cromwell, op. cit. vol. I, 359. For a similar opinion of Lord Randolph Churchill, see E. T. Raymond, op. cit. 104.
48. Bertie, op. cit. vol. II, 269–315. In the more favorable atmosphere of the 1930's, Capt. Liddell Hart openly regretted the absence of a negotiated peace in 1918. Such a peace, he felt, would have constituted the 'British' way of war rather than that of Clausewitz. *When Britain Goes to War, Adaptability and Mobility* (London, 1932), 45. And consistent with his earlier implicit advocacy of limited war, in 1939 David Lloyd George would also favor a negotiated peace with Hitler. Cooper, op. cit. 266–7; Beaverbrook, *Men and Power*, xxxvii–xxxviii, 308.
49. Fuller, *The Second World War*, 130–31; Donald Sanders, 'Stalin Plotted a Separate Peace,' *The American Mercury* (New York, 1947), 519–25; *Hitler's Table Talk*, 184; Dallin, op. cit. 178–81; Mourin, op. cit. chap. IX; Higgins, Loc. cit. 1202.
50. Fuller, op. cit. 215; Sherwood, op. cit. chap. xxx; Ehrman, op. cit. 555. It would be interesting to know in this connection just how much more the fear of a separate peace by Russia in 1943 evoked the final decision at Teheran for Overlord than had the earlier and far graver threat of her collapse. See, especially, Forrestal, op. cit. 283.
51. Grigg, op. cit. 394–5; cf. Thomas Jones, *A Diary with Letters, 1931–1950*, 505; Butler, op. cit. 562.
52. So far none of the recent Soviet attacks on Stalin's early war leadership have controverted the considerable weight of Western evidence showing his steady growth in military understanding. But there is no

doubt that, like Hitler's, Stalin's death rather than his crimes made him a momentarily useful scapegoat for his former subordinates. In addition to Sherwood's *Roosevelt and Hopkins*, see Maj. Gen. John Deane, *The Strange Alliance — The Story of Our Efforts of Wartime Cooperation with Russia* (New York, 1947), 41ff., 156ff., 224; and Krushchev, loc. cit. 12ff.

53. *Marlborough, His Life and Times*, vol. III, 95–6; cf. Adm. Sir R. H. Bacon, *The Life of Lord Fisher of Kilverstone* (London, 1929), vol. I, 207, vol. II, 142 ff.; J. E. Tyler, *The British Army and the Continent, 1904–1914* (London, 1937), 18ff.

54. Arthur Schlesinger, Jr., *The Vital Center, The Politics of Freedom* (Boston, 1949), 20ff.; cf. Isaiah Berlin's 'Mr. Churchill,' *The Atlantic Monthly*, September 1949, and Carl Burckhardt's 'On Reading Churchill's "Memoirs,"' *Measure*, Fall 1951, vol. II, no. 4.

55. Victor Germains, *The Tragedy of Winston Churchill* (London, 1931), 41; Sidney Hook, *The Hero in History — A Study in Limitation and Possibility* (London, 1945), 91–3; Lt. Col. C. à Court Repington, *The First World War, 1914–1918, Personal Experiences* (Boston, 1920), vol. I, 204, 352; Lord Riddell, *More Things That Matter* (London, 1925), 37; Bertie, op. cit. vol. I, 142ff.; Bryant, op. cit. 415–25; 'Flag Officer,' loc. cit. 261ff.; Lloyd George, op. cit. vol. III, 1067ff.; Richmond *Papers*, 100; Templewood, op. cit. 98; and especially the well-known indictment of Mr. Churchill's role at the Dardanelles by C. E. W. Bean, the official Australian historian, Bean, op. cit. vol. I, 20.

56. *The Grand Alliance*, 429.

57. Asquith, op. cit. vol. II, 55; cf. Stimson, op. cit. 430.

58. *The Hinge of Fate*, 825.

59. *The Story of My Early Life, A Roving Commission*, 116–17.

60. *Mr. Broderick's Army*, 23; Sir Edward Marsh, *A Number of People, A Book of Reminiscences* (London, 1939), 151; Lt. Col. T. S. Baldock, *Cromwell as a Soldier* (London, 1899), chap. XXIX; Maj. Gen. Sir Frederick Maurice, *Principles of Strategy — A Study of Application of the Principles of War* (New York, 1930), 150–51; *Marlborough, His Life and Times*, vol. III, 126.

61. Burke, op. cit. vol. III, 104–6.

62. Cromwell, op. cit. vol. I, 303–14. The distaste which Winston Churchill has expressed over Cromwell's tendencies toward absolute war, manifested in his murder of prisoners of war in Ireland, may be compared with Mr. Churchill's own acceptance of area bombing at the expense of Axis civilians when he, in turn, was faced with the cruel temptations of a prolonged and desperate struggle. Winston Churchill, *A History of the English Speaking Peoples*, vol. II, *The New World* (New York, 1956), 288ff.; *Amid These Storms*, 263.

63. *The World Crisis, 1915*, 37.

64. Gordon Craig, 'Delbruck: The Military Historian,' *Makers of Modern Strategy*, 272ff. It is notable that when in the autumn of 1942 Hitler adopted a strategy of exhaustion, it was because he no longer saw a more direct means of obtaining victory.

65. Victor Germains, 'The Military Lessons of the War,' *Contemporary Review*, no. 896 (London, August 1940), 154; cf. Irving Gibson, 'Maginot

and Liddell Hart: The Doctrine of Defense,' *Makers of Modern Strategy,* 381–3; *The Gathering Storm,* 415–16; Ellis, op. cit. 2; Capt. B. H. Liddell Hart, *The Times,* loc. cit.; de Guingand, op. cit. 112.

66. Capt. H. M. Curteis, 'The Doctrine of Limited Liability,' *Journal Royal United Service Institution,* vol. LXXXIII, no. 532 (London, November 1938), 697; cf. *Mr. Broderick's War,* 23.

67. *The World Crisis, 1915,* 37.

68. Rothfels, loc. cit. *Makers of Modern Strategy,* 111; cf. Clausewitz, op. cit. vol. III, 210.

69. *The World Crisis, 1915,* 538; cf. Lt. Col. C. à Court Repington, 'Churchillian Strategy,' *Blackwoods,* vol. CCXIV (London, July–December 1923), 835; Robertson, op. cit. 277.

70. Viscount Grey of Fallodon, *Twenty-five Years 1892–1916* (New York, 1925), 74–5; cf. Crutwell, op. cit. 90, and Callwell, op. cit. vol. I, 215–16.

71. *The World Crisis, 1911–1914,* 253; *The World Crisis, 1916–1918,* vol. II, 267; *While England Slept,* 142–3. For the case for Haig's battles along the Somme as opposed to Mr. Churchill's rather one-sided presentation of this basic issue, see Haig, op cit. 152–8; Sir Charles Oman in *The World Crisis by Winston Churchill — A Criticism,* chap. II, 'The German Losses on the Somme, July–December 1916'; Ralph Lutz, *The Causes of the German Collapse in 1918,* Hoover War Library Publication no. 4 (Stamford, 1934); Gen. Sir Frederick Maurice, *The Last Four Months, How The War Was Won* (Boston, 1919), 218ff.; Brig. Sir James Edmonds, 'Was Germany Defeated in 1918?', *Journal Royal United Service Institution,* vol. LXXXIII, no. 530 (London, May 1938), 394ff. Duff Cooper, *Haig* (Garden City, 1936), 97–121, 159–76.

72. *The World Crisis, 1915,* 36; cf. Lt. Col. Alfred Burne, *Strategy in World War II, A Strategical Examination of Land Operations* (Harrisburg, Penn., 1947), 22–3; cf. Morgan, op. cit. 25, 87.

73. Rothfels, loc. cit. *Makers of Modern Strategy,* 107; cf. *On War,* vol. III, 209–12, and Callwell, op. cit. vol. I, 215–16.

74. Only after the invasion of Sicily did the Prime Minister impart to the Commons the opinion that 'a decision by the Italian Government and people will not seriously affect the general course of the war. Still less will it alter its ultimate result. . . .' *House of Commons Debates,* fifth series, vol. 391, 1398. For parallel conclusions regarding Italy's role in the First World War, see a review by Herman Wendt, 'The Military Importance of the Italian Theatre of War,' *Army Quarterly,* vol. XXI, no. 1 (London, April 1938), 50ff.; and Haig's Memorandum, Lloyd George, op. cit. vol. IV, 2435–9.

75. Gen. Sir Hastings Ismay, 'Letter to the Editor,' *The Daily Telegraph and Morning Post* (London, Nov. 26, 1948).

76. Bacon, op. cit. vol. II, 258; cf. Beaverbrook, *Politicians and the War,* vol. I, 80.

77. Leahy, op. cit. 157–8; cf. Butcher, op. cit. 442ff.; Eisenhower, op. cit. 138. That is, the invasion to be entitled Overlord, as Roundup was already scuttled. Brooke still disagrees with Eisenhower's understanding. Bryant, op. cit. 636–40.

78. Ehrman, op. cit. 107ff., 176ff.; cf. Hanson Baldwin, 'Churchill Was

Right,' *The Atlantic Monthly* (July 1954), 29ff.; and Bryant, op. cit. 361, 636.

79. Eisenhower, op. cit. 167–8.
80. Butcher, op. cit. 319.
81. Ehrman, op. cit. 108–9. Ehrman's argument in the official British War History on behalf of Mr. Churchill's sincerity toward Overlord would appear to rest chiefly upon his refusal to consider just what the Prime Minister meant by the term. To be sure, with his deep understanding of Overlord as the 'keystone of the arch of Anglo-American cooperation,' Mr. Churchill could never have been so crude or literal as to have accepted Smuts' suggestion for a frank opposition to the cross-Channel operation so late as 1944. Ehrman, op. cit. 112ff.
82. Stimson, op. cit. 433–7. For Sir Alan Brooke's post-war effort to explain away Stimson's reactions, see Bryant, op. cit. 674ff.
83. Guedalla, *The Duke*, 169–70.
84. Hudleston, op. cit. 8.
85. Morgan, op. cit. 112; cf. Sir John Fortescue, *A History of the British Army* (London, 1935), vol. II, 305ff., 577ff.; Lawrence Gipson, *The Great War for the Empire*, vol. 2, *The Victorious Years 1758–1760* (New York, 1949), chaps. I, IV; *The United States and World Sea Power*, 73ff., 215ff.
86. See above and also Friedel, op. cit. 310ff.; Bryant, op. cit. 619.
87. *The Grand Alliance*, 673; cf. Winston Churchill, 'The American Mind and Ours,' *The Strand Magazine*, vol. LXXXII (London, August 1931), 150; *The Story of My Early Life, A Roving Commission*, 28; Ehrman, op. cit. vol. I, 115ff.; Bryant, op. cit. 25, 201, 618.
88. William Wordsworth in F. V. Maccunn, *The Contemporary English View of Napoleon* (London, 1914), 232.
89. Morgan, op. cit. 25–70; cf. Clausewitz, *On War*, vol. III, 154; Robertson, op. cit. 319ff.; Ehrman, op. cit. 357.
90. Eisenhower, op. cit. 157–60; cf. Leighton and Coakley, op. cit. 139; Bryant, op. cit. 574, 712–13; Richmond *Papers*, 92.
91. Harrison, op. cit. 42; Leighton and Coakley, op. cit. 673; Bryant, op. cit. 619.
92. *The Grand Alliance*, 102, 540.
93. Harrison, op. cit. chap. I. As the Italian Army Chief of Staff also recognized in a warning to Mussolini in May 1943. *Mémoires de Mussolini 1942–1943* (Paris, 1948), 38.
94. Marshall, op. cit. 159; cf. Callwell, op. cit. vol. I, 249; Bryant, op. cit. 673; and Leighton and Coakley, op. cit. 673.
95. Fuller, op. cit. 267; Badoglio, op. cit. 98; Eisenhower, op. cit. 159–60; Kesselring, op. cit. 159.
96. Morgan, op. cit. 6; *The Hinge of Fate*, 678; *Closing the Ring*, 24; Bryant, op. cit. 557ff., 670n.1.
97. Sherwood, op. cit. 688–9; Leighton and Coakley, op. cit. 672–3.
98. *While England Slept*, 311.
99. Fuller, op. cit. 268; cf. Clark, op. cit. 2; and Kesselring, op. cit. 198.
100. It is hardly surprising that Sir Arthur Bryant has finally discovered a happier synonym for an 'eccentric' strategy in his term 'concentric.' Bryant, op. cit. 670.

101. Arnold, op. cit. 278.
102. Eisenhower, op. cit. 61, 241; cf. Bryant, op. cit. 302n.1, 336–50; Butler, op. cit. 249–50, 310–11; Roskill, op. cit. 202; Haldane, *An Autobiography*, 246ff.; Playfair, op. cit. vol. i, 200–201.
103. Asquith, op. cit. vol. ii, 67–100; Richmond *Papers*, 254, 363.
104. Sherwood, op. cit. 257.
105. Sydenham of Combe, *The World Crisis — A Criticism*, 20; cf. *The Hinge of Fate*, 89ff.; and Byrum Carter, *The Office of Prime Minister* (Princeton, 1956), 316ff.
106. *Onwards to Victory*, 127–30; cf. John Ehrman, *Grand Strategy*, vol. vi, *October 1944–August 1945* (London, 1956), 322–34.
107. *Their Finest Hour*, 21; cf. Bacon, op. cit. vol. ii, chaps. xix and xx and especially postscript no. 1.
108. *The Gathering Storm*, 627; Bryant, op. cit. 21–6, 320; Butler, op. cit. 561–2.
109. De Weerd, *Makers of Modern Strategy*, 289; Lloyd George, op. cit. vol. vi, 3404ff.; Winston Churchill, 'Men Who Have Influenced or Impressed Me,' *The Strand Magazine*, vol. lxxxi (London, February 1931), 140–41; Josephus Daniels, *The Wilson Era — Years of War and After, 1917–1923* (Chapel Hill, 1946), 332; Georges Clemenceau, *Grandeur and Misery of Victory* (London, 1930), chap. vii; Beaverbrook, *Men and Power*, chap. vi; Adm. Fisher, *Correspondence*, vol. ii, 214ff.; Butler, op. cit. 529–31.
110. A conflict foreshadowed so early as 1911 with the British expert and by 1917 with the U. S. expert. Elting Morison, *Admiral Sims and the Modern American Navy* (Boston, 1942), 404–5; Butler, op. cit. 130; Bryant, op. cit. 299; Sir Frederick Maurice, *Haldane 1856–1915, The Life of Viscount Haldane of Cloan* (London, 1937), 284ff.; Adm. Fisher, *Correspondence*, vol. ii, 443.
111. Harris, op. cit. 153.
112. Guedalla, *Mr. Churchill*, 312ff.; Lloyd George, op. cit. vol. ii, 640ff., vol. iv, 1846.
113. *The Gathering Storm*, 411; *The World Crisis* (revised edition), chaps. v and xix; René Kraus, *Winston Churchill: A Biography* (Philadelphia, 1940), 163–82; Adm. Fisher, *Correspondence*, vol. ii, 407.
114. *On War*, vol. iii, 125.
115. Mr. Churchill probably did not help his cause at this time by advocating the logistic absurdity of a last-minute switch of Anvil from the Riviera to Bordeaux. Ehrman, op. cit. vol. v, 363–4.
116. See Eisenhower, op. cit. 291–4, and Clark, op. cit. 3, for differing U. S. Army opinions on this issue; and *Triumph and Tragedy*, vol. v, book i, chaps. iv–x and 691–723; Ehrman, op. cit. vol. v, 349–57; Pogue, op. cit. chaps. xi, xii; Lukacs, op. cit. 533ff.; Nicholas Kallay, *Hungarian Premier, A Personal Account of a Nation's Struggle in the Second World War* (New York, 1954), chap. xvi.
117. Pogue, op. cit. chaps. xxiii–xxiv; Eisenhower, op. cit. 194, 396–402; cf. *Triumph and Tragedy*, book ii, chaps. viii–xi; Edward Collins, 'Clausewitz and Democracy's Modern War,' *Military Affairs*, xix, no. 1 (Washington, Spring 1955), 15ff.; Esher, op. cit. vol. iv, 132–7; Truman, op. cit. vol. i, 211ff.; Forrestal, op. cit. 264–77, 496.

118. Craig, op. cit. 204ff.
119. *Closing the Ring*, 311; cf. Leahy, op. cit. 153–63; Bryant, op. cit. 415, 702ff.; Stimson, op. cit. 428–39; Eisenhower, op. cit. 138–67; and *Triumph and Tragedy*, 267.
120. 'Marshall Decries Stand by MacArthur,' *The New York Times* (New York, May 9, 1951), 14; cf. Bryant, op. cit. 414.
121. Sherwood, op. cit. 780–81.
122. See Byron Dexter, 'Clausewitz and Soviet Strategy,' *Foreign Affairs* (October 1950), 43–7; Wilmot, op. cit. 711, and Arnold, op. cit. 481, for interpretations along this line.
123. In the spring of 1942 British war production equaled American; by 1944 the United States was producing approximately six times as much as the sadly overburdened British war economy. Postan, op. cit. 244.
124. Sherwood, op. cit. 779; George Fischer, *Soviet Opposition to Stalin — A Case Study in World War II* (Cambridge, Mass., 1952).
125. *The Story of My Early Life, A Roving Commission*, 331.

Appendix

WAR PLANS

These definitions are as accurate as possible within the limitations of unclassified sources.

ABC–1:   Agreement concluded March 27, 1941, between the United States and Britain, designed to emphasize a European rather than an Asiatic offensive if the United States entered the war.

ABC–2:   Air side of above agreement designed to increase U.S. bomber production and employ much of it in Britain.

AIDA: German plan for an assault of the Afrika Korps against Egypt in late spring 1942.

ALBION: German cover plan for Barbarossa in 1941, involving an ostensible threat against Britain.

ANVIL: Allied plan to invade southern France from the Mediterranean in summer 1944.

ARCADIA: The first general Anglo-American conference after Pearl Harbor, meeting in Washington, December 1941–January 1942.

ATTILA: German plan of 1941–42 to seize unoccupied France in the event of an Allied threat in French North Africa.

AUFBAU OST: Preliminary German plan of summer 1940 for attacking Russia in 1941.

BARBAROSSA: Final German plan of December 1940 to attack Russia in May 1941.

BOLERO: American logistic build-up in Britain to sustain a cross-Channel operation at any date.

251

D or DOG: U. S. Navy plan of autumn 1940 to emphasize the Atlantic rather than the Pacific theater in the event of war.

EAST WIND RAIN: Japanese plan to attack the United States in December 1941.

FELIX: German plan of autumn 1940 to aid Spanish assault on Gibraltar in January 1941.

GREAT PLAN: German plan of spring 1942 which included both plan HERCULES to seize Malta and plan AIDA to attack Egypt in that order.

GRAY: U. S. plan to occupy the Azores in spring of 1941.

GYMNAST: Allied plan to invade French North Africa in 1942. This name was changed to TORCH in July 1942.

HARLEQUIN: Army side of a simulated British threat against France staged in the Channel in September 1943.

HERCULES: German plan to seize Malta in spring 1942.

INFLUX: British plan to invade Sicily in 1941.

JUPITER: British plan to invade Norway in 1942.

MAGNET: U. S. plan of December 1941 to send American troops to Northern Ireland to relieve British troops there for duty in the Middle East.

MANDIBLES: British plan to seize Rhodes in spring 1941.

MARITA: German plan of December 1940, involving the invasion of frequently altered targets in the Balkans and Middle East, but finally including Greece and Yugoslavia in the spring of 1941.

MENACE: British-de Gaullist plan to seize Dakar and French West Africa in September 1940.

MILLENNIUM: Evidently a British Army plan for a cross-Channel invasion in 1942.

OVERLORD: Final Allied cross-Channel invasion of June 1944.

PILGRIM: British plan to seize the Canaries in 1941 if the Germans entered Spain.

POT-OF-GOLD: U.S. plan to prevent German attack on or infiltration of Brazil in spring 1940.

RAINBOW NO. 5: U. S. plan to emphasize the defeat of the European Axis in collaboration with Britain and, if possible, with France.

RANKIN: British variant plans for a cross-Channel invasion in 1943 in the event of a distintegration of German power.

ROUNDUP: Allied plan to cross the Channel in strength in May 1943.

SEA-LION: German plan for the invasion of Britain in summer 1940.

SLEDGEHAMMER: Allied plan to cross the Channel in September 1942.

SUNFLOWER: First German plan for the embryonic Afrika Korps to aid the Italians in Libya in early 1941.

SUPER-GYMNAST: Early Allied plan to occupy French North Africa in the spring of 1942.

WHIPCORD: British plan to invade Sicily in 1942.

WORKSHOP: British plan to seize Pantelleria in 1941.

BIBLIOGRAPHY

Bibliographical note: *This bibliography does not pretend to be exhaustive in material on the Axis, especially in the great wealth of primary sources in Italian. The most serious omission on the Allied side involves the still unpublished third and fourth volumes on Grand Strategy of the British Official History of the Second World War. These volumes may modify judgments of Sir Winston Churchill's policies to some extent. The author has, of course, seen material and heard interpretations which he is not at liberty to cite directly, but which have influenced him considerably.*

Acknowledgment for their assistance or advice is made to Isaiah Berlin, Gordon Craig, Wesley Craven, David Dallin, the late E. M. Earle, Victor Hunt, Gerritt Judd, Captain T. B. Kittredge, Basil Rauch, Herbert Rosinski, Arthur Schlesinger, Jr., the late Robert Sherwood, General Walter Bedell Smith, Hans Trefousse, and Nathaniel Weyl.

I. OFFICIAL AND SEMI-OFFICIAL HISTORIES, DOCUMENTS, AND PAPERS

Aspinwall-Oglander, Brigadier C. F. *History of the Great War, Military Operations: Gallipoli.* London: Heinemann, 1929.

Bean, C. E. W. *The Official History of Australia in the War of 1914–1918.* Sydney: Angus and Robertson, 1937.

Behrens, C. B. A. *History of the Second World War, United Kingdom Civil Series.* Edited by Sir Keith Hancock. *Merchant Shipping and the Demands of War.* London: H.M. Stationery Office and Longmans, Green, 1955.

Bulletins U. S. Department of State. Washington: U. S. Govt. Printing Office, 1946.

Butler, J. R. M. *History of the Second World War, United Kingdom Military Series.* Edited by J. R. M. Butler. *Grand Strategy,* vol. ii, *September 1939–June 1941.* London: H.M. Stationery Office, 1957.

Ciano, Count Galeazzo. *Diplomatic Papers.* Edited by Malcolm Muggeridge. London: Odhams Press, 1948.

Cline, Ray. *United States Army in World War II.* Edited by K. R. Greenfield. *The War Department, Washington Command Post: The Operations Division,* Office of the Chief of Military History, Dept. of the Army. Washington: U. S. Govt. Printing Office, 1951.

Craven, Wesley and Cate, James. *The Army Air Forces in World War II.* vol. i, *Plans and Early Operations, January 1939 to August 1942;*

vol. II, *Europe: Torch to Pointblank, August 1942 to December 1943.* Chicago: University of Chicago Press, 1948–49.

Dardanelles Commission, First Report of. London: H.M. Stationery Office: By Authority, 1917.

Documents on German Foreign Policy 1918–1945 from the Archives of the German Foreign Ministry, Series D. vol. I, *From Neurath to Ribbentrop;* vol. II, *Germany and Czechoslovakia 1937–1938;* vol. III, *Germany and the Spanish Civil War 1936–1939;* vol. VIII, *The War Years September 4, 1939–March 18, 1940.* Washington: U. S. Dept. of State, U. S. Govt. Printing Office, 1949–54.

Documents on International Affairs 1939–1946. Edited by the Royal Institute of International Affairs under Arnold Toynbee. New York: Oxford University Press, 1951.

Ehrman, John. *History of the Second World War, United Kingdom Military Series.* Edited by J. R. M. Butler. *Grand Strategy,* vol. V, *August 1943–September 1944;* vol. VI, *October 1944–August 1945.* London: H.M. Stationery Office, 1956.

Ellis, Major L. F. *History of the Second World War, United Kingdom Military Series.* Edited by J. R. M. Butler. *The War in France and Flanders 1939–1940.* London: H.M. Stationery Office, 1953.

Falsifactors of History. Soviet Information Bureau, Soviet Embassy. Washington: February 1948.

Fortescue, Sir John. *A History of the British Army.* vols. I–XIII, London: Macmillan, 1910–35.

Fuehrer Conferences: German Navy (Abbrev.). *Fuehrer Conferences on Matters Dealing with the German Navy.* Naval Intelligence, Navy Dept. Washington: U. S. Govt. Printing Office, 1947.

Greenfield, Kent, Palmer, Robert, and Wiley, Bell. *United States Army in World War II.* Edited K. R. Greenfield. *The Army Ground Forces, The Organization of the Ground Combat Troops.* Office of the Chief of Military History (formerly Historical Division), Dept. of the Army. Washington: U. S. Govt. Printing Office, 1947.

Hall, H. D. *History of the Second World War, United Kingdom Civil Series.* Edited by Sir Keith Hancock. *North American Supply.* London: H.M. Stationery Office and Longmans, Green, 1955.

Hancock, W. K., and Gowing, W. W. *History of the Second World War, United Kingdom Civil Series.* Edited by Sir Keith Hancock. *British War Economy.* London: H.M. Stationery Office and Longmans, Green, 1949.

Harrison, Gordon. *United States Army in World War II.* Edited by K. R. Greenfield. *The European Theater of Operations, The Cross-Channel Attack.* Office of the Chief of Military History, Dept. of the Army. Washington: U. S. Govt. Printing Office, 1951.

Hitler Directs His War. The Secret Records of the Daily Military Conferences. Edited by Felix Gilbert from manuscript, University of Pennsylvania Library. New York: Oxford University Press, 1950.

Hitler's Table Talk. Introduced by H. B. Trevor-Roper. London: Weidenfeld and Nicolson, 1953.

Leighton, Richard, and Coakley, Robert. *The United States Army in World War II.* Edited by K. R. Greenfield. *The War Department, Global*

Logistics and Strategy 1940–1943. Office of the Chief of Military History, Dept. of the Army. Washington: U. S. Govt. Printing Office, 1955.

Les Lettres secrètes échangées par Hitler et Mussolini. Editions du Pavois. Paris, 1946.

Long, Gavin. *Greece, Crete and Syria.* Australian War Memorial. Canberra: 1954.

Marshall, General of the Army George C. (cited under only), General of the Army H. H. Arnold, Fleet Admiral Ernest J. King. *The War Reports, 1939–1945.* New York: Lippincott, 1947.

Matloff, Maurice, and Snell, Edwin. *United States Army in World War II.* Edited by K. R. Greenfield. *The War Department, Strategic Planning for Coalition Warfare 1941–1942.* Office of the Chief of Military History, Dept. of the Army. Washington: U. S. Govt. Printing Office, 1953.

Morison, Samuel Eliot (titles abbreviated in text). *History of United States Naval Operations in World War II.* vol. i, *The Battle of the Atlantic, September 1939–May 1943;* vol. ii, *Operations in North African Waters, October 1942–June 1943;* vol. iii, *The Rising Sun in the Pacific, 1931–April 1942;* vol. v, *The Struggle for Guadalcanal, August 1942–February 1943;* vol. ix, *Sicily, Salerno, Anzio, January 1943–June 1944.* Boston: Little, Brown, 1947–54.

N.C.A. (Abbrev.). *Nazi Conspiracy and Aggression.* Office of the United States Chief of Counsel for Prosecution of Axis Criminality (See War Trials). Washington: U. S. Govt. Printing Office, 1946.

N-S.R. (Abbrev.). *Nazi-Soviet Relations 1939–1941.* Documents from the Archives of the German Foreign Office. Edited by Raymond Sontag and James Beddie. Dept. of State. Washington: U. S. Govt. Printing Office, 1948.

O'Brien, Terence. *History of the Second World War, United Kingdom Civil Series.* Edited by Sir Keith Hancock. *Civil Defense.* London: H.M. Stationery Office and Longmans, Green, 1955.

Official Munition Production of the United States July 1, 1940–August 31, 1945. Prepared by the War Production Board and Civilian Production Administration. Washington: May 1, 1947.

Palmer, Robert. *Reorganization of Ground Troops for Combat.* See Greenfield, Palmer, and Wiley.

Palmer, R., Wiley, B., and Keast, W. *United States Army in World War II.* Edited by K. R. Greenfield. *The Army Ground Forces, Procurement and Training of the Ground Combat Troops.* Office of the Chief of Military History (formerly Historical Division), Dept. of the Army. Washington: U. S. Govt. Printing Office, 1947.

Pearl Harbor Attack. Hearings before the Joint Committee in Investigation of the Pearl Harbor Attack. First Session, 79th Congress. Washington: U. S. Govt. Printing Office, 1946.

Playfair, Major General I.S.O., with Stitt, Commander G.M.S., Molony, Brigadier C.J.C., and Toomer, Air Vice-Marshall S.E. *History of the Second World War, United Kingdom Military Series.* Edited by J. R. M. Butler. *The Mediterranean and Middle East.* Vol. i, *The*

Early Successes against Italy (to May 1941); vol. II, authors as above except Flynn, Captain F.C., instead of Stitt, Commander G.M.S., *The Germans Come to the Help of Their Ally, 1941.* London: H.M. Stationery Office, 1954–56.

Pogue, Forrest. *United States Army in World War II.* Edited by K. R. Greenfield. *The European Theater of Operations, The Supreme Command.* Office of the Chief of Military History, Dept. of the Army. Washington: U. S. Govt. Printing Office, 1954.

Postan, M. M. *History of the Second World War, United Kingdom Civil Series.* Edited by Sir Keith Hancock. *British War Production.* London: H.M. Stationery Office and Longmans, Green, 1952.

Richards, Denis. *Royal Air Force 1939–1945,* vol. I, *The Fight at Odds;* vol. II, Richards, Denis, with Saunders, Hilary St. George, *The Fight Avails.* London: H.M. Stationery Office, 1953–54.

Romanus, Charles, and Sunderland, Riley. *United States Army in World War II.* Edited by K. R. Greenfield. *China-Burma-India Theater, Stilwell's Mission to China.* Office of the Chief of Military History, Dept. of the Army. Washington: U.S. Govt. Printing Office, 1953.

Roskill, Captain S. W. *History of the Second World War, United Kingdom Military Series.* Edited by J. R. M. Butler. *The War at Sea,* vol. I, *The Defensive.* London: H.M. Stationery Office, 1954.

Ruppenthal, Roland. *United States Army in World War II.* Edited by K. R. Greenfield. *The European Theater of Operations, Logistical Support of the Armies,* vol. I, *May 1941–September 1944.* Office of the Chief of Military History, Dept. of the Army. Washington: U. S. Govt. Printing Office, 1953.

Stacey, Colonel C. P. *Official History of the Canadian Army in the Second World War,* vol. I, *Six Years of War — The Army in Canada, Britain and the Pacific.* Ottawa: Queens Printer, 1955.

Statistical Digest of the War. History of the Second World War, United Kingdom Civil Series. Edited by Sir Keith Hancock. London: H.M. Stationery Office and Longmans, Green, 1951.

Statistics Relating to the War Effort of the United Kingdom. Presented by the Prime Minister to Parliament. London: H.M. Stationery Office, 1944.

Strategic Bombing Survey (Abbrev.). *The United States Strategic Bombing Survey, The Effects of Strategic Bombing on the German War Economy.* Overall Economic Effects Division. Washington: U. S. Govt. Printing Office, 1945.

The German Campaigns in the Balkans (Spring 1941). Dept. of the Army, Historical Study. Washington: U. S. Govt. Printing Office, November 1953.

War Trials (Abbrev.). *Trial of the Major War Criminals before the International Military Tribunal.* Secretariat of the Tribunal. Nuremberg: 1947–48 (See N.C.A.).

Watson, Mark. *United States Army in World War II.* Edited by K. R. Greenfield. *The War Department, Chief of Staff: Prewar Plans and Preparations.* Office of the Chief of Military History, Dept. of the Army. Washington: U. S. Govt. Printing Office, 1950.

Wellington, the Duke of. *The Dispatches of Field Marshal the Duke of Wellington during His Various Campaigns 1799–1818.* Compiled by Lieutenant Colonel Gurwood. London: J. Murray, 1837–39.
Wiley, Bell. 'The Building and Training of Infantry Divisions.' See Palmer, Wiley, and Keast.
Wilson, Field Marshal Sir Henry Maitland. *Report by the Supreme Allied Commander Mediterranean to the Combined Chiefs of Staff on the Italian Campaign, 8 January to 10 May 1944.* London: H.M. Stationery Office, 1946.

II. BOUND SPEECHES

Burke, Edmund. *Select Works.* Edited by E. J. Payne. Oxford: Clarendon Press, 1892.
Churchill, Winston. *Arms and the Covenant.* London: Harrap, 1938.
———. *Blood, Sweat and Tears.* With preface and notes by Randolph Churchill. New York: Putnam, 1941.
———. *Mr. Broderick's Army.* London: Arthur Humphreys, 1903.
———. *Onwards to Victory.* Compiled by Charles Eade. Boston: Little, Brown, 1944.
———. *Secret Session Speeches.* New York: Simon and Schuster, 1946.
———. *Step by Step 1936–1939.* London: Odhams Press, 1949.
———. *The Dawn of Liberation.* Compiled by Charles Eade. Boston: Little, Brown, 1945.
———. *The End of the Beginning.* Compiled by Charles Eade. Boston: Little, Brown, 1943.
———. *The Unrelenting Struggle.* Compiled by Charles Eade. Boston: Little, Brown, 1942.
———. *The War Speeches.* In three volumes. Compiled by Charles Eade. Cambridge, Mass.: Houghton Mifflin, 1953.
———. *While England Slept. A Survey of World Affairs.* New York: Putnam, 1938.
———. *The Parliamentary Debates: House of Commons 1901–1945.*
The Writings and Speeches of Oliver Cromwell, vols. I–III. Edited by W. C. Abbott with the assistance of C. D. Crane. Cambridge: Harvard University Press, 1939.
Hitler, Adolf. *My New Order, Speeches 1922–1941.* Edited by Raoul de Roussey de Sales. New York: Reynal and Hitchcock, 1941.
Roosevelt Papers (Abbrev.). *The Public Papers and Addresses of Franklin D. Roosevelt.* Edited and compiled by Samuel Rosenman. New York: Harper, 1950.

III. MEMOIRS, DIARIES, AUTOBIOGRAPHY, AND PERSONAL CORRESPONDENCE

Adams, Henry. *The Education of Henry Adams.* New York: Random House, Modern Library Edition, 1931.

Amery, L. S. *My Political Life.* vol. i, *England before the Storm 1896–1914;* vol. ii, *War and Peace 1914–1929;* vol. iii, *The Unforgiving Years 1929–1940.* London: Hutchinson, 1953–55.

———. 'The Great War Leaders,' *Servant of Crown and Commonwealth.* London: Cassell, 1954.

Arnold, General of the Army H. H. *Global Mission.* New York: Harper, 1949.

Ashmead-Bartlett, Ellis. *The Uncensored Dardanelles.* London: Hutchinson, 1928.

Asquith, Herbert Henry, Earl of Oxford and Asquith (cited as Asquith). *Memoirs and Reflections 1852–1927.* Boston: Little, Brown, 1928.

Attlee, C. R. *As It Happened.* London: Heinemann, 1954.

Badoglio, Marshall Pietro. *Italy in the Second World War — Memoirs and Documents.* New York: Oxford University Press, 1948.

The Diary of Lord Bertie of Thane 1914–1918. Edited by Lady Algernon Lennox. New York: George Doran, undated.

Beaverbrook, Lord. *Men and Power, 1917–1918.* London: Hutchinson, 1956.

———. *Politicians and the War, 1914–1916.* vol. i, London: Thornton Butterworth, 1928. Vol. ii, London: The Lane Publications, 1932.

Blount, Wilfred. *My Diaries — Being a Personal Narrative of Events 1888–1914,* parts i and ii. New York: Knopf, 1921.

Brabazon of Tara, Lord. *The Brabazon Story.* London: Heinemann, 1956.

Bradley, General of the Army Omar N. *A Soldier's Story.* New York: Holt, 1951.

Butcher, Captain Harry. *My Three Years with Eisenhower, The Personal Diary of Captain Harry C. Butcher, U.S.N.R., Naval Aide to General Eisenhower, 1942 to 1945.* New York: Simon and Schuster, 1946.

Cavallero, General Ugo. *Commando Supremo, diario 1940–1943 del Capo di Stato.* Bologna: Cappelli, 1948.

Churchill, Winston. *Amid These Storms — Thoughts and Adventures.* New York: Scribner, 1932.

———. *The Second World War:* vol. i, *The Gathering Storm;* vol. ii, *Their Finest Hour;* vol. iii, *The Grand Alliance;* vol. iv, *The Hinge of Fate;* vol. v, *Closing the Ring;* vol. vi, *Triumph and Tragedy.* Boston: Houghton Mifflin, 1948–53.

———. *The Story of My Early Life, A Roving Commission.* New York: Scribner, 1945.

———. *The World Crisis,* vols. i–v. New York: Scribner, 1923–29; revised edition in one vol. New York: Scribner, 1949.

Ciano, Count Galeazzo. *Die Stellung italiens zum internationales Konflikt, Rede des Grafen Galeazzo Ciano.* Basel: Verlag Birkhauser, 1939.

———. *The Ciano Diaries 1939–1943.* Edited by Hugh Gibson. New York: Doubleday, 1946.

Ciechanowski, Jan. *Defeat in Victory.* New York: Doubleday, 1947.

Clark, General Mark. *Calculated Risk.* New York: Harper, 1950.

Clemenceau, Georges. *Grandeur and Misery of Victory.* London: Harrap, 1930.

Cooper, Duff (Viscount Norwich). *Old Men Forget.* London: Rupert Hart-Davis, 1954.

Cunningham of Hyndhope, Admiral of the Fleet. *A Sailor's Odyssey.* London: Hutchinson, 1951.

Daniels, Josephus. *The Wilson Era — Years of War and After, 1917–1923.* Chapel Hill: University of North Carolina Press, 1946.

Deane, Major General John. *The Strange Alliance. The Story of Our Efforts at Wartime Cooperation with Russia.* New York: Viking, 1947.

de Gaulle, General Charles. *War Memoirs,* vol. i, *The Call to Honor 1940–1942.* New York: Viking, 1955.

de Guingand, Major General Sir Francis. *Operation Victory.* New York: Scribner, 1947.

Edwards, Commander Kenneth, R. N. *Operation Neptune.* London: Collins, 1946.

Eisenhower, General of the Army Dwight. D. *Crusade in Europe.* New York: Doubleday, 1948.

Esher, Reginald, Viscount. *Journals and Letters,* vols. i–iv. Edited by M. V. Brett and O. Esher. London: Nicholson and Watson, 1934–38.

Fear God and Dread Nought. The Correspondence of Admiral of the Fleet Lord Fisher of Kilverstone. Edited by Arthur Marder. vol. i, *The Making of an Admiral 1854–1904;* vol. ii, *Years of Power, 1904–1914.* London; Jonathan Cape, 1952–56.

Fisher, Admiral of the Fleet Lord. *Memories.* London: Hodder and Stoughton, 1919.

The Forrestal Diaries. Edited by Walter Millis with E. S. Duffield. New York: Viking, 1951.

French, Field Marshal Viscount of Ypres. *1914.* Boston: Houghton Mifflin, 1919.

Gafencu, Grigore. *Prelude to the Russian Campaign August 21, 1939–June 22, 1941.* London: Frederick Muller, 1945.

Galland, Adolf. *The First and The Last. The Rise and Fall of the German Fighter Forces 1938–1945.* New York: Holt, 1954.

Gibbs, Philip. *More That Must Be Told.* New York: Harper, 1921.

Grey of Fallodon, Viscount. *Twenty-Five Years 1892–1916.* New York: Frederick Stokes, 1925.

Grigg, Sir James. *Prejudice and Judgment.* London: Jonathan Cape, 1948.

Guderian, General Heinz. *Panzer Leader.* London: Michael Joseph, 1952.

The Private Papers of Douglas Haig 1914–1919. Edited by Robert Blake. London: Eyre and Spottiswoode, 1952.

Haldane, Viscount. *An Autobiography.* New York: Doubleday Doran, 1929.

———. *Before the War.* New York: Funk & Wagnalls, 1920.

Halder, General Franz. *Hitler als Feldherr.* Munich: Dom Verlag, 1949.

———. *War Diary.* Office of the Chief of Counsel for the Prosecution of War Crimes. Unbound manuscript, courtesy of The Council on Foreign Relations in New York City, undated and unplaced.

Hamilton, General Sir Ian. *Gallipoli Diary.* New York: George Doran, 1920.

Harris, Air Marshal Sir Arthur. *Bomber Offensive.* London: Collins, 1947.

Hassell, Ulrich von. *The Von Hassell Diaries 1938–1944. The Story of the Forces against Hitler inside Germany.* New York: Doubleday, 1947.

Hayes, Carlton. J. *Wartime Mission in Spain 1942–1945.* New York: Macmillan, 1945.

Hitler, Adolf. *Mein Kampf.* New York: Reynal and Hitchcock, 1939.

Hoare, Sir Samuel (Viscount Templewood). *Complacent Dictator.* New York: Knopf, 1947.

Hull, Cordell. *The Memoirs of Cordell Hull*. New York: Macmillan, 1948.
The Secret Diary of Harold L. Ickes, vol. III, *The Lowering Clouds 1939–1941*. New York: Simon and Schuster, 1954.
Ingersoll, Ralph. *Top Secret*. New York: Harcourt, Brace, 1946.
Jodl, General Alfred. *War Diary*. Unbound manuscript in German, courtesy of Princeton University Library, undated and unplaced.
Jones, Thomas. *A Diary With Letters 1931–1950*. London: Oxford University Press, 1954.
Kallay, Nicolas. *Hungarian Premier — A Personal Account of a Nation's Struggle in The Second World War*. New York: Columbia University Press, 1954.
The Memoirs of Field Marshall Kesselring. London: William Kimber, 1953.
King, Fleet Admiral Ernest, and Whitehill, Walter. *Fleet Admiral King, A Naval Record*. New York: W. W. Norton, 1952.
Leahy, Fleet Admiral William. *I Was There. The Personal Story of the Chief of Staff to Presidents Roosevelt and Truman Based on His Notes and Diaries Made at the Time*. New York: Whittlesey House, 1950.
Lloyd George, David. *War Memoirs*, vol. I–VI. London: Nicholson and Watson, 1933–37.
Ludendorff's Own Story August 1914–November 1918. New York: Harper, 1919.
MacClean, Fitzroy. *Eastern Approaches*. London: Jonathan Cape, 1949.
Mannerheim, Field Marshal Gustav. *The Memoirs of Field Marshal Mannerheim*. New York: Dutton, 1954.
Marsh, Sir Edward. *A Number of People, A Book of Reminiscences*. London: Heinemann, 1939.
Maugeri, Admiral Franco. *From the Ashes of Disgrace*. New York: Reynal and Hitchcock, 1948.
Morgan, Lieutenant General Sir Frederick. *Overture to Overlord*. New York: Doubleday, 1950.
Morgenthau, Henry. *Ambassador Morgenthau's Own Story*. Garden City: Doubleday, Page, 1919.
Mémoires de Mussolini 1942–1943. Paris: René Julliard, 1948.
Nelson, Donald. *Arsenal of Democracy*. New York: Harcourt, Brace, 1946.
Oliver, F. S. *Ordeal by Battle*. New York: Macmillan, 1915.
Papagos, General Alexander. *The German Attack On Greece*. London: Greek Information Office, 1946.
Perkins, Frances. *The Roosevelt I Knew*. New York: Viking, 1946.
Rauschning, Herman. *The Voice of Destruction*. New York: Putnam, 1940.
Repington, Lieutenant Colonel C. à Court. *The First World War 1914–1918. Personal Experiences*. Boston: Houghton Mifflin, 1920.
Reynaud, Paul. *In the Thick of the Fight 1930–1945*. New York: Simon and Schuster, 1945.
Richmond, Admiral Sir Herbert. *Portrait of an Admiral. The Life and Papers of Sir Herbert Richmond*. Edited by Arthur Marder. Cambridge, Mass.: Harvard University Press, 1952.
Riddell, Lord. *More Pages from My Diary 1908–1914*. London: Country Life, 1934.
———. *War Diary 1914–1918*. London: Nicholson and Watson, 1933.

The Rommel Papers. Edited by Capt. B. H. Liddell Hart. London: Collins, 1953.

Robertson, Field Marshal Sir William. *From Private to Field Marshal.* Boston: Houghton Mifflin, 1921.

————. *Soldiers and Statesmen.* London: Cassell, 1926.

Roosevelt, Elliott. *As He Saw It.* New York: Duell, Sloan and Pearce, 1946.

Roosevelt Letters (Abbrev.). *F.D.R., His Personal Letters 1928–1945.* Edited by Elliott Roosevelt. New York: Duell, Sloan and Pearce, 1950.

Hyde Park Papers of President Roosevelt. Secretary's File. Hyde Park, N.Y.: Roosevelt Library Archives.

Rougier, Louis. *Mission secrète à Londres, les accords Pétain-Churchill.* Paris: Les Editions du Cheval Ailé, 1947.

Schmidt, Paul. *Hitler's Interpreter.* New York: Macmillan, 1951.

Slessor, Sir John. *The Central Blue. Recollections and Reflections.* London: Cassell, 1956.

Smalley, George. *Anglo-American Memories.* Second series. New York: Putnam, 1912.

Speidel, Lieutenant General Hans. *Invasion 1944, Rommel and the Normandy Campaign.* Chicago: Regnery, 1950.

Spender, J. A. *Life, Journalism and Politics.* New York: Frederick Stokes, 1927.

Spears, Brigadier General Sir Edward. *Prelude to Victory.* London: Jonathan Cape, 1939.

Spears, Major General Sir Edward. *Assignment to Catastrophe.* Vol. i, *Prelude to Dunkirk July 1939–May 1940;* vol. ii, *The Fall of France June 1940.* New York: A. A. Wyn, 1955.

Standley, William, and Ageton, Arthur. *Admiral Ambassador to Russia.* Chicago: Regnery, 1955.

Stettinius, Edward, Jr. *Roosevelt and the Russians. The Yalta Conference.* Garden City: Doubleday, 1949.

Stilwell, General Joseph. *The Stilwell Papers.* Edited by T. H. White. New York: William Sloan Associates, 1948.

Stimson, Henry, and Bundy, McGeorge. *On Active Service in Peace and War.* New York: Harper, 1947.

Suñer, Serrano. *Entre les Pyrénées et Gibraltar. Notes et réflexions sur la politique Espagnole depuis 1936.* Geneva: Les Editions du Cheval Ailé, 1948.

Templewood, Viscount (Sir Samuel Hoare). *Nine Troubled Years.* London: Collins, 1954.

Truman, Harry. *Memoirs,* vol. i, *Year of Decisions.* New York: Doubleday, 1955.

Truscott, Lieutenant General L. K., Jr. *Command Mission — A Personal Story.* New York: Dutton, 1954.

Weizäcker, Ernst von. *Memoirs.* London: Victor Gollancz, 1951.

Werth, Alexander. *The Year of Stalingrad.* London: Hamish Hamilton, 1946.

Weygand, General Maxim. *Recalled to Service.* New York: Doubleday, 1952.

Wilson of Libya, Field Marshal Lord. *Eight Years Overseas 1939–1947.* London: Hutchinson, 1950.

Wright, Captain Peter. *At the Supreme War Council.* London: Everleigh Nash, 1921.

IV. BIOGRAPHY

Ashley, Maurice. *Oliver Cromwell, The Conservative Dictator.* London: Jonathan Cape, 1937.

Bacon, Admiral Sir Reginald. *The Life of Lord Fisher of Kilverstone, Admiral of the Fleet.* London: Hodder and Stoughton, 1929.

Baker, R. S., *Woodrow Wilson, Life and Letters,* vols. I–VIII, New York: Doubleday, Doran, 1939.

Baldock, Lieutenant Colonel T. S. *Cromwell as a Soldier.* London: Paul Trench, Trubner, 1899.

Begbie, Harold. *The Mirrors of Downing Street. Some Political Reflections.* New York: Putnam, 1921.

Blumentritt, General Guenther. *Von Rundstedt, The Soldier and the Man.* London: Odhams Press, 1952.

Broad, Lewis. *Winston Churchill.* London: Hutchinson, 1950.

Brome, Vincent. *Aneurin Bevan.* London: Longmans, Green, 1953.

Bryant, Sir Arthur. *The Turn of the Tide. A Study Based on the Diaries and Autobiographical Notes of Field Marshal the Viscount Alanbrooke.* London: Collins, 1957.

Callwell, Major General Sir C. E. *Field Marshal Sir Henry Wilson, His Life and Diaries.* New York: Scribner, 1927.

Churchill by His Contemporaries. Edited by Charles Eade. London: Hutchinson, 1953.

Churchill, Winston. *Great Contemporaries.* New York: Putnam, 1932.

――――. *Marlborough, His Life and Times,* vols. I–VI. New York: Scribner, 1933–38.

――――. *Lord Randolph Churchill,* vols. I–II. New York: Macmillan, 1906.

Colvin, Ian. *Master Spy. The Incredible Story of Admiral Wilhelm Canaris,* New York: McGraw Hill, 1951.

Cooper, Duff, *Haig.* Garden City: Doubleday, Doran, 1936.

Cowles, Virginia. *Winston Churchill — The Era and the Man.* New York: Harper, 1953.

Davis, Richard Harding. *Real Soldiers of Fortune.* New York: P. F. Collins, 1906.

Davenport, John, and Murphy, Charles. *The Lives of Winston Churchill, A Close Up.* New York: Scribner, 1945.

Deutscher, Isaac. *Stalin, A Political Biography.* New York: Oxford University Press, 1949.

Driberg, Tom. *Beaverbrook, A Study in Power and Frustration.* London: Weidenfeld and Nicolson, 1956.

Dugdale, Blanche. *Arthur James Balfour, First Earl of Balfour.* London: Hutchinson, 1936.

Feiling, Keith. *The Life of Neville Chamberlain.* London: Macmillan, 1947.

Ferté, Air Chief Marshal Sir Philip Joubert de la 'Churchill the Airman,' in *Churchill by His Contemporaries* above.

Friedel, Frank. *Franklin D. Roosevelt, The Apprenticeship.* Boston: Little, Brown, 1952.

Germains, Victor. *The Tragedy of Winston Churchill*. London: Hurst and Blackett, 1931.

Guedalla, Philip. *Mr. Churchill*. New York: Reynal and Hitchcock, 1942.

———. *The Duke*. London: Hodder and Stoughton, 1946.

Hart, Captain B. H. Liddell. *Reputations*. London: John Murray, 1928.

Heiden, Konrad. *Der Fuehrer. Hitler's Rise to Power*. Boston: Houghton Mifflin, 1944.

Himmelfarb, Gertrude. *Lord Acton — A Study in Conscience and Politics*. Chicago: University of Chicago Press, 1952.

Hodges, Arthur. *Lord Kitchener*. London: Thornton Butterworth, 1936.

Hudleston, F. J. *Gentleman Johnny Burgoyne. Misadventures of an English General in the Revolution*. Indianapolis: Bobbs-Merrill, 1927.

Hughes, Emrys. *Winston Churchill, British Bulldog. His Career in War and Peace*. New York: Exposition Press, 1955.

Jones, Thomas. *Lloyd George*. Cambridge, Mass.: Harvard University Press, 1951.

Keynes, John Maynard. *Essays in Biography*. New York: Harcourt, Brace, 1933.

Kraus, René. *Winston Churchill. A Biography*. Philadelphia: Lippincott, 1940.

Mahan, Captain A. T. *The Life of Nelson. The Embodiment of the Sea Power of Great Britain*. Boston: Little, Brown, 1897.

Maurice, Major General Sir Frederick. *Haldane 1856–1915, The Life of Viscount Haldane of Cloan*, vols. I–II. London: Faber and Faber, 1937–39.

Nicolson, Harold. *Curzon: The Last Phase 1919–1925. A Study in Post-war Diplomacy*. London: Constable, 1934.

Owen, Frank. *The Tempestuous Journey. Lloyd George, His Life and Times*. London: Hutchinson, 1954.

Paul, Robert. *The Lord Protector. Religion and Politics in the Life of Oliver Cromwell*. London: Lutterworth Press, 1955.

Raymond, E. T. *Portraits of the Nineties*. New York: Scribner, undated.

———. *Uncensored Celebrities*. New York: Holt, 1919.

Rowse, A. L. *The Early Churchills. An English Family*. New York: Harper, 1956.

———. 'The Summing Up — Churchill's Place in History,' in *Churchill by His Contemporaries* above.

Sencourt, Robert. *Winston Churchill*. London: Faber and Faber, 1941.

Sherrard, O. A. *Lord Chatham, A War Minister in the Making. Pitt and the Seven Years War*. London: The Bodley Head, 1952–55.

Sherwood, Robert. *Roosevelt and Hopkins, An Intimate History*. New York: Harper, 1948.

Spender, J. A., and Asquith, Cyril. *Life of Herbert Henry Asquith, Lord Oxford and Asquith*. London: Hutchinson, 1932.

Watson, S. J. *Carnot*. London: The Bodley Head, 1954.

Whitney, Major General Courtney. *MacArthur, His Rendezvous with Destiny*. New York: Knopf, 1956.

Wrench, John. *Geoffrey Dawson and Our Times*. London: Hutchinson, 1955.

Young, B. G. M. *Stanley Baldwin*. London: Rupert Hart-Davis, 1952.

Young, Desmond. *Rommel*. London: Collins, 1950.

V. PERIODICALS AND PRESS

'American Forces Land in French Africa . . . Effective Second Front, Roosevelt Says,' *The New York Times*. New York: November 8, 1942.

Assmann, Vice Admiral Kurt. 'Hitler and the German Officer Corps,' *United States Naval Institute Proceedings*. Annapolis: May 1956.

———. 'The Battle for Moscow, Turning Point of the War,' *Foreign Affairs*, vol. xxviii, no. 2. New York: January 1950.

Baldwin, Hanson. 'Churchill Was Right,' *The Atlantic Monthly*. Boston: July 1954.

Baratier, General. 'A French View of the *Times* Article: "Defence or Attack",' *Army Quarterly*, vol. xxxvi, no. 1. London: April 1938.

Barclay, Brigadier C.N. 'British Generalship,' *Army Quarterly*, vol. lix, no. 2. London: January 1950.

Beardon, Colonel R.H. 'Reply to "Does Defence Mean Defeat?",' *Journal Royal United Service Institution*, vol. lxxxiii, no. 531. London: August 1938.

———. 'Some Strategical Theories of Captain Liddell Hart,' *Journal Royal United Service Institution*, vol. lxxxi, no. 524. London: November 1936.

Berlin, Isaiah. 'Mr. Churchill,' *The Atlantic Monthly*. Boston: September 1949.

Brooks, Russell. 'The Unknown Darlan,' *United States Naval Institutute Proceedings*, vol. 81, no. 8. Annapolis: August 1955.

Burckhardt, Carl. 'On Reading Churchill's Memoirs,' *Measure, A Critical Journal*, vol. ii, no. 4. Chicago: Regnery, Fall 1951.

Burne, Lieutenant Colonel Alfred. 'The Development of British Strategic Thought,' *Army Quarterly*, vol. lxxii, no. 4. London: April 1956.

Churchill, Winston. 'Let the Tyrant Criminals Bomb,' *Collier's*. New York: January 14, 1939.

———. 'Men Who Have Influenced or Impressed Me,' *The Strand Magazine*, vol. lxxxi. London: February 1931.

———. 'The American Mind and Ours,' *The Strand Magazine*, vol. lxxxii. London: August 1931.

———. 'The Hinge of Fate,' *The New York Times*. New York: October-November 1950.

Collins, Edward. 'Clausewitz and Democracy's Modern War,' *Military Affairs*, vol. xix, no. 1. Washington: Spring 1955.

Curteis, Captain H. M. 'The Doctrine of Limited Liability,' *Journal Royal United Service Institution*, vol. xxxiii, no. 532. London: November 1938.

De Weerd, H. A. 'Marshall, Organizer of Victory,' *Infantry Journal*, vol. lix, no. 1, and vol. lv, no. 1. Washington: December 1946 and January 1947.

———. 'On Overestimating the Enemy,' *The Reporter*, vol. iii, no. 4. New York: August 15, 1950.

Dexter, Bryan. 'Clausewitz and Soviet Strategy,' *Foreign Affairs*, vol. xxix, no. 1. New York: October 1950.

Dinerstein, Herbert. 'The Impact of Air Power on International Security

1933–1940,' *Military Affairs*, vol. xix, no. 2. Washington: Summer 1955.

'Editorial,' *Army Quarterly*, vol. xxxiv, no. 1. London: April 1937.

Edmonds, Brigadier Sir James. 'Was Germany Defeated in 1918?' *Journal Royal United Service Institution*, vol. lxxxiii, no. 530. London: May 1938.

Erle-Drax, Admiral Sir Ernle. 'The British War Effort,' *Journal Royal United Service Institution*, vol. xxxvii, no. 548. London: November 1942.

Flag Officer, 'Lest We Forget — The Tragedy of the Dardanelles,' *National Review*, vol. lxxxvi. London: October 1925.

Fraccaroli, Aldo. 'The Italian Navy in the Late War,' *Journal Royal United Service Institution*, vol. xciii, no. 571. London: August 1948.

Gallery, Admiral D. V. 'An Admiral Talks Back to the Airmen,' *The Saturday Evening Post*. Philadelphia: June 25, 1949.

Garvin, J. L. 'Mr. Churchill and the War of Empires,' *The English Review*, vol. xxvii. London: 1923.

Germains, Victor. 'Some Problems of Imperial Strategy,' *National Review*, vol. lx, no. 663. London: May 1938.

———. 'The Army in War,' *National Review*, vol. lxii, no. 676. London: June 1939.

———. 'The Military Lessons of the War,' *Contemporary Review*, no. 896. London: August 1940.

———. 'To Be or Not To Be,' *National Review*, vol. cxi, no. 667. London: September 1938.

'Goering's Unpublished Interview.' Edited by Brigadier General W. W. Quinn. *U. S. News and World Report*. Washington: May 14, 1954.

Greenberg, Martin. 'Winston Churchill, Tory Democrat,' *Partisan Review*. New York: March-April 1951.

Greer, Thomas. 'Air Arm Doctrinal Roots, 1917–1918,' *Military Affairs*, vol. xx, no. 4. Washington: Winter 1956.

Halle, Louis. 'Strategy versus Ideology,' *The Yale Review — A National Quarterly*, vol. xlvi, no. 1. New Haven, September 1956.

Hart, Captain B. H. Liddell. 'Our Military Correspondent,' *The Times*, London, October 25–27, 1937.

———. 'The Defence of the Empire,' *Fortnightly Review*, new series, no. 853. London: January 1938.

———. 'War, Limited,' *Harper's Magazine*, vol. 192, no. 1150. New York: March 1946.

Higgins, Trumbull. 'East Wind Rain,' *United States Naval Institute Proceedings*, vol. 81, no. 11. Annapolis: November 1955.

Horan, Rear Admiral H. E. 'Combined Operations 1939–1945,' *Journal Royal United Service Institution*, vol. xcviii, no. 589. London: February 1953.

Howarth, Herbert. 'Behind Winston Churchill's Grand Style,' *Commentary*. New York: June 1951.

Ismay, Lord. 'Letter to the Editor,' *The Daily Telegraph and Morning Post*, London: November 26, 1948.

Jacob, Lieutenant General Sir Ian. 'The High Level Conduct and Direction of World War II,' *Journal Royal United Service Institution*, vol. ci, no. 603. London: August 1956.

Kittredge, Captain T. B. 'A Military Danger, The Revelation of Secret Strategic Plans,' *United States Naval Institute Proceedings*, vol. 81, no. 7. Annapolis: July 1955.

Krushchev, Nikita. 'Stalin Depicted as Savage Despot,' *The New York Times*. New York: June 5, 1956.

Langer, William. 'Political Problems of a Coalition,' *Foreign Affairs*, vol. XXVI, no. 2. New York: October 1947.

Leighton, Richard. 'Preparation for Invasion,' *Military Affairs*, vol. X, no. 1. Washington: Spring 1948.

MacClean, Fitzroy. 'Tito: A Study,' *Foreign Affairs*, vol. XXVIII, no. 2. New York: January 1950.

MacMillan, Captain Norman. 'The Influence of Air Forces on the Course of the War,' *Journal Royal United Service Institution*, vol. LXXXVI, no. 541. London: February 1941.

McCloy, John. 'The Great Military Decisions,' *Foreign Affairs*, vol. XXVI, no. 1. New York: October 1947.

McDermott, Eric. S. J. 'The Elder Pitt and His Admirals and Generals,' *Military Affairs*, vol. XX, no. 2. Washington: Summer 1956.

'Marshall Decries Stand by MacArthur,' *The New York Times*. New York: May 9, 1951.

'Marshall Scores "Back Door" Forces,' *The New York Times*. New York: May 19, 1949.

Matloff, Maurice. 'Military Planning of '39–41 Held Hazy,' *The New York Times*. New York: December 31, 1951.

———. 'The Soviet Union and the War in the West,' *United States Naval Institute Proceedings*, vol. 82, no. 3. Annapolis: March 1956.

Maurice, Major General Sir Frederick. 'Intrigues of the War, Important Military Secrets Now Disclosed,' *Westminister Gazette*. London: June 1922.

———. 'Unity of Policy among Allies,' *Foreign Affairs*, vol. XXI, no. 2. New York: January 1943.

Miller, John Jr. 'The Casablanca Conference and Pacific Strategy,' *Military Affairs*, vol. XIII, no. 4. Washington: Winter 1949.

Osmanski, Lieutenant Colonel Frank. 'The Logistical Planning of Operation Overlord,' Part III, *Military Review*, vol. XXIX, no. 10. Command and General Staff School. Fort Leavenworth: January 1950.

Pettee, George. 'Strategic Intelligence, Part I — Faults and Errors in World War II,' *Infantry Journal*, vol. LIX, no. 4. Washington: October 1946.

Poole, De Witt Clinton. 'Light on Nazi Foreign Policy,' *Foreign Affairs*, vol. XXV, no. 1. New York: October, 1946.

Repington, Colonel C. à Court. 'Churchillian Strategy,' *Blackwood's Magazine*, vol. CCXIV. London: July-December 1923.

Rosinski, Herbert. 'Strategic Diplomacy,' *Infantry Journal*, vol. LX, no. 2. Washington: February 1947.

———. 'Strategy of Fear,' *Infantry Journal*, vol. LVIII, no. 6. Washington: June 1946.

———. 'The Mediterranean and Near East,' *Infantry Journal*, vol. LX, no. 2. Washington: February 1947.

Robinson, Major General H. Rowan. 'Defence or Attack?' *Army Quarterly*, vol. XXXV, no. 2. London: January 1938.

Robinson, Major General H. Rowan. 'The Strategic Situation in the Near East,' *Journal Royal United Service Institution*, vol. LXXXV, no. 540. London: November 1940.

Salvemini, Gaetano. 'Pietro Badoglio's Role in the Second World War,' *The Journal of Modern History*, vol. XXI, no. 4. Chicago: December 1949.

Sanders, Donald. 'How Stalin Plotted a Separate Peace,' *The American Mercury*, vol. LXV, no. 287. New York: November 1947.

Schlesinger, Arthur, Jr. 'Wilmot's War, or "Churchill Was Always Right," ' *The Reporter*, vol. VI, no. 9. New York: April 29, 1952.

Schmitt, Bernadotte. 'Italian Diplomacy 1939–1941,' *The Journal of Modern History*, vol. XXVII, no. 2. Chicago: June 1955.

Sheppard, Major E. W. 'Does Defence Mean Defeat?' *Journal Royal United Service Institution*, vol. LXXXIII, no. 530. London: May 1938.

Slessor, Wing Commander J. C. 'Gold Medal Essay,' *Journal Royal United Service Institution*, vol. LXXXII, no. 527. London: August 1937.

Sommers, Martin. 'Why Russia Got the Drop on Us,' *The Saturday Evening Post*. Philadelphia: February 8, 1947.

Storry, Richard. 'Fascism in Japan,' *History Today*, vol. VI, no. 11. London: November 1956.

Straus, Dr. E. B. 'The Psychological Effects of Bombing,' *Journal Royal United Service Institution*, vol. XXXIV, no. 534. London: May 1939.

Thomas, T. H. 'British War Policy and the Western Front,' *Foreign Affairs*, vol. I, no. 4. New York: June 1923.

Wendt, Herman. 'The Military Importance of the Italian Theatre of War,' *Army Quarterly*, vol. XXXVI, no. 1. London: April 1938.

White, D. F. 'Soviet Philosophy of War,' *Political Science Quarterly*, vol. LI, no. 3. New York: September 1936.

VI. BOUND SECONDARY SOURCES

Assmann, Vice Admiral Kurt. *Deutsche Schiksalsjahre, historische Bilder aus dem zweiten Welkrieg und seiner Vorgeschichte*. Wiesbaden: Brockhaus, 1950.

Baldwin, Hanson. *Great Mistakes of the War*. New York: Harper, 1950.

———. *Strategy for Victory*. New York: W. W. Norton, 1942.

Beloff, Max. *The Foreign Policy of Soviet Russia 1929–1941*, vols. I–II. Under the auspices of the Royal Institute of International Affairs. New York: Oxford University Press, 1949.

Belot, Rear Admiral Robert de. *La Guerre aéronavale en Méditeranée 1939–1945*. Geneva: Payot, 1947.

Bruun, Geoffrey. *Europe and the French Imperium*. Rise of Modern Europe Series, edited by William Langer. New York: Harper, 1938.

Burckhardt, Jacob. *Force and Freedom. Reflections on History*. Edited by James Nichols. New York: Pantheon Books, 1943.

Burne, Lieutenant Colonel Alfred. *Strategy in World War II, A Strategical Examination of Land Operations*. Harrisburg: The Military Service Publishing Company, 1947.

Callwell, Major General Sir C. E. *The Dardanelles*. Boston: Houghton Mifflin, 1924.

Carter, Byrum. *The Office of Prime Minister*. Princeton: Princeton University Press, 1956.
Challener, Richard. *The French Theory of the Nation in Arms 1866–1939*. New York: Columbia University Press, 1955.
Charlton, Air Commodore L. E. O. *The Menace of the Clouds*. London: William Hodge, 1937.
Churchill, Winston. *Ian Hamilton's March*. London: Longmans, Green, 1900.
————. *The River War*. London: Eyre and Spottiswoode, 1951.
————. *The Unknown War — The Eastern Front*. New York: Scribner, 1931.
————. *A History of the English Speaking Peoples*, vol. II, *The New World*. New York: Dodd, Mead, 1956.
Clausewitz, Carl von. *On War*. London: Paul French, Trubner, 1911.
Corbett, Sir Julian. *England in the Mediterranean. A Study of the Rise and Influence of British Power within the Straits 1603–1713*. London: Longmans, Green, 1917.
————. *England in the Seven Years War — A Study in Combined Strategy*, vols. I–II. London: Longmans, Green, 1907.
————. *Some Principles of Maritime Strategy*. London: Longmans, Green, 1911.
Craig, Gordon. 'Delbrück: The Military Historian,' in *Makers of Modern Strategy*.
————. *The Politics of the Prussian Army*. Oxford: The Clarendon Press, 1955.
Crutwell, C. R. M. *The Role of British Strategy in the Great War*. Cambridge: Cambridge University Press, 1936.
Dallin, David. *Soviet Russia and the Far East*. New Haven: Yale University Press, 1948.
De Weerd, H. A. 'Churchill, Lloyd George, Clemenceau: The Emergence of the Civilian,' in *Makers of Modern Strategy*.
Douhet, Guilo. *The Command of the Air*. New York: Coward-McCann, 1942.
Dulles, Allen. *Germany's Underground*. New York: Macmillan, 1947.
Dunlop, Colonel John. *The Development of the British Army 1899–1914*. London: Meuthen, 1938.
Ellison, Lieutenant General Sir Gerald. *The Perils of Amateur Strategy as Exemplified by the Attacks on the Dardanelles Fortress*. London: Longmans, Green, 1916.
Fay, Sidney. *The Origins of the World War*, vol. I, *Before Sarajevo: Underlying Causes of the War*. New York: Macmillan, 1928.
Feis, Herbert. *The Spanish Story. Franco and the Nations at War*. New York: Knopf, 1948.
Fischer, George. *Soviet Opposition to Stalin — A Case Study in World War II*. Cambridge, Mass.: Harvard University Press, 1952.
Forrest, Sir George. *The Life of Lord Roberts*. New York: Frederick Stokes, undated.
Fortescue, Sir John. *Following the Drum*. London: William Blackwood, 1931.
————. *Wellington*. New York: Dodd, Mead, 1925.
Fuchida, Mitsuo, and Okumiya, Masatake. *Midway — The Battle That Doomed Japan — The Japanese Navy's Own Story*. Annapolis: United States Naval Institute, 1955.

Fuller, Colonel J. F. C. *On Future Warfare*. London: Sifton Praed, 1928.
———. *The Reformation of War*. New York: Dutton, 1923.
Fuller, Major General J. F. C. *A Military History of the Western World*, vols. I–III. New York: Funk and Wagnalls, 1953–1956.
———. *The Second World War 1939–1945, A Strategical and Tactical History*. New York: Duell, Sloan and Pearce, 1949.
Garthoff, Raymond. *Soviet Military Doctrine*. Glencoe, Ill.: The Free Press, 1953.
Gaulle, General Charles de. *The Army of the Future*. New York: Lippincott, 1941.
Germains, Victor. *The Mechanization of War*. London: Sifton Praed, 1927.
Gibson, Irving: 'Maginot and Liddell Hart: The Doctrine of Defense,' in *Makers of Modern Strategy*.
Gilbert, Felix. 'Ciano and His Ambassadors,' *The Diplomats, 1919–1939*. Edited by F. Gilbert and G. Craig. Princeton: Princeton University Press, 1953.
Gipson, Lawrence. *The Great War for the Empire*, vol. 2, *The Victorious Years 1758–1760*. New York: Knopf, 1949.
Goerlitz, Walter. *History of the German General Staff 1657–1945*. New York: Frederick Praeger, 1953.
Grenfell, Captain Russell. *Main Fleet to Singapore*. London: Faber and Faber, 1951.
Guillaume, General Auguste. *Soviet Arms and Soviet Power*. Washington: Infantry Journal Press, 1949.
Hamilton, General Sir Ian. *The Soul and Body of an Army*. London: E. Arnold, 1921.
Hankey, Lord. *Politics, Trials and Errors*. Chicago: Regnery, 1950.
Hart, Captain B. H. Liddell. *Defense of the West*. New York: William Morrow, 1950.
———. *The British Way in Warfare*. New York: Macmillan, 1933.
———. *The Current of War*. London: Hutchinson, 1941.
———. *The Defence of Britain*. London: Faber and Faber, 1939.
———. *The German Generals Talk*. New York: William Morrow, 1948.
———. *The Strategy of the Indirect Approach*. London: Faber and Faber, 1946.
———. *The War in Outline*. New York: Modern Library Edition, Random House, 1936.
———. *When Britain Goes to War, Adaptability and Mobility*. London: Faber and Faber, 1932.
Hilger, Gustav, and Meyer, Alfred. *The Incompatible Allies. A Memoir History of German-Soviet Relations 1918–1941*. New York: Macmillan, 1953.
Hinsley, F. H. *Hitler's Strategy*. Cambridge: Cambridge University Press, 1951.
Hirst, Francis. *The Consequences of the War to Great Britain*. London: Oxford University Press, 1934.
Hook, Sidney. *The Hero in History — A Study in Limitation and Possibility*. London: Secker and Warburg, 1945.
Iseley, Jeter, and Crowl, Philip. *The U. S. Marines and Amphibious War. Its Theory and Practice in the Pacific*. Princeton: Princeton University Press, 1951.

Jones, F. C. *Japan's New Order in East Asia, Its Rise and Fall.* Under the auspices of the Royal Institute of International Affairs. London: Oxford University Press, 1954.

Kennan, George. *American Diplomacy 1900–1950.* Chicago: University of Chicago Press, 1951.

Kennedy, John. *Why England Slept.* New York: Wilfred Funk, 1940.

Kernan, Colonel M. F. *Defense Will Not Win the War.* Boston: Little, Brown, 1942.

King, Jere. *Generals and Politicians — Conflict between France's High Command, Parliament and Government 1914–1918.* Berkeley: University of California Press, 1951.

Kingston-McCloughery, Air Marshal E. J. *The Direction of War — A Critique of Political Direction and High Command in War.* New York: Frederick Praeger, 1955.

Kleist, Peter. *Zwischen Hitler und Stalin 1939–1945.* Bonn: Athenaeum Verlag, 1950.

Langer, William. *Our Vichy Gamble.* New York: Knopf, 1947.

Langer, William, and Gleason, S. E. *The Challenge to Isolation 1937–1940.* New York: Harper, 1952.

———. *The Undeclared War 1940–1941.* New York: Harper, 1953.

Lee, Wing Commander Asher. *The German Air Force.* New York: Harper, 1946.

Lukacs, John. *The Great Powers and Eastern Europe.* Chicago: Regnery, 1953.

Lutz, Ralph. *The Causes of the German Collapse in 1918.* Stanford: Hoover War Library Publication no. 4, 1934.

Maccuun, F. V., *The Contemporary English View of Napoleon.* London: G. Bell and Sons, 1914.

Mahan, Captain A. T. *The Influence of Sea Power upon the French Revolution and Empire 1793–1812.* Boston: Little, Brown, 1898.

Marder, Arthur. *The Anatomy of British Sea Power — A History of British Naval Policy in the Pre-Dreadnought Era 1880–1905.* New York: Knopf, 1940.

Makers of Modern Strategy. Military Thought from Machiavelli to Hitler. Edited by E. M. Earle, with the collaboration of Gordon Craig and Felix Gilbert. Princeton: Princeton University Press, 1943.

Martienssen, Anthony. *Hitler and His Admirals.* New York: Dutton, 1949.

Maurice, Major General Sir Frederick. *The Last Four Months of the War. How the War Was Won.* Boston: Little, Brown, 1919.

———. *Principles of Strategy — A Study of the Application of the Principles of War.* New York: Richard Smith, 1930.

McNeill, William. *Survey of International Affairs 1939–1946. America, Britain and Russia, Their Co-operation and Conflict 1941–1946.* Under the auspices of the Royal Institute of International Affairs. New York: Oxford University Press, 1953.

Meinecke, Friedrich. *The German Catastrophe — Reflections and Recollections.* Translated by Sidney Fay. Cambridge, Mass.: Harvard University Press, 1950.

Mendelssohn, Peter de. *Design for Aggression. The Inside Story of Hitler's Plans.* New York: Harper, 1946.

Morison, Elting. *Admiral Sims and the Modern American Navy.* Boston: Houghton Mifflin, 1942.

Mourin Maxime. *Les Tentatives de Paix dans la seconde guerre mondiale, 1939–1945.* Paris: Payot, 1949.

Munro, Ross. *Gauntlet to Overlord. The Story of the Canadian Army.* Toronto: Macmillan, 1946.

Nef, John. *War and Human Progress. An Essay on the Rise of Industrial Civilization.* Cambridge, Mass.: Harvard University Press, 1953.

Nickerson, Hoffman. *The Armed Horde 1795–1939. A Study of the Rise, Survival and Decline of the Mass Army.* New York: Putnam, 1940.

Oman, Sir Charles. 'The German Losses on the Somme, July–December 1916,' in *'The World Crisis' by Winston Churchill — A Criticism.* See below.

Puleston, Captain W. D. *The Influence of Sea Power in World War II.* New Haven: Yale University Press, 1947.

Rauch, Basil. *Roosevelt from Munich to Pearl Harbor — A Study in the Creation of a Foreign Policy.* New York: Creative Age Press, 1950.

Rauschning, Hermann. *The Revolution of Nihilism — Warning to the West.* New York: Alliance, 1939.

Richmond, Admiral Sir Herbert. *Statesmen and Sea Power.* Oxford: The Clarendon Press, 1946.

————. *The Navy as an Instrument of Policy 1558–1727.* Cambridge: Cambridge University Press, 1953.

Riddell, Lord. *More Things That Matter.* London: Hodder and Stoughton, 1925.

Rose, J. H. *The Indecisiveness of Modern War and Other Essays.* New York: Harcourt, Brace, 1927.

Rossi, A. *The Russo-German Alliance August 1939–June 1941.* Boston: The Beacon Press, 1951.

Rothfels, Hans. 'Clausewitz,' in *Makers of Modern Strategy.*

Schlesinger, Arthur, Jr. *The Vital Center. The Politics of Freedom.* Boston: Houghton Mifflin, 1949.

Seton-Watson, R. W. *Britain in Europe 1789–1914. A Survey of Foreign Policy.* Cambridge: Cambridge University Press, 1937.

Seversky, Major Alexander de. *Victory through Air Power.* New York: Simon and Schuster, 1942.

Shulman, Milton. *Defeat in the West.* New York: Dutton, 1948.

Swift, Jonathan. *The Conduct of the Allies and of the Late Ministry in the Beginning and Carrying on the Present War.* Edinburgh: Freebair, 1711.

Sydenham of Combe, Lord, 'Mr. Churchill as Historian,' in *'The World Crisis' by Winston Churchill — A Criticism.* See below.

Taylor, Telford. *The Sword and Swastika. Generals and Nazis in the Third Reich.* New York: Simon and Schuster, 1942.

The United States and World Sea Power. Edited by E. B. Potter and others of the U. S. Naval Academy. Englewood Cliffs: Prentice-Hall, 1955.

'The World Crisis' by Winston Churchill — A Criticism, with Lord Sydenham of Combe, Sir Charles Oman, and other contributors. London: Hutchinson, undated.

Trefousse, H. L. *Germany and American Neutrality*. New York: Bookman Associates, 1951.

Trevelyan, G. M. *England under Queen Anne*, vol. I, *Blenheim*. London: Longmans, Green, 1930.

Tyler, J. E. *The British Army and the Continent 1904–1914*. London: E. Arnold, 1938.

Vagts, Alfred. *A History of Militarism — Romance and Realities of a Profession*. New York: W. W. Norton, 1937.

Wavell, Field Marshal Earl. *Soldiers and Soldiering, or Epithets of War*. London: Jonathan Cape, 1953.

Weinberg, G. L. *Germany and the Soviet Union 1939–1941*. Leiden: E. J. Brill, 1954.

Wells, H. G. *Men Like Gods*. New York: Macmillan, 1923.

Werner, Max. *Attack Can Win in 1943*. Boston: Little, Brown, 1944.

Wheeler-Bennett, John. *Munich: Prologue to Tragedy*. New York: Duell, Sloan and Pearce, 1948.

———. *The Nemesis of Power. The German Army in Politics 1918–1945*. New York: St. Martin's Press, 1954.

White, D. F. *The Growth of the Red Army*. Princeton: Princeton University Press, 1944.

Wilmot, Chester. *The Struggle for Europe*. New York: Harper, 1952.

Wiskemann, Elizabeth. *The Rome-Berlin Axis, A History of the Relations between Hitler and Mussolini*. New York: Oxford University Press, 1949.

Woodward, David. *The Tirpitz and the Battle for the North Atlantic*. New York: W. W. Norton, 1954.

Wright, Quincy. *A Study of War*. vol. I–II. Chicago: University of Chicago Press, 1942.

Ziff, William. *The Coming Battle of Germany*. New York: Duell, Sloan and Pearce, 1942.

Judex

275